A Victorian American
Henry Wadsworth Longfellow

By

Herbert S. Gorman

KENNIKAT PRESS, INC./PORT WASHINGTON, N. Y.

Copyright 1926 by George H. Doran Company
Copyright renewed 1954 by Herbert S. Gorman
Reissued in 1967 by Kennikat Press by arrangement with
Doubleday and Company

Manufactured in the United States of America

Library of Congress Catalog Card No: 66- 25915

PREFACE

Biography is essentially one individual's conception of another individual as deduced and illustrated from factual information, writings, letters and the color of the time involved. It is impossible to write about any man (no matter how recently snatched from this earth) and to offer the portrait to the public with the unqualified assertion, "This *is* the man." All that the biographer can safely say is, "This is the man as I see him." After all, there is even a bias in the impartiality of facts. The chapters which follow, therefore, are Henry Wadsworth Longfellow as I see him. Of necessity, I have been somewhat selective, drawing from the copious reservoir of Longfellowana those particulars which appeared most fitting for the objective I had in mind. At the same time, I have tried to be impartial, to study both sides of the medal and to reflect, as clearly as I could, the Longfellow who dominated American poetry for so many decades. It was impossible not to be selective for there is hardly a book concerned with American letters of the nineteenth century that does not deal with Longfellow in some way. The *Life of Henry Wadsworth Longfellow with Extracts from his Journals and Correspondence*, edited by Samuel Longfellow, runs to three volumes alone. There are a multitude of essays, critical studies, anecdotes, memoranda, reminiscences, correspondences, appreciations, and miscellaneous citations concerned with the poet of Craigie House. To use everything would have resulted in a work of Gargan-

vii

tuan proportions. It remained, therefore, for me to
go through this huge mass of material—and I do not
pretend to have gone through all of it, for there are
portions safely shut away from the unbiased student
—and glean from it the revelatory facts and gestures
that adumbrate the real Longfellow. The period,
also, has been studied afresh in concordance with the
individual and the result is, I hope, a picture of the
Time-Spirit as well as of the poet who rode it so
well.

The query possibly arises: Why write a life of
Longfellow at all? There are several reasons for so
astonishing a procedure in this era of literary innovation, and not the least of them is the intrinsic interest
of the subject in itself. Longfellow is representative
of many urges. He was the first figure in American
letters to discover Europe as a rich mine, and it is
part of the thesis of this book, so far as a biography
may be saddled with a thesis, to show that the greater
part of his mental and intellectual sustenance was
drawn from the Old World. He antedated Henry
James in some broad particulars, although he was
never so completely cut off from what may be denominated the American common touch. Unlike the novelist, he was never able to observe America with the
faintly surprised curiosity and detached analysis of the
denationalized student. Longfellow played an important part in the development of American letters in that
he was one of the floodgates through which rushed a
European culture that for a time swept before it any
incipient autochthonous urges the effete East may have
possessed. He undoubtedly believed in his heart that
he was an American and so far as birth and tradition go
he was one, but he had no conception of the duties—and

they were duties—that devolved upon the American littérateur in those years of scanty culture when the basis of a national literature was being formed. Margaret Fuller knew. Poe suspected it. Walt Whitman gave dynamic evidence of it. But Longfellow, without being quite conscious of it, was as much English as he was American. He was our great Victorian.

Indeed it is as a Victorian that I see him; not, perhaps, an American Tennyson, but, in some ways, an American Victoria. It would be decidedly frivolous to dub him "our late dear Queen" and yet his didactic obsessions, his insistence upon the purities of living, his careful abstention (congenitally necessary, of course) from passion of any sort, and the adulation bestowed upon him by vast masses of the American public and, in particular, by his ever-zealous personal friends, would seem to offer ample opportunity for so considering him. All this may be set down without losing sight of the facts that he was essentially lovable as a personality, valuable as an ornament to the American scene of his time, and, to some degree, distinguished as a scholar. It is unnecessary to insist too strongly on the many demerits and few virtues of his poetry, that unceasing output which percolated throughout the civilized world, for it is as a man that I choose to consider him, a representative figure of the dominant urge of his time. There is but little critical consideration—in the true sense of the word—of his work in this biography, therefore, and only is any extended attention paid to his books when it seems to add to the revelation of the man's nature.

It is possible that various Longfellow disciples will take umbrage at some of the points indicated in these chapters, but I can do no more than bow my head (a bit bloodied, perhaps) and merely reiterate, "This is the man as I see him." He is a fascinating man. He offers opportunity for an observation of a critical epoch in American history. He ties up his country with Europe. He is no more dead than the era between 1830 and 1880 in New England is dead. It is necessary to understand him and his age if we are to understand our own and ferret out why we are what we are and from what curious urges we evolved.

The impossibility of duly acknowledging the multitudinous sources that made this work not wholly without some authority stares me in the face. I could with some flippancy wave an airy thanks to the entire literary and historical output of the nineteenth century but that would suggest a profound comprehension which I do not possess and of which I am not capable. But there are few important works I have not consulted for some fact, some note, some word, some date. To the Houghton Mifflin Company, publishers of Longfellow as well as of so many New England figures of the nineteenth century, and Mr. Ferris Greenslet I am indebted for various copyright permissions, which indebtedness I acknowledge with all grateful thanks. Samuel Longfellow's arrangement of his brother's letters and diaries was necessarily drawn upon for a vast number of facts and parallelisms. I might also mention *Henry Wadsworth Longfellow: His Life, His Works, His Friendships* by George Lowell Austin, *The Life of Henry Wadsworth Longfellow* by Francis H. Underwood, *Henry Wadsworth Longfellow* by Thomas Wentworth Higginson, and *Random Memories* by Ernest Wadsworth Longfellow. These books but head the list and it is impossible to enumerate others without enumerating all of them, a

P R E F A C E

task which would fill too much space and mean but little after all. The unnamed sources, therefore, must accept my general thanks.

New York,
May 9, 1926.

HERBERT S. GORMAN.

CONTENTS

ILLUSTRATIONS

A VICTORIAN AMERICAN
HENRY WADSWORTH LONGFELLOW

CHAPTER ONE
Drums and Dreams

Mists rise, sucked up by the early sun. The boy runs to keep pace with the sturdy old gentleman whose square-toed, silver-buckled shoes clack on the stones as he hurries up the steep incline of the hill. Before them the Observatory squats like an infant giant and stares out over the Bay. There is the rushing of feet, the shifting of many forms, the babble of excited voices. On Indian Point the tall pine trees stand like feathered sachems and the fish-hawks circle high above them. The shore back of the Neck is deserted except for the crying curlews, the plovers, and the sand-birds. There are no boys there now. Wideeyed and vociferating, they are swarming about Munjoy's Hill, calling to one another through the early morning sunlight, gathering round the black tar-barrel which hangs like an unsightly wasps' nest on its tall pole, and darting along the fortifications. They are waiting for the hollow thunder of cannon to drift in from the sea. The elders are more subdued. They have heard the sound of guns before and know what it means. Standing in small groups or eddying along the eminence of the hill they wait impatiently, casting frequent glances at the apex of the Observatory where several men stare seaward through spy glasses.

The old gentleman hurries forward, his glittering shoe-buckles reflecting the silver glare of the sun. He carries himself with a martial air, his full ruffled bosom swelling and the powdered club of his hair thrusting out behind from beneath his cocked hat. Clutching his gnarled stick tightly he makes his way through the various groups which part for him. He is greeted respectfully and more than one hand is raised in the

19

military salute. The small boy, hurrying at his side, has chestnut hair, lively blue eyes, a delicate complexion and rosy cheeks. He dances with excitement as they approach the Observatory and listens attentively to the conversation that ensues between his martial-appearing companion and the stout man in uniform who advances from the door. There has been no word from William Burroughs as yet. The *Enterprise* must be off Pemaquid Point somewhere. Perhaps the little fishing boat so hurriedly transformed into a brig-of-war has already come to grips with the English vessel. The stout man calls the old gentleman General. The General's eyes flash and he grips his stick in a fiercer grasp. Perhaps he is thinking of that not-so-distant day when he was captured by British soldiers and imprisoned in Fort George at Castine. The English troopers, more than a score, had surrounded his house at night and the General, guarded by six men, had defended himself vigorously until, shot through the arm and weak from loss of blood, he succumbed. But he had escaped, evading the bloodhounds and pursuing his course through the wilderness by a pocket compass. The small boy beside him had heard the story and thrilled to it.

There is a shout from the apex of the Observatory. Captain Moody, his eye glued to the telescope, has seen something in the distance. The population of Portland press forward on Munjoy's Hill and stare seaward. Is it imagination or did they hear a faint rumble that was not the rumble of thunder? Then three or four puffs of smoke rise in the air far out on the horizon and are slowly dispersed by the wind. It is half-past seven in the morning. The mass of people wait impatiently and Time passes in calm silence. The wind has veered to the east. A triumphant surmise spreads like a lighted trail of gunpowder through the expectant watchers and presently a loud and contagious cheer assaults the sun-splashed morning. There can be no doubt about it. The *Enterprise* has driven the Britisher back to mid-sea where he belongs. The Maine coast is clear. If it were not so there would be more puffs of smoke and the grumbling fierceness of cannon for Burroughs is adventurous, dogged and brave. He would never run before the fire of the enemy however hell-raking it might be. The crowd disperses, streaming back into Portland, wandering along Washington Street with its long alternating lines of Lombardy poplars and balm-of-gileads, dotting the Back Fields, circling through the sunburnt pasture west of High Street where swamp joins huckleberry patch, and wandering up State Street where mansions stand with the bayberry bushes growing to the very fences.

The General turns homeward, too, clutching his stick in one hand and the shoulder of the boy with the other. At the corner of Preble Street he pauses and observes the brick mansion occupied by the widow of the dead Commodore. He thinks of his seventh child, young Henry Wadsworth, who died in the fire-ship before the walls of Tripoli while serving under the Commodore. That was in 1804. He thinks, too, of Alexander, his ninth son, who was second lieutenant on the *Constitution* only a year ago when that frigate captured the British *Guerrière*. And now it is 1813 and another Henry Wadsworth, unexpected in 1804, is walking at his side. The General looks down at his small grandson and notes the lively intelligent face with satisfaction. This six-year-old lad so martial-minded (had he not powdered his hair and gone about with a tin gun but a year ago?) is part of the heritage of the

21

Wadsworths and Longfellows to this new and barbarous
country that is being defended so strenuously from the
repeated onslaughts of the English. Born on the Atlantic seaboard with three thousand miles of wilderness
behind him he has come at a lucky moment. He is to
grow up with his country, to broaden with it, to enunciate it to the world. He is the child of men of action,
of pioneers, of builders, of warriors. Is it too much to
expect that he will be a man of action and a builder?
Is it not possible that he may be a soldier? The General wonders to himself as he passes the mansion of
the widow of Commodore Preble and turns in at the
brick residence built by him and now occupied by
Stephen Longfellow, the father of this grandson who
steps so excitedly beside the silver-buckled shoes. The
old veteran thinks of many things as he walks up the
path to the door where Zilpah, his daughter, stands, but
there is one thing that does not enter his mind and
that is poetry. The Wadsworths and Longfellows do
not feel the creative urge. They are too busy creating
a country.

II

There are three important factors in the formulation
of the individual. They are hereditary influences, immediate surroundings, and the color of the time. In
the particular case of General Peleg Wadsworth's
grandson they were all unusual and extraordinarily picturesque—for Henry's ancestors were a pioneer breed,
his surroundings were the immature unfoldings of a
new nation, and the time was colored by gigantic and
destructive influences over all the civilized world. It
is decidedly important to orientate Henry if we are
to understand how far he succeeded, how badly he
failed, and in what measure he reflected his era. We

must study the chrysalis from which this engaging personality emerged.

The long line of Longfellows starts at Newbury, a pleasant old town in northeastern Massachusetts, and the year is approximately 1676. This first American ancestor was William Longfellow, the son of William Longfellow of Hosforth, near Leeds, in Yorkshire, England. He was born in 1651 and was therefore a young man when he settled in Newbury. In November, 1678, he married Anne Sewall, the daughter of Henry Sewall and sister to Chief Justice Samuel Sewall. Even as William was the first of the Longfellows to settle in America, so was he the first of Henry's ancestors to die in action, for in 1690 he joined Sir William Phips' unfortunate expedition against Quebec as an ensign of the Newbury Company, leaving six small children behind him. The story of this ill-fated gesture against the Canadian stronghold is an old one. The fleet commanded by Phips sailed from Boston Harbor on the 9th of August, 1690, the thirty-two vessels carrying twenty-two hundred soldiers, and arrived before Quebec during the early part of October. The attempt to capture the city proved futile and Phips abandoned the project, turning his prows toward home. While passing through the Gulf of St. Lawrence a furious storm came up and the ships were scattered. That one having on board the Newbury Company was driven on the forsaken shore of Anticosti and during the storm Ensign William Longfellow and nine companions were drowned. In Judge Sewall's *Diary* for 1690 is written: " 'Twas Tuesday, the 18th of November, that I heard of the death of Capt. Stephen Greenleaf, Lieut. James Smith, and Ensign Wm. Longfellow, Serjt. Increase Pilsbury, who with Will Mitchell, Jabez Musgro, and four more were drown'd at Cape Britoon [this is an error] on Friday night the last of October."

Among the six children left by William Longfellow was a boy of five named Stephen, a name that was to recur in each succeeding generation of the family. This Stephen (the name came originally from his mother's grandfather, Stephen Dummer) apparently was a quiet-living man who passed his whole life in Newbury content to earn his livelihood by manual labor. He was a blacksmith and he may be pictured as a knotty-muscled fellow tending his forge and swinging his sledgehammer in the semi-rural calmness of the New England village. We may guess that he was not too bright or too ambitious. Life, for him, was not bounded by perplexing horizons but assumed the semblance of an unperturbed pool of domesticity in the tangled greenness of a virgin land. On March 25, 1714, he married Abigail Thompson, the daughter of Rev. Edward Thompson of Marshfield and by her had ten children. Perhaps it was this ministerial blood that induced ambitions beyond the forge in Stephen junior, born in 1723, for this youth developed such a fondness for books and gave such intellectual promise that his father sent him to Harvard College, where he received his diploma in 1742. Young Stephen became a school teacher in the village of York but apparently he did not last long there for in 1744 Thomas Smith, the venerable minister of Falmouth, as Portland, Maine, was then called, invited him to the northern town to open a school there.

Here we have the first connection between the Longfellows and Portland, for Stephen went there, opened his school and fared well. This educational enterprise was "in a building on the corner of Middle Street and School, now Pearl Street," and among the pupils were many youths who were to become prominent in life later. On October 19, 1749, Stephen was married to Tabitha Bragdon of York, whereby we learn that his brief tenure in that village was not without results. It was shortly after this marriage that Stephen deserted his boarding-place at the parsonage of Thomas Smith and installed himself in a house of his own in Fore Street, transferring his school there and continuing to teach until 1760 when he was appointed a clerk of the judicial court. The family fortunes, it will be observed, are beginning to rise. Scholarship—brief and sketchy perhaps—is making its inroads on manual labor, the text-book having succeeded the forge as a means of livelihood. And yet one can not but feel a warm glow for the older Stephen, who died in 1764, leaving his schoolmaster son a small legacy. This son waived material considerations for sentiment and despatched the legacy of silver coin to Boston that it might be made into a permanent memorial, but, alas, the vessel was lost and the coin permanently banked on the bottom of the Atlantic Ocean. Stephen, junior, rose magnificently to the occasion and making up an equal amount of his own silver coin—the rewards of hammering ABC into the minds of Falmouth children —sent it to Boston where it arrived safely and was manufactured into a tankard, a can and two porringers by John Butler, the silversmith. This is important for it is one of the most revelatory facts concerning Stephen and gives us a clew to a sentimental idealism that was to be a part of the Longfellow family's characteristics from that time on. Indeed, the breed (and how admirable it was!) had obviously developed and the history of the family becomes the history of that impressive New England strain that furnished the new land its civic, military, and ethical leaders.

Three sons and one daughter were born to Tabitha
and Stephen, and it is the eldest of these offspring, a
third Stephen, who is to carry on the Longfellow line.
This third Stephen was born in 1750 (on August 3rd,
to be exact) and in 1773 he married Patience Young
of York (that village of his father's youth which had
now produced two wives for Longfellows) and passed
the greater part of his life in Gorham where he died
on May 28, 1824. But long before this date the martial atmosphere known of old by the first American
Longfellow had again made its impress on the family.
In the journal of Thomas Smith, that venerable pastor,
for 1775 (momentous date!) we read: "October 16,
a fleet of five or six vessels of war anchored at the
Island with Mowat, a cat bomb ship, two cutter schoon-
ers and a small bomb sloop. On the 17th, they came
up before the town, P. M.; sent word that in two
hours they should fire upon the town, which was res-
pited. On the 18th, at nine A. M. they began and
continued until dark, with their mortars and cannon,
when with marines landing, they burnt all the lower
part of the town and up as far as Mr. Bradbury's, excepting Mrs. Ross' two houses, and son Thomas' shop
and stores, my house being included." Among the
Falmouth houses to be so burned by the British was
the home of Stephen Longfellow on Fore Street. It
was never rebuilt. Perhaps Stephen thought he was
altogether too near the ocean for safety's sake while
the American Revolution ran its course. Anyway the
committee appointed to liquidate the accounts of those
who suffered in the burning of the town granted him
£1,119 and he removed to Gorham with other townsmen, there to live until his death in 1790. It does not
appear that this second Stephen's ardor flung him
into military duties, but we must remember that he

was fifty-two years old in 1775. Beside that, he was a schoolmaster and schoolmasters make notoriously bad soldiers. We get an idea of him from a brief sketch of his life by N. P. Willis wherein we note: "Mr. Longfellow filled many important offices in the town to universal acceptance. He was about fifteen years grammar-school master, town clerk twenty-two years, many years clerk of the proprietors of the common land, and from the establishment of the county in 1760 to the commencement of the Revolution in 1775 he was register of probate and clerk of the judicial courts. His handwriting, in beautiful characters, symbolical of the purity and excellence of his own moral character, is impressed on all the records of the town and county through many successive years." With a handwriting symbolical of a pure moral character and the memory of that legacy melted up into memorial porringers added to the fact that his early years were molded in the schoolroom we begin to get a clear idea of the second Stephen.

There remains that third Stephen who was, among other things, the grandfather of Henry. It has already been pointed out that he discovered York to be an excellent place wherein to find a wife. His residence in Gorham was undoubtedly due to his father's removal there after the British had destroyed the Falmouth house on Fore Street. Stephen, the third, profiting by his father's incumbency of the clerkship of the judicial court, possibly, concentrated on the local public life of his day. He started as a surveyor but was soon holding various public offices. For eight years he represented Gorham in the General Court of Massachusetts, and, later, he was a senator from Cumberland County. From 1797 to 1811 he was judge of the Court of Common Pleas. The Longfellow family fortunes continue to rise, it will be observed. Black smith to schoolmaster to judge were the first three jumps. We may picture this third Stephen as the practical-minded old gentleman who consolidated the family position. Driving into Portland in his old square-top chaise, making his way into the courthouse escorted by the sheriff, he must have presented an appearance of small-town authority. According to one account he was "a fine-looking gentleman, with the bearing of the old school; was erect, portly, rather taller than the average, had a strongly marked face, and his hair was tied behind in a club with a black ribbon. To the close of his life [don't forget that he lived until 1824] he wore the old-style dress—knee-breeches, a long waistcoat and white-top boots. He was a man of sterling qualities of mind and heart, great integrity, and sound common sense." The closing sentence of this description appears to be pretty much of a formula but we may guess that Stephen followed his conscience closely and that the idealism implicit in his father descended to him.

From the union of this third Stephen and Patience Young of York came six children. The second child and first son, still another Stephen, is important to us for he was the father of Henry. But before any examination of him is made it will be more logical to turn to the maternal ancestry of Henry and trace it down to Zilpah, who was to be the wife of the fourth Stephen and mother of Henry. Then, having brought the two parents together, they may be studied in their relation to the son, their influence gauged and the results weighed. If two such pioneer strains are to culminate in a gentle-minded poet there must be obvious molding influences and they may best be found where the Wadsworth and Longfellow bloods meet and fuse.

CHAPTER ONE

This Wadsworth blood becomes a part of the New England heritage more than forty years before William Longfellow settled in Newbury. Christopher Wadsworth sailed into Boston Bay on the ship *Lion* and landed September 16, 1632, according to the most logical assumptions. There is even an ancient Bible extant with this declaration in it and such a medium of evidence is peculiarly appropriate, for the Wadsworths developed into a line of Puritan deacons. It is well to remember that the Puritans and Pilgrims were distinct religious sects. The Pilgrims were mainly of the laboring caste, poor people meagerly endowed with educations and fired by a fanatic urge. They were complete Separatists from the National Church of England. The Puritans, on the other hand, were still connected with the National Church, although not observing all of its services and rituals. They were educated folk, for the most part, men who had attended colleges in England and who had commanded various trades and professions. The Massachusetts Colony was populated mainly by the Puritans, who, to a certain degree, swallowed up those earlier Pilgrims who had first dared the wildernesses of the rock-bound savage land. Christopher Wadsworth was obviously a Puritan. He must have been, or he could not have held public office, as he did, in the community. Settling in Duxbury, soon after he landed he became an acquaintance and neighbor to such leaders as Captain Miles Standish, Elder Brewster and John Alden. We may be sure that the doughty Christopher was a man of parts who enjoyed the confidence of his community, for in January, 1634, he was elected constable of Duxbury. Now in those days this office was a sort of high sheriffship, an important post, and Christopher must

29

have developed dynamic potentialities to be so exalted at the close of a brief two years' residence.

There is little extant about him but that little is significant. The mere fact that he was an equal in that grave body of early settlers is something. We note mention of him in the early records. These notations are not important but they do show that he was a personality in the commonwealth. He possessed a temper, too. There is a story (which may or may not be legend) that shows the caliber of his rage. One summer he had gotten all his hay piled in the barn-yard and was about to pitchfork it into the barn when a terrific thunderstorm came up and a bolt of lightning set fire to the hay and entirely consumed it. Christopher probably tramped back into the house extremely wet and not too sure about the designs of Providence. The next year when he had gotten his hay in exactly the same place and was about to wield the pitchfork another fearful tempest came up. Christopher, who was along in years at this time, took one look at the dark and threatening clouds, heard the muttering of the thunder, and flinging down his pitchfork, rushed into the house, secured a flaming brand, ran back through the rain and set all his hay on fire, swearing as he did so that he meant to get ahead of God Almighty that time! Whereby we may learn that even Puritans lost their tempers occasionally.

Christopher's will was dated July 31, 1677, and it was filed in September, 1678, so it is obvious that he died during the latter part of the thirteen months intervening between those two dates. His wife was Grace Cole, but whether he married her before or after his arrival in America is uncertain. We know nothing about her except that she bore Christopher four children—Samuel, Joseph, Mary and John—outlived her husband and left John the bulk of the family estate at Duxbury. All that Joseph, the eldest son, got was "a Dutch settle," while his wife received a "red petticoat, with three laers, besides the two pewter dishes and Bible which they have heretofore received." It would be pleasant to trace the career of Samuel, who was killed at the Sudbury fight while combatting the Indian braves of King Philip, the Narragansett chieftain, but it is with John that we are concerned, for John carried on that direct line that will bring us to Henry's mother. John was born in 1638, and he lived and died on the homestead built up by Christopher at Duxbury. For many years he was a deacon, and, setting down so much, we gain an adequate idea of the man; inasmuch as deacons in Puritan days were a breed in themselves. He just managed to touch the new century, dying in 1700. In 1667 he married Abigail Andrews and the issue of this marriage numbered eleven children. The third child and first son was another John, born in 1671. He, too, lived in Duxbury, and there is little in the records about him. We may imagine him leading the industrious, semi-primitive life of those days with an adequate ardor in his labors. We know that he had two wives and six children, the fifth and last by his first wife being Peleg, who was born in 1715. This Peleg was a deacon also, and, like his father, grandfather and great-grandfather, lived all his days in Duxbury. His life-span reached as far as 1774, almost to the fiery moment when the Colonies rose in wrath against the unjust oppressions of the British government. Peleg had ten children and as we note some of their names (Zilpah, Cephas, Jephthah, Zilpha, Peleg, Uriah and Ira) the whole of that old New England, based so firmly upon a Biblical foundation, flashes back upon us.

We see the sturdy little communities steadily expanding, the squares of cultivated land stretching farther and farther into the wildernesses which retreat before them, the dark-garmented, horny-handed toilers with their bold noses and thin mouths shifting into that type which we are to dub the "New Englander," the blue shadows of the pines upon the fields of snow, the tumbling walls marking off the stony pastures, the hook-nosed Indians retreating beyond the Connecticut River and toward the north where the land is dotted with ice-covered ponds and great splashes of red and yellow upon the hunched hills in the autumn. And through the streets of the towns and along the muddy roads we see the deacons riding or walking. They are the backbone of this new life that has sprung up so fiercely in this land of maize and murder. So from the first we see the Wadsworths becoming a part of the infant civilization of the United States, growing up with the country, absorbing and being absorbed by it.

It is with Peleg, the son of Peleg, that we reach a nationalistic flavor, for this man, born in 1748, is to become a Revolutionary general. He is the fifth son of a fifth son if that means anything to the conjunction of stars that twinkled in the frosty New England heavens at his birth. He was graduated from Harvard College in 1769 and, after teaching for a short time, engaged in mercantile pursuits. But the feverish time-spirit was not to permit him to remain a sedentary character. In 1775 a new nation spoke in the scattered fire of muskets at Lexington and Concord and within a brief period Peleg Wadsworth had raised a company of minute men of which the Continental Congress commissioned him captain in September, 1775. In 1776 we find him laying the defenses of Roxbury under General Thomas and later he is in Colonel Cotton's regiment on Dorchester Heights. His value as an officer must have become apparent to his superiors for he was appointed an aid to General Ward when the heights were occupied in March, an occupation, by the way, which discomfited Howe so much that his fleet left Boston Bay post haste. In 1778 Peleg was made Adjutant-General of his State.

It is no part of these paragraphs to retell a portion of the American Revolution and therefore Peleg's subsequent career during the fighting must be glanced at in the most cursory manner. It is enough to affirm that he proved himself a brave and far-sighted commanding officer and that it was in the two years following his appointment as an Adjutant-General that he reached his apogee as a military commander. He was sent to Maine as second in command during the inglorious Penobscot Expedition when the vain attempt was made to dislodge the British fleet from Bagaduce, and, according to the accounts of the men under him, would have changed that defeat into a victory if he had been in command instead of the slow and wavering Saltonstall who would not show the proper spirit. Anyway, the General Court in its enquiry afterward adjudged: "That Commodore Saltonstall be incompetent ever after to hold a commission in the service of the State, and that Generals Lovell and Wadsworth be honorably acquitted." And to prove their trust in Peleg he was given command of the whole eastern department between the Piscataqua and St. Croix. For a time the General had to do with the vexatious stamping out of Tories and then in 1781 Peleg was caught unawares by the British and captured. He fought bravely against the red-coats until he was shot through the arm when, weak from loss of blood, he was set

on a horse and taken to Fort George at Castine. His
escape from that British prison has already been noted.
After that he followed his family to Boston and took
no further part in the war which had now almost run
its course in New England.

In 1772 Peleg had married Elizabeth Bartlett of
Plymouth and by her he had eleven children. These
children, through the strains that had come down
through their mother and grandmother Wadsworth
inherited the blood of five of the *Mayflower* Pilgrims,
including Elder Brewster and John Alden. Peleg
lived in Plymouth until 1784 when he removed to
Falmouth, the town which was to be called Portland
and where his daughter, Zilpah, met Stephen Longfellow. Regarding her father's appearance Zilpah
wrote years later: "Perhaps you would like to see my
father's picture as it was when we came to this town
after the war of the Revolution, in 1784. Imagine
to yourself a man of middle size, well proportioned,
with a military air, and who carried himself so truly
that many thought him tall. His dress, a bright scarlet coat, buff small clothes and vest, full ruffled bosom,
ruffles over the hands, white stockings, shoes with
silver buckles, white cravat bow in front; hair well
powdered and tied behind in a club, so called . . ."
The picture is decidedly fascinating. Peleg's remaining
years may be disposed of easily enough. He built the
Wadsworth house in Portland where Henry was to pass
his boyhood, purchased from the State of Massachusetts 7,500 acres of land in Hiram township on the Saco
River, was elected to the Massachusetts Senate in 1792
and in the same year was elected a Representative to
Congress, a post which he held until 1806 when he refused to serve any longer. He then retired to Hiram
where he became the patriarch of the town, serving as

selectman, town treasurer and magistrate. He was eighty-one years old when he died in 1829. In this man we observe the high-water mark of the Wadsworth family. He was the fine flowering of the New England blood that had striven so masterfully in the up-building of the country.

We come now to those two personages, man and woman, who were to be the parents of Henry. General Wadsworth's daughter, Zilpah, his third child, was born at Duxbury, January 6, 1778, while her father was absent, fighting the British. Her infancy was obviously an excited and nerve-racking period, for the commonwealth, in the midst of the turmoil of war, could have paid but small attention to the gentler amenities of living. Bearing a child in a war-torn land while the father is absent and in imminent danger of losing his life must have done something to the nervous system of Elizabeth Bartlett, and perhaps this something had its shaping influence on the character of Zilpah. The little girl was eight years old when she first occupied the brick house in Portland and in after years she recalled the discomforts of existing in the unfinished building. In 1799, when she was twenty-one years old, we hear of her presenting a standard to the Federal Volunteers, the first uniformed military command in Maine, which, by the way, was as yet a part of Massachusetts. Zilpah was beautiful. She was slight but upright and though in later years she was to be the victim of invalidism she was always animated. Her youth was lively with social gayety and dancing. Music appealed to her strongly and so, too, did poetry. Nature was a passion. She would sit by the window during a thunderstorm thrilling to the flashes of lightning and the dashing rain. Threading all her days was an unquestioning religious urge, a simple piety that expressed itself in church-going, attentiveness to sermons, and enthusiastic partaking in hymns. It was this charming, slight, gay, religious, sentimental creature who met young Stephen Longfellow and, on January 1, 1804, was united to him by marriage.

And now who was this young man who brought the sturdy blood of the Longfellows to, perhaps, the still sturdier blood of the Wadsworths? Stephen was a second child and he was born in Gorham on March 23, 1776. He was therefore two years older than Zilpah. His boyhood was passed in Gorham where the proximity of war must have excited him as a lad although he did not possess the intimate knowledge of the trials of campaigns that Zilpah Wadsworth must have carried in the back of her mind. In 1794 he went to Harvard College. A picture of him at this time has been drawn by Daniel Appleton White, whose middle name is to mean so much to Henry in the years to come. Mr. White noted: "He [Stephen] was evidently a well-bred gentleman when he left the paternal mansion for the University. He seemed to breathe an atmosphere of purity, as his natural element, while his bright intelligence, buoyant spirits, and social warmth diffused a sunshine of joy that made his presence always gladsome." These extraordinary stilted sentences are revelatory in that they express in some measure the sort of attitude toward life that maintained at that time. People who "diffused a sunshine of joy" were more "gladsome" than the older Puritan type that had partially vanished with the primitive struggle for existence. Stephen, while a favorite with his classmates, did not neglect his studies and we learn that he was an exemplary student and departed from the halls of knowledge with a full share of its honors. In 1798 Stephen entered the law office of Salmon Chase, an uncle of that

Salmon Portland Chase who was to become a chief justice of the United States. The year 1801 discovered
Stephen as a member of the bar and embarking on an
extensive and lucrative practice. Moving, as he did, in
the foremost social circles of his environment (we must
never forget that he came from a "paternal mansion"
and not a mere house) it was not long before he met
Zilpah Wadsworth, who was certainly one of Portland's
most charming belles. Three years after his admission
to the bar he was married to her and the young couple
went to live in the Wadsworth house on Congress Street.
They remained there for a year, their first-born,
Stephen, Junior, was ushered into the world and then
Zilpah and Stephen decided to set up housekeeping
for themselves and they moved to a small two-story
wooden house on the corner of Congress and Temple
Streets. They were not installed here for long. Samuel Stephenson, a well-to-do Portland merchant who
had married Stephen's sister, Abigail, was called to the
West Indies on business and the wife invited Zilpah and
Stephen to share the Stephenson home with her. The
young couple were here during the winter season of
1806-7 and it was here on February 27, 1807, that a
boy, a second son, was born and christened for Zilpah's
brother, Lieutenant Henry Wadsworth, who died in the
fireship in the harbor of Tripoli on the night of September 4, 1804. In the spring of 1807 General Peleg
Wadsworth removed to Hiram where he was to pass his
remaining days and Zilpah and Stephen and their two
infants became heirs to the brick house on Congress
Street.

The young Henry is excellently placed, it will be
observed. His grandparents are plentifully endowed
with the goods of this world. Their social status is
unquestioned. The father is a successful lawyer and

soon to be entrusted with public offices. He is State Legislator, presidential elector and member of Congress in turn. He is the official welcomer of Lafayette to Portland. He is a trustee of Bowdoin College and the recipient of an LL.D. from that institution. He is Recording Secretary and then President of the Maine Historical Society. He is to live until 1849, surrounded and bulwarked by the good will and respect of Portland burghers. He is intelligent, religious, a trifle strict, perhaps, essentially didactic. Henry's mother is the complement to this nature. She is sensitive, a lover of nature, of music, of poetry, of religion. The mind of Henry is evolved from the imbedded urges and instincts of these two people. The home life that shapes him will be noted later but that home life, it may be remarked here, is wholly dependent upon the spiritual emanations of Zilpah and Stephen. We may guess that Zilpah had the most to do with it. It is from her, if from anybody, that Henry gets those inborn inclinations that are to divert him from the law office and fashion him into a lifelong disciple of letters. There have been teachers before in both the Longfellow and Wadsworth families. We must not forget the first Stephen Longfellow who came to Portland. And neither must we forget that even the General, Peleg Wadsworth himself, taught for a time at Plymouth. But in spite of these stray straws that show which way the new wind is to blow there are insufficient clews to prognosticate a poet. Henry partially evolves from hereditary urges that would seem to direct him toward a differing goal than that which he is to pursue. And it is these hereditary urges that weaken him accordingly.

THE OLD LONGFELLOW HOMESTEAD AT NEWBURY, MASS.

LONGFELLOW'S BIRTHPLACE AS IT APPEARED IN 1882,
THE YEAR OF THE POET'S DEATH

GEN. PELEG WADSWORTH AND ELIZABETH BARTLETT, HIS WIFE

III

Turning from Henry's hereditary influences, influences, it must be repeated, that are hardly to mold the boy into the figure which his inheritance would suggest, we are faced by the color and "feel" of the time, a time which may not have been out of joint but was assuredly but recently *in* joint. Especially are we concerned with Portland, the "beautiful town that is seated by the sea," for it was in Portland that Henry's eyes first opened on the world. Here it was that his youth waked to the sensory world and it is in the forgotten streets, in the old faded houses, in the meadows and woods adjacent, in the childhood trips to his grandfather Wadsworth's house at Hiram or his grandfather Longfellow's house at Gorham or to the images at Lake Sebago (where the taciturn Hawthorne dreamed in the cavern) that we begin to get the "feel" of that immediately surrounding element called daily life which was to fashion Henry into the peculiar personality he was to be. This land of his begetting was part and parcel of his begetters. The two fitted. The Longfellows, certainly, *were* Portland, Maine. And if the Wadsworths, in one case, at least, transcended parochial standards and assumed a national tone we must remember that nationalism and parochialism were extremely close during the first decade of the nineteenth century. As for Henry himself, in spite of his scholastic internationalism, he remained Portland to the end but the pioneer instinct was so weak in him that he could not rediscover Portland, much less America, as a phenomenon of unsuspected aspects, urges, and contradictory developments. He could do no more than regurgitate a pleasantly Germanic Europeanism, the result of vivid impressions during his most formative years. For the present we are concerned with the Portland of the docile but lively small boy, the Portland that existed between 1807 and 1820.

Built upon a narrow peninsula called the "Neck" Portland lay in a depression between two hills, Munjoy and Bramhall. On the south was the harbor and on the north, the calm expanse of Back Cove. There were but three houses on Munjoy's Hill, if we except those in old Fort Sumner, and a thick growth of alder bushes overspread the greater part of it. Bramhall's Hill was a far-away wilderness and the distant sound of Caleb Young's fife could be heard from it at the sunset hour although the distance was at least two miles. Along the streets of the town proper stood the square old-fashioned mansions of the merchants, their noble fronts gazing benignly at the road. Behind them in the large high-fenced gardens the fruit trees flourished. War and politics wrought its irreparable damage here for the non-intercourse policy of 1806 had been followed by an embargo in 1807 (the year of Henry's birth) and commerce had suspended. An almost total destruction of shipping followed and in two years the trade at the port fell off nine thousand tons. Grass grew on the wharves and men out of employment roamed the streets. Commercial houses failed; payments were stopped; distress and poverty reigned. In 1812 privateers were fitted out here and shortly after the conclusion of the second war with England the commerce revived. Trade with the West India Islands developed and the low-decked brigs, manned by tanned New Englanders, carried out Maine lumber and dried fish and returned with sugar, rum and molasses. Long Wharf and Portland Pier were stages for a vigorous and spectacular life and it is evident that Henry knew of this life and, boy-like, was caught up in its romance. There

to great noise and the resounding songs of negro steve-
dores the hogsheads of molasses were hoisted from the
dark holds of the brigs. Heavy wagons dragged
by straining horses passed, the drivers snapping their
long whips. Drunken sailors and truckmen roystered
about. And adding to the tumult of the shipping were
the teams coming into the town by way of Deering's
Bridge or by Horse Tavern, charcoal carriers from
Waterborough, shook-loads from Fryeburg and Hiram
and Baldwin, hoop-poles, cord-wood and screwed hay
from towns to the West. Vermonters with their sunburnt faces and in their blue woolen frocks, surveyors
rushing about with a shingle in one hand and a rule-
staff in the other, West India negroes, Spanish sailors,
Revolutionary veterans, a dozen varieties of men contributed to the confusion. There were also the lumber-
yards, the distilleries, the tanneries, the rope-walks,
adding to the general "hustle" of this young town.

One must insist on this "hustle" for it marks the
death of something fine and unadulterated in the old
Colonial life. Business with a big B was lifting an
infant head and stepping out for the first time. Of
course this was true of the entire New England seaboard. The clipper-ship era was at the ports and soon
the white bellying canvas was to fleck the Northern sea.
In the streets of Portland the Revolutionary period
was fading away under the influences of this new democratic, business-immersed life. Pantaloons were super-
seding knee-breeches and the cocked hats and bush wigs
were already archaic. It was only the old men who
clung tenaciously to the habits of the past and wandered out in their queues and spencers and displayed
their shrunken shanks in silk stockings. The daily
speech was far from literary, for Portland was not much
concerned with culture. It was sufficient to call the

old men "daddies," the old women "marms," the ship-masters "skippers," and the teachers "masters." Open fires and brick-ovens still took the place of stoves, and the fires, carefully raked up at night, were kindled the next morning with flint, steel and tinder boxes. Most of the houses had barns behind them and at night-fall the boys drove the cows through the town streets. Carriages were unusual and even as late as 1825 when General Lafayette visited Portland the ball in his honor was meagerly attended because of a sudden storm and the lack of equipages. People walked in those days. The currency was chiefly Spanish dollars, halves, quarters, pistareens, eighths and sixteenths. Portland merchants, cagey as New Englanders are, placed small faith in Federal money and most of the prices were reckoned in shillings and pence. It took two days to get to Boston by accommodation stage and the cost was between eight and ten dollars. Two papers, the old *Portland Gazette* and the *Eastern Argus,* supplied most of the news although the town-crier still went his daily rounds. Portland did not have much time for amusements. Theatrical performances were prohibited under heavy penalties, for the old Puritan prejudices still maintained in some measure. Now and again itinerant players would venture into the town and set up their tawdry scenery in Union Hall. In 1830 a theater was built but the town weakened and it was soon converted into a church. Such amusements as there were proved to be those that did not tax the brain. In the summer there were excursions by sailing boats and in the winter there were sleighing parties, suppers and square dances. All the year around there was rum, cold in the hot months and made up into flips and punches in the winter, for sobriety, one is led to believe, was rather the exception than the rule. There was also church attendance all the year round.

In spite of a certain primitive tinge, the result of a raw newness and a dynamic intensity of growth, there must have been a modicum of culture in this town by Casco Bay. Those merchants, the Matthew Cobbs, the Ebenezer Stores, the Joseph H. Ingrahams, the élite of Congress and Middle Streets, were not altogether business machines. They were the immediate descendants of Pilgrim and Puritan blood, the heirs of Cotton Mather, and though the decorative and emotional arts may have been thrust behind them with a "Retro me, Sathanas!" there was a moral earnestness in their attitude toward life that demanded some sustenance for the soul. A fervent didacticism colored their mental existence but it was surcharged with a sincerity that carried its own emphasis. Since Christopher Leavett first set foot here in 1623 (and how close that is to the first square-toed shoe clattering on Plymouth Rock!) this portion of New England had been an integral part of Pilgrim development. There had been Indian massacres and wars and ambushed assaults on the little corn boats that crept into the bay. In 1690 Lieutenant Thaddeus Clark and thirteen men had been shot down on Munjoy's Hill by the painted Indians. In 1717 Lieutenant-Governor Dummer had reared his spacious tent on this same eminence and entered into a treaty with the red men who came "with French colors and made a great show." It was all a part of the first border history of this country. The breed of men that developed here must be obvious to the reader. Hardheaded, religious, self-assertive, reticent, and, as the years followed and commerce became an end in itself and not merely a means of self-existence, sly, full of

gumption (there is no other word for it), shrewd, inured to adventure through generations of hardship,
these men form Henry's background. The background
had begun to fade when he came but it was still there,
still strong enough to formulate in some measure his
attitude toward life.

Of course, there was also the great outside world.
There was the rest of the Colonies. But it is fairly
evident that they did not impinge too drastically upon
one another. New England was New England just
as New York and Pennsylvania were New York and
Pennsylvania and the South was the South. The arteries of travel were a difficult matter because communication and the diffusion of ideas were almost an impossibility. A group of diverse commonwealths were tied
together in Philadelphia in 1776 and it was to be years
before they partook of a common homogeneity. Portland, therefore, was a city in itself except for its common relationship with the rest of New England. Boston
may have wafted its influences, for Boston was already
crystallizing into that Athens of America that was to
reach across the Charles River and include Henry
for so many decades but outside of Boston there was
little cultural or nationalistic development in New
England. The far-flung towns were working out
their own destinies. The steadily mounting shipping
undoubtedly brought a sense of the broadness of the
earth but it is doubtful if it brought more than that,
for the shipmasters were hardly concerned with abstrac-
tions or the climbing progress of time. The fact that
East Indians might walk the streets of Salem and Spanish sailors might royster in the dock taverns of Portland
without occasioning surprise in the matter-of-fact citizens is not so remarkable.

Yet great things were happening in that outside

world. If we attach ourselves to a date (and 1813 is as good as any for in that year the autumn was ushered in by the sea fight between Captain Stephen Burroughs' brig *Enterprise* and the British *Boxer* off Pemaquid Point and inside Monhegan) and take a swift view of Europe we shall see that much was occurring which was to influence Henry in years to come in so far as it affected *his* Europe. It was in January of this year that Napoleon's shattered "Grande Armée" recrossed the Niemen in full retreat from the Russian forces of Czar Alexander I. On September 4 (the day that the population of Portland massed on Munjoy's Hill to witness the outcome of Burroughs' venture) the Emperor of the French was at Dresden anxiously waiting for the expected onslaught of the Army of Bohemia. Maréchal Ney was advancing Northward from Wittenberg at the head of the army of Berlin. The battle of Leipzig was but a month away and this is important, for Leipzig was the tombstone of Napoleon. It was there that his fortunes shattered and his star was eclipsed. It was God's period set to the long nightmare story that began at Montenotte. In September, 1813, the eagle's wings were bedraggled and the golden bees were tarnished, for the loss of all Germany loomed as a specter over the squat Emperor. In London the mad, blind and melancholy George III mumbled to himself while the Prince Regent varied his love affairs with an amateur diplomacy somewhat clipped by his ministers. There was repression everywhere in the "tight little isle" and an ominously approaching sound of cracking walls and tumbling idols. The British armies of Arthur Wellesley, Duke of Wellington, were pushing hard against the Spanish forces of that wavering puppet, Joseph Bonaparte. In Ireland the ferocious war for the Catholic Emancipation continued.

45

Eugene Beauharnais, the debonair Prince Eugene, was viceroy of Northern Italy and in the south of the boot Joachim Murat was King, little suspecting that execution was already knocking at his door. It was an era of fixed bayonets and the thrones of pretender Kings were shaking in this fierce whirlwind that was rushing over the length and breadth of Europe in the shape of a concerted onslaught against the French Empire. It was, however, more than a war against a single man. It was a vast readjustment and reconstruction. On September 4, 1813, we find Sir Charles Stewart writing to Lord Castlereagh: ". . . However great and formidable the alliance against France now appears, however zealous and cordial all the Powers are for the common cause, still it is impossible the great leaders of the different armies should not have their military opinions in some degree governed by the immediate interests of the power which they serve. It is Russia's interest to act in Saxony inasmuch as she may be looking to it. It is Austria's to rouse the Tyrolese to recover Italy; the movements of Bavaria upon the Danube are more congenial to her objects and make her feel more secure. It is Prussia's to drive the war from Silesia and regain her strong places. All these objects would be accomplished by the overthrow of the enemy, but it ever has and will be the nature of a great alliance that the powers concerned cannot divest themselves of their immediate interests, or forego their future objects during the progress of military operations. No commander-in-chief ever had before two Emperors and a King superintending and controlling not only movements in agitation but also operations decided on . . ."

Society was debauched. Lord Byron was preëminent in the drawing-rooms of London. He was yet to

marry, and, perhaps, already engaged in that alleged in-
cestuous relationship with his half-sister, Augusta
Leigh, which was to be the secret cause of the rift between him and Lady Byron and to afford Harriet
Beecher Stowe so much material for indignation half a
century later. Shelley, hurrying between Bracknell and
London, was suffering from strange delusions and finding sympathy in his new friend, Peacock. Coleridge
was squandering the proceeds of his play, "Remorse,"
on drugs and alienating his superior friends. It was on
this much repeated 4th of September, 1813, that Sir
Walter Scott refused the Poet Laureateship in succession to the poetical Pye in a courteous letter to the
Marquis of Hertford. Robert Southey was to receive
the coveted post and gulp down the annual tun of
wine. Wordsworth, having been appointed distributor
of stamps in the county of Westmorland, had but
recently removed to Rydal Mount and was beaming in
the unexpected luxury of a commodious house. At
Somersby the four-year-old Alfred Tennyson wandered about the ancient Norman cross and saw "the
golden globes lying in the dewy grass among those
apple trees."

In Europe a host of children stood at the closed
door of maturity waiting for it to open. Born in the
thunder of Napoleon's guns the Empire was to be no
more to them than a childish dream. They were to be
christened to this monstrous music, however, and it was
to echo in their blood and brains. These children
were to be contemporaries of Henry and yet how different in development and achievement! In Paris
the eleven-year-old Victor Hugo waited for the sound
of those spiritual trumpets that were to ring in his
ears all through his life. Alexandre Dumas was eight
years old and a romantic child at Villers-Cotterets and

Michelet had reached the ripe age of fifteen. Honoré de Balzac was a boy of fourteen, Prosper Merimée was ten and Gautier was but two. George Sand was nine, Alfred de Vigny was sixteen and De Musset was three. The old era still lingered in Bernardin de St. Pierre who was to live another year and Madame de Staël who survived until 1817. But their work was done. They did not belong to this era. Chateaubriand was at the height of his powers and a young man of twenty-three; Alphonse de Lamartine was at the threshold of fame. In Weimar the old Goethe sat translating Oriental poetry from Hafiz.

Such, in the briefest and most stark terms, was the world into which Henry was inducted, the world that he was to travel and observe in the immediate years that followed 1813. Born from the mingled strains of Pilgrim and Puritan blood, set down in a parochial town just entering upon a vast commercial activity, carefree in so far as the vexing material hardships of life were concerned, correctly placed in the "social swim" of his era, surrounded by such comforts as his time proffered and hedged from the exigencies of self-reliance, he would seem to be particularly adjusted to one of those mansions that faced Preble Street, Portland, in the opening years of the nineteenth century. He must be followed now as well as may be from the distance of a century.

IV

Henry is martial-minded. At the age of six we can hardly attribute any degree of retrospection to his nature, now such fallow soil for impressions, but if we could assemble the memorabilia of his babyhood it would hardly be distinctive. After all, there are few children who are more than the blind reflexes of their

48

environment. The first glimpse of him is in a letter written by his mother when he was eight months old and there we find the fond parent stating: "I think you would like my little Henry W. He is an active rogue and wishes for nothing so much as singing and dancing. He would be very happy to have you raise him up to see the balls on the mirror. . . ." His martial spirit becomes manifest in a letter written by his aunt, Lucia Wadsworth, on May 6, 1812. The war with England had already broken out and a proposed invasion of Canada was in the air. The shade of William Longfellow of Newbury must have been hovering above the writer when she penned: "Canada must be subdued before that time [the Fourth of July] or the opportunity will be lost. Our little Henry is ready to march; he had his tin gun prepared and his head powdered a week ago." But before Henry could march the war came to his very door. Standing on Munjoy's Hill, clutching the sturdy hand of the General, he had seen the white puffs of smoke go up and heard the exultant cries of the townsmen. And there was more to follow.

Three days after Henry had seen those puffs of smoke and heard those cries there were muffled drums in the streets of Portland. There were long faces and subdued voices and the shuffle of slow feet. For the *Enterprise* had come in to port. She had come in with her unwilling prisoner, the British brig *Boxer*, and there had been joy at the triumphant spectacle but the joy had been dampened when the body of Captain William Burroughs had been borne from the deck of his little vessel. It had been dampened, too, when a moment later the body of the British commander, Captain Samuel Blythe, had been placed beside the American officer's remains, for Captain Blythe had been a young

49

and brave antagonist. Ten-oared barges brought the dead commanders ashore. Minute-guns had added their sonorous peals to the day of solemnity. There had been a solemn procession through the streets of Portland the next day when the two dead captains had been carried to the cemetery at the foot of Munjoy's Hill and buried side by side in the cold amity of the grave. Henry was undoubtedly excused from school, if there was any school, for this occasion, and we may see him observing the funereal procession with grave blue eyes. The General has undoubtedly come over from Hiram again and he stands beside his daughter and grandchildren, his clubbed pigtail thrust out, watching and sensing the ghosts that stand by his side watching, too.

The days pass and Henry (whether or no his hair be powdered and his tin gun ready) continues to acquire what is popularly termed an education. His martial ardor persists in some measure, for four months after the sea fight he writes to his father who is on a visit to Boston, requesting a drum, and the agreeable parent responds: ". . . I have found a very pretty drum, with an eagle painted on it, but the man asks two dollars for it; and they do not let any vessels go from Boston to Portland now. But if I can find any opportunity to send it down I shall buy it. . . ." It is to be hoped that Henry got his drum, for it must have made fine music on Munjoy's Hill in the afternoon when the sun slanted westward behind the distant peak of Mount Washington. The desire for this drum is curious, as Henry from the very beginning had been violently averse to loud sounds. He had even, on one Fourth of July, begged the maid most privately to put cotton in his ears so that the sound of the cannon might be muffled. Not

ZILPAH WADSWORTH LONGFELLOW

Courtesy of Margaret E. Harding
Photo by Adams Studio, Inc., of Portland, Maine

that he was afraid! He indignantly denied that allegation.

This martial flurry indubitably made a deep impression on Henry's sensitive nature, and, perhaps, destroyed for a time the routine of his childish days. It flung him out of the parochial atmosphere wherein he existed and which was circumscribed by his home life and his days at school, for he had been at school since he was three years old. This home life and these days at school are important for they are the shell from which Henry's mind was hatched. We have already noted the varied aspects of color that Portland had to offer the boy and now it is time to step within the old Wadsworth house and discover what sustenance was there for a growing mind that was as yet a tangle of unformulated urges.

v

Henry's household was not small. Besides his father and mother and Aunt Lucia, there came to be three brothers and four sisters. There is Stephen, born in 1805; Elizabeth, born in 1809; Anne, born in 1810; Alexander, born in 1815; Mary, born in 1816; Ellen, born in 1818; and Samuel, born in 1819. Not all of these children, it will be observed, form a portion of the milieu of Henry's small boyhood. But there is Stephen and Elizabeth and Anne, and perhaps, Alexander and Mary, although Henry has progressed past the ripe age of eight when they arrive. It was still the era of large families, the period of a generous fecundity. Life, being a matter of severe duties, implied certain unescapable things. For instance, the woman's sphere was emphatically within the home and the bear-

ing and upbringing of offspring was the chief duty
for which she had been placed upon a more or less
goodly earth. Henry's seven brothers and sisters,
therefore, were not indicative of an exceptional fondness for children, any more than they were proof positive of parents who fitted (as they certainly did) most
decisively into the best traditions of their contemporary
current of living. Stephen and Zilpah loved their children. There is ample evidence to show that the father
was kindly, open-handed, tolerant, and blessed with
a natural aptitude for the best in life, while Zilpah, in-
valid though she was for the greater part of her days,
was all that is implied in the word mother. Henry's
home, therefore, was a pleasant abode untarnished of
the usual vexations and impregnated with whatsoever
culture the times had to offer. The boy could play
whatever games he chose as long as he did not play
them on Sunday. Upon that day, the day about which
the New England social scene of the time revolved so
self-consciously, profane books and diversions were set
aside. The family "went to meeting" twice, and we
may picture the small Henry walking beside his frail
mother, carrying her little foot-stove of hot coals on
cold days, for the First Parish Meeting-House must
have been a draughty place. Already the moderate
Calvinism of the old preachers had shifted into the
early form of Unitarianism preached by the Reverend
Ichabod Nichols, who, according to various accounts,
was a man of some intellectual powers, but who hid
his light under the bushel-basket of timidity. It is well
to emphasize the New England Sunday for it was
undoubtedly partially because of this day that Henry's
mind became so ingrained with that didactic disposition
that was to weaken his poetical powers. The pros and
cons of the New England Sabbath would require a com-

plete study in itself.   There is ample argument to be
adduced as to its necessity in a land where the material
struggle toward an established commonwealth was so
overwhelming.   It may be viewed from an economic
aspect.   Its relation to the fine arts is another matter
entirely.   It was on this day that Henry was never permitted to forget that he was a humble creature of God.
He, as well as his ancestors, had been preserved by a
Divine Power.   Sandwiched between the "meetings"
was Bible-reading, generally conducted by Zilpah, and
the sober inspection of atrocious engravings of Scrip-
tural scenes, scenes so badly drawn as to put the fear
of God into any youngster, as an inspection of the
illustrated Bibles of that time will show.   There were
also the "family records," always an important adjunct
to the family Bible, wherein one might note the deaths
and births.   These records were pegs upon which hung
histories in little of New England development.   Then,
in the evening, there were hymns to be sung, psalmody
from the *Bridgewater Collection.*   We may imagine
Henry's voice piping up in that old favorite:

> While Thee I seek, protecting Power,
> Be my vain wishes stilled.

Certainly Henry's "vain wishes" did not include that
tin gun and drum.

The tolerance of Henry's father may have lessened
the rigors of the usual New England Sunday for it is
believed that it was at his urging that the covenant of
the First Parish was modified.   Stephen may have been
the unalloyed product of Pilgrim and Puritan bloods
but he also possessed a sense of humor and an integrity
that would not permit him to subscribe to doctrinal
statements that were too stark and illuminated by Hell

Fire. He thought about religious matters for himself and did not rely on the preachers implicitly. And as Stephen was an important figure in Portland and a valued parishioner the church managed to see things his way. Henry, it is to be suspected, did not regard his Sundays as too onerous. He probably liked the Bible pictures and took some pleasure in the hymns, for he was of a naturally religious disposition and not at all analytic about it.

It was not always Sunday, however, and the six remaining days of the week could be filled with a thousand and one things. Outside of school hours there were ball, kite-flying, and swimming in the summer, and snowballs, coasting and skating in the winter. Henry partook of these boyish pastimes rather moderately for he was never in love with rough sports. We shall see that his being was not of the sort that mingled promiscuously; a certain fastidiousness was implicit in his nature from the first. It revealed itself in his unusual neatness as a child and became almost emphatic in the near-foppishness of his young manhood. Although the circus and the menageries might lure him from his home he was probably more at ease among the books in his father's library or listening to music, especially after his sister had replaced the mother's spinet with a real piano. This question of books is extremely important for books edged so into Henry's life as to nullify a portion of its natural existence. An important part of his being was sustained by books and the major part of his inspiration, such as it was, was to rise from the printed page throughout the long years that followed his first readings. His father's library was not large—it must be remembered that it was not an era of particular culture —but it was well selected, for Stephen Longfellow was animated by a natural bent toward the best. On the shelves, therefore, Henry might find Shakespeare, Milton, Pope, Dryden, Thomson and Goldsmith. Then there was *The Spectator*, the *Rambler*, the *Lives of the Poets*, *Dr. Johnson's Rasselas*, *Plutarch's Lives*, and the histories of Hume, Gibbon, Gillies and Robertson. All this reading, of course, remained untouched on Sunday for it would never do to read, for example, *Hamlet* on that blessed day. Instead of the bard of Avon, Henry must content himself with Hannah More's choice and moral works. For some obscure theological reason Bunyan's *Pilgrim's Progress* was banished from these shelves on week-days as well as Sundays. John Bunyan, probably, was not an incipient Unitarian, but the prophet of a false gospel. So Henry contented himself with such books as were persona grata and evidently got great pleasure from them. Cowper was a particular favorite and so, too, was Thomas Moore's *Lalla Rookh*. Then there were *Robinson Crusoe*, the *Arabian Nights* (in a carefully expurgated edition), *Don Quixote* (a curious and admirable choice for Henry to make) and *Ossian*. The hollow and windy bombast of this last afforded the boy ample opportunity to let off the steam of his lively nature as he went about the house declaiming it. It is impossible, of course, to estimate the influence of this reading on Henry's impressionable nature. He, himself, asserted in after years: "Every reader has his first book; I mean to say, one book among all others which in early youth first fascinates his imagination, and at once excites and satisfies the desires of his mind. To me, this first book was the *Sketch-Book of Washington Irving*." The influence of the *Sketch Book* will be noted hereafter when Henry has emerged from Bowdoin into his father's law office and is casting about for some pleasant avocation to lighten the dull passages of Blackstone. But, for the present, it may be dismissed as one of many pricks that awakened the mild creative instincts in the boy.

It has been said that there was music in this household. Besides the hymns there were such bouncing pieces (not on Sunday!) as *The Battle of Prague, Governor Brook's March, Washington's March,* and other sonorous trifles. The songs, of course, were the usual favorites of the day, *Henry's Cottage Maid, Brignal's Banks, Bonnie Doon, The Last Rose of Summer,* and *Oft in the Stilly Night.* Henry, who by this time was an attendant at singing school, entered lustily into these vocal renditions. Whether or not he possessed a good voice is one of the mysteries of Time. It is probable that the singing lessons, guided by the old-fashioned tuning fork, may have smoothed out some of the roughness. Then there was dance music, too, which is in itself a proof of the broadness and tolerance of the father. Indeed, what with his attitude toward a softened doctrine, his piano and Henry's attendance at dancing school, it becomes apparent that Stephen was one of the most progressive-minded Portlanders of his time. He was a private pleasure as well as a public servant. And because he was so we catch a glimpse of Henry stepping out in the *Money Musk, The Haymakers,* or *The Fisher's Hornpipe.*

The evenings (and whoso has lived in New England will remember the winter evenings) were occupied with lessons first of all. The small satchels were opened and the worn books disgorged to the table and the little heads bowed over the creaky slates. Outside the long blast of the evening mail horn might sound and in the great fireplace the burning logs might sing and crackle, but the Longfellows were immersed. They were getting educated. And after the slates and books were put away there were games until the tolerant Stephen, intent upon his law papers, shooed them out, whereupon the children pattered to the kitchen where the black crane, disporting a fish baked in effigy upon its back, hung over the fireplace. And after the frolic in the kitchen there was the dreary procession upstairs from the lighted rooms to the unwarmed bed-chambers where the frost freaked white arabesques upon the panes, and there was a hurried snuggling into the huge featherbeds, those soft stuffed whales that were the pride of New England once. Outside the bitter wind might whistle and the New England winter snarl at the rattling windows but Henry was safe for the time being. And in the morning there was the breaking of ice in the pitchers for water wherewith to wash one's drowsy face. There was the big blazing breakfast. There was the grinning face of old Dick Richards, Stephen's colored man, to carry Henry off to school, the servant promising all the while to bequeath his cottage on Munjoy's Hill to the small boy.

Yes, of course, there was school.

VI

Henry, reaching the ripe age of three, became a pupil of Ma'am Fellows, who conducted a small brick schoolhouse in Spring Street. Although the influence of the school mistress extended over a brief period it is well to pause and regard Ma'am Fellows, for she belonged to that ancient type of terror that is the natural sworn enemy of every small boy. Her ideas of rigid discipline extended to the fervent belief that "one should never smile in school hours" and we may guess that nobody wanted to smile when she was about. Her prime function appears to have been to teach letters and respect for one's elders. It would be pleasant to ascribe a sort of boyhood familiar to some of Dickens' youths to Henry if only to inject a sympathetic note into these paragraphs but there is no evidence that the boy had a particularly bad time at Ma'am Fellows. "My recollections of my first teacher," stated Henry in after years, "are not vivid; but I recall that she was bent on giving me a right start in life; that she thought that even very young children should be made to know the difference between right and wrong; and that severity of manner was more practical than gentleness of persuasion. She inspired me with one trait,— that is, a genuine respect for my elders." This appears to be an extremely graceful way of saying that Ma'am Fellows carried a switch. If Ma'am Fellows' school was a sort of Dotheboys Hall one would like to hear more about it, but any knowledge of New England schools of a century ago will show that severity was not an unusual part of the curriculum. Ma'am Fellows, perhaps, was a trifle more austere than the general run of schoolmarms but it must be remembered that she had reached the vinegary age and was gray in service by the time Henry sidled into a bench before her. Anyway, the boy did not remain there long; after the first vacation he was transferred to the town-school on Love Lane, near Centre Street. It was quite near his home and Henry, now about five, would seem to be "set" as far as his primary education was concerned. But, not so. Complications ensued.

After one week of the public school Henry was removed from it and sent to a private establishment conducted by one Nathaniel H. Carter. The reason was simple: the school boys in Love Lane were too rough. Apparently the name of the thoroughfare had no psy-

chological influence on adolescent natures. There is
much that is revelatory of Henry's nature in this knowledge of his hasty removal. It shows that Henry was
not a public school boy. He was a born private school
boy in spite of his tin gun and drum. There is no implication here that Henry was a hot-house rose although
it may be inferred that he was much nearer the hot-
house in nature than the playing field. He was undoubtedly that type of boy who is so unhappy and lonely
in the generous roughness of the public school. Sensitive, quick to anger, not especially entertained by the
idea of sports, a little mollycoddled by his home life,
he did not possess the powers of adjustment for a successful entry into a lively camaraderie with boys of his
own age. It is possible that he could not stand teasing.
Among other things it is reported that Henry came
home from Love Lane one day with his cheeks burning
with indignation because the master had accused him
of telling a lie. This incident may be dismissed as of
no importance, for if he did not tell a lie he should
have.

Possibly Henry's parents were too hasty in removing
him from the public school and installing him in a
private one, for a boyish knocking about with young-
sters of all sorts and conditions would have benefited
him more than the sole companionship of boys in the
same social set as himself. This lad who remembered
the "Spanish sailors with bearded lips" so well would
possibly have had more vital memories of his boyhood
if it had not been placed upon such a genteel plane.
And yet one cannot speculate too drastically about his
hasty removal from public school life. The boy may
have suffered too much, although his one term with the
switch-wielding Ma'am Fellows should have inured
him to the give-and-take of the public school yard. It

must be remembered, also, that he was extremely young. Anyway, to Nathaniel Carter's private school he went, to stay for a short time, and then, in 1813, to follow the satisfactory Mr. Carter to the Portland Academy where he remained until he was ready for college.

Having observed the life led by the small boy during those hours passed at home we may assume that this ran parallel with the early part of these school days and divide up the years of Henry's primary education into three divisions: his studies, his play-time and his literary excursions. Starting therefore with his studies it may be set down immediately that "co-education" existed without question in those days. Portland Academy housed girls as well as boys. Just before entering the Academy Henry had brought home a "billet."

Master Henry Longfellow is one of the best boys we have in school. He spells and reads very well. He can also add and multiply numbers. His conduct last quarter was very correct and amiable.

June 30, 1813.   N. H. CARTER.

Henry is six years old when he brings home this proud paper. During the next spring he goes "half through his Latin Grammar" and is standing "above several boys twice as old as he." But by this time Henry has lived a lot. He has powdered his hair and gotten his tin gun ready. He has seen the two dead captains carried through the streets of Portland. And he has written his first letter to his father requesting a drum. There has even been a fire in the Longfellow home when the excited Henry has seen flames bursting through the roof, Dr. Weed rushing through the door with Zilpah in his arms and a blanket wrapped about her, and the firemen darting to and fro in obedience to

the orders issuing from the brass trumpet of the chief
perched on a post of the front fence. The years pass
and Henry continues to imbibe an education. He must
have been willing and strenuous and we may guess that
learning was more of a pleasure than anything else.
In 1817 (Henry is now ten years old) the boy goes
under a new preceptor, a gentleman rejoicing in the
name of Bezaleel Cushman and who has been for two
years headmaster of Portland Academy. Except for
"occasional levity" Bezaleel finds Henry's deportment
good. Henry, being of a lively and nervous disposition, probably got the giggles now and then when something particularly funny came up. And then, of course,
there were always those small red-cheeked Portland
damsels sitting opposite. Perhaps Henry was one of
the boys who pierced holes in their desk covers through
which to inspect these same tiny Maine Cleopatras.
Bezaleel was a nervous excitable man, smelling of
tobacco, india rubber and pencils, and it is possible that
he had small patience with youthful philanderers.

Elijah Kellogg, one of Henry's schoolmates, has
left a picture of the boy as he was during these years at
the Portland Academy, and, allowing for the roman-
tico-sentimental aura of the hero worshiper, it may be
accepted as authentic enough. "He was a very handsome boy," wrote Mr. Kellogg of Henry. "Retiring,
without being reserved, there was a frankness about
him that won you at once. He looked you square in
the face. His eyes were full of expression, and it
seemed as though you could look down into them as into
a clear spring. . . . He had no relish for rude sports;
but loved to bathe in a little creek on the border of
Deering's Oaks; and would tramp through the woods
at times with a gun, but this was mostly through the
influence of others; he loved much better to lie under

a tree and read. . . . If he was a thoughtful, he certainly was not a melancholy, boy . . ." It was Stephen, Henry's elder brother, who was fond of hunting and there is an account that Henry came home one day greatly upset from a gunning expedition with his brother. He had shot a robin and the spectacle of the dead bird had brought tears to his eyes.

During the frequent vacations from school (the terms at Portland Academy were divided into quarters with a week's freedom at the end of each, and, perhaps, two weeks in the summer months) Henry made visits to his grandfather Longfellow's house in Gorham, a few miles from Portland, or he went to Hiram, still farther from Portland, where General Peleg Wadsworth had built himself a residence in the midst of his seven-thousand-acre estate, "Wadsworth's Grant," between the Saco and Ossipee rivers. Henry came into close touch with the Revolutionary era, with the old fighters, during these visits. He touched hands with the iron that was the backbone of New England. There in the pleasant untrammeled wildernesses of Maine he discovered and knew that quiet rural life that was filled with the cool ardors of country living. He saw nature there untouched by any false overlays of a rapidly sprouting civilization. To Gorham he went through a dreary deserted road that was reputed to be haunted and a little of the somber taciturnity of the stone-flawed land must have impressed itself upon his imaginative mind. There were elm trees about the homestead at Gorham and beneath the windows grew syringa and sweetbriar and the blood-hued damask roses. Across the road was the blacksmith's shop, and, as the heavy-hoofed farm horses trampled in to be shod, memories of the first Stephen Longfellow, Stephen the blacksmith, must have permeated the air. There was a brook and a creaky wooden bridge and a one-story schoolhouse sitting forlornly at the turn of the road. Three miles away was the village of Gorham Corner where the farmers rode in for supplies. Still nearer, in fact next door, was the farm of Samuel Stephenson, who had married Stephen Longfellow's sister and was therefore uncle to Henry. It is easy enough to recreate Henry's vacation days at Gorham. He followed the mowers, drove in the cows, observed the cheese presses in the dairy, reddened his fingers and mouth with wild strawberries, took part in the fall corn-husking, and filled the quills for the looms. There were meadows rich in pennyroyal wherein to lie and there were the seasons whereon to feed, the late spring with its young greens and sprouting buds, the summer with its heavy-headed luxuriance, the autumn in its bewildering array of colors, and the warm windless magic of the Indian summer, that season of all seasons in New England.

At Hiram he found the same country magic on a larger scale. He found, too, the old General with his tales of war, his accounts of the redcoats, his narrative of escape by night. The General must be emphasized again and again for he was of such dynamic stuff as to have shaped in some measure the youthful mind of Henry. It was the General who, as a recent graduate from Harvard College, had protested in 1771 at the "servile reception" tendered by the educational institution to the Royal Governor, Hutchinson. He had even written some verses at that time entitled, *On the Decay of Virtue and Increase of Politeness and Servility at Harvard College.* He belonged to the old breed and he must have filled Henry with awe and admiration and martial thoughts. There were other inducements to martial thoughts near Hiram, too, for not so far away was the town of Fryeburg, and in this town was a small clear lake called Lovewell's (or Lovell's) Pond. It was here that an Indian fight took place that was to form the subject of Henry's first published poem.

The youthful writings of Henry were, without exception, extraordinarily bad and imitative. He entered literature with those weaknesses that were to be with him all through his life, weaknesses of dependence, weaknesses of didactic emphasis, weaknesses of prosiness, weaknesses of the creative instinct. It is naturally to be assumed that the boyish writer would be handicapped by innumerable puerilities but it is certainly to be expected that the mature writer would eradicate them to a greater extent than Henry ever did. The attention paid to his early productions therefore is more to show a juvenile fecundity than anything else. It is also to illustrate that itching urge upon which Henry's life was based, and which, in spite of the universality of his fame, he fumbled so badly. He was like his era, blessed with a few good points and cursed with innumerable bad ones that were the result of a slovenly adjustment toward life. The first prong of a double-horned theses may be prophesied here, although it is as yet too early to actually take it up. It is that actual achievement in literature between 1820 and 1880 in America was in direct ratio to the writer's power to shake himself clear of the American spirit as then exemplified in print. Success in American letters was quite another thing. One had but to jump into the mediocre tide and float along with it. Of course, there were exceptions, half a dozen, perhaps, but these figures only prove the rule. Henry was partially representative of this mediocre tide although foreign influences unmistakably molded the huge and imposing edifice which he reared upon such a shallow vein of gentle talent. Time has already lamentably breached this edifice but from the ruins we may observe an entire period in American letters.

Henry, by his ninth year, had given his adoring parents some reason to believe that he possessed an aptitude for letters, although it is fairly evident that the idea of a professional literary career was far from their thoughts. The boy was destined to become a lawyer like his father. Traditions about the boyhood of famous men are generally untrustworthy, for the hero-worshiper unconsciously enlarges upon and overemphasizes them in after years. Therefore the turnip story about Henry may be taken for what it is worth. The tradition is that Henry upon being requested to write a composition modestly shrunk from the ordeal. The teacher thereupon asked him if he could not write words and Henry averred that he could. "Then, you can put words together?" "Yes, sir." "Then you may take your slate, and go out behind the schoolhouse, and there you can find something to write about; and then you can tell what it is, what it is for, and what is to be done with it; and that will be a composition." Henry took his slate and wandered off, presumably somewhat dubiously. He went behind Mr. Finney's barn and there he chanced to see a most excellent turnip growing in all its pristine glory. Intense concentration must have convinced the boy that he knew what it was, what it was for and what would be done with it. Anyhow, he based his first composition upon it and took it back to his teacher, who, according to the tradition, was properly surprised. It is difficult to conceive the reason for the teacher's surprise at this accomplishment. One would think that the surprise would have been more logical if Henry had *not* been able to set down what the turnip was, what it was for and what would be done with it.

Henry's first real composition in verse form appears to have been "Venice, an Italian Song," written when he was thirteen years old and still a student at the Portland Academy. His first publication followed close upon this and the date may be set down. It was November 17, 1820. Certainly the Indian fight at Lovewell's (or Lovell's) Pond was the inspiration. This skirmish made a deep impression on the boy and it is to be expected that he set the line down with some excitement in the achievement. It was with fear and trembling that he carefully copied the verses, slipped out of the house and ran down to Mr. Shirley's printing office at the foot of Exchange Street where he cautiously slipped the poem into the letter box. The evening before the next issue of the semi-weekly *Portland Gazette* appeared he stood shivering in the November twilight before the office, watching the windows shake as the small press printed the paper. We may imagine his excitement the next morning when he secured the sheet and saw printed in real type:

THE BATTLE OF LOVELL'S POND

Cold, cold is the north wind and rude is the blast
That sweeps like a hurricane loudly and fast,
As it moans through the tall waving pines lone and drear,
Sighs a requiem sad o'er the warrior's bier.

The war-whoop is still, and the savage's yell
Has sunk into silence along the wild dell;
The din of the battle, the tumult, is o'er
And the war-clarion's voice is now heard no more.

The warriors that fought for their country—and bled,
Have sunk to their rest; the damp earth is their bed;
No stone tells the place where their ashes repose,
Nor points out the spot from the graves of their foes.

They died in their glory, surrounded by fame,
And Victory's loud trump their death did proclaim;
They are dead; but they live in each Patriot's breast,
And their names are engraven on honor's bright crest.

HENRY.

Time and again the boy read his performance and each time it seemed to him more perfect. But he was desirous of adult criticism and that very evening at the home of Judge Mellen, a friend of his father's, he received it. "Did you see the piece in to-day's paper?" asked the Judge. "Very stiff, remarkably stiff; moreover, it is all borrowed, every word of it." Alas, for the hopes of the ambitious adolescent! Henry had come into direct contact with "the critic" for the first time in a career that was to extend over sixty years. Somewhere in the world a little boy named Edgar Allan Poe must have burst out laughing at that moment. But sanguineness, always a characteristic of Henry, offered its comfortable shoulder and the boy proceeded with his literary endeavors. From time to time during Henry's last year at Portland Academy various "efforts" appeared in the *Portland Gazette,* and the family, certainly "in" on the secret by this time, must have offered both praise and criticism. Henry even started a sort of literary partnership with a school chum named William Browne. In this friend's letters to Henry we may observe such telling bits as "I think your lines were excellent," "As to your Epigram, which you pronounce so bad, I find no fault in it," "I hope you will send me the whole of your Tragedy, *in partibus,* i.e., by inches," and "Concerning that thing you call a Comedy, I shall not send it you, *quia non habeo;* in plain Greek, ωλεται; anglicé, it is destroyed." From which we observe that Henry and William are learned youths who have paid some attention to their Greek and Latin. By 1821 the two friends are considering a series of papers to be written by them alternately, for which "the less assuming name of *The Spectator*" is suggested.

All of this, of course, is unimportant except in so far as it reveals to us the natural inclinations of Henry. He is, we see, a boy with an instinctive leaning toward sedentary and scholarly pursuits, rather averse to the sportive intercourse of the usual type of New England boy. There is no particular illumination of brilliancy here. It is true that Henry is but thirteen when he starts writing poetry but we must remember that he was three years old when he started to go to school, that he enjoys the pleasant culture of an adequate home, that he is not the harum-scarum sort of lad, that his imagination has been kindled by martial fires and memories, and that he has been fed on good books since he first learned to read. His father is what used to be denominated "a pillar of the Commonwealth" and his mother is a gracious creature with instinctive leanings toward culture. And so Henry passes through his short boyhood (children apparently aged more rapidly in those early days) rather sheltered from the outrageous usages of the world and, because of this protection, a bit "stuffy" in the schoolboy sense of the word. This "stuffiness" becomes more noticeable when he enters Bowdoin College and it is more properly considered at that point of his career.

It is in September, 1821, at the age of fourteen years and six months, that Henry matriculates at Bowdoin. To all intents and purposes his boyhood is ended.

CHAPTER TWO
The Wilderness College

THE brown logs spin and churn in the river while the boys in their quaint, old-fashioned garments stand on the green bank. There is a sharp bite in the north wind that comes tearing through the tall trees, for it is late autumn and the early winter is already whipping the lean hounds of cold before it. The pines, the birches and the bushes stand desolately, shivering in anticipation of driving sleet and heavy snows. New England crouches like a giant with head bowed between his knees and granite shoulders uplifted against the gales which are muttering ominously from the Canadian border. This New England, this twilight-land of snow and stone and shade, so magically transformed into a dawn-land, into a Land of Promise by a weather-beaten horde of pioneers, is like one of the graven gods in the prophetic books of William Blake. The boys who stand, arms entwined, on the bank of the Androscoggin are unaware of the gigantic aspects implicit in the nature of their rocky corner of the world. They are standing on the threshold of manhood but before they may step over the lintel they must clear their minds of childish things, even, perhaps, of a national childishness. Before them stretch certain years of intellectual cultivation, years wherein they must pore over musty books and attain some comprehension of the finer pursuits of living. The fare to be fed them is dubious but they are unconscious of this for they possess no standards by which to gauge its limitations. This primitive corner of the world is no Athens, no Salamanca, no Sorbonne, no Cambridge. It is rough-hewn, untutored, traditionless, unconscious of the sweeping perspective of life. There is nothing established here, no mellowed aspects of experience. The years have yet to

69

pour a scholastic atmosphere over the humble buildings which have translated Brunswick into a college town. The boys stand silently and watch the rushing river while the wind tears at the branches above their heads. One of them does not know it but he has already set his feet on a long path which is to lead him across seas and into the great cities of the world and raise him apart from his fellow men.

II

This Bowdoin College to which Henry and his older brother, Stephen, are admitted requires some attention. It is certainly not to be mentioned in the same breath with that Harvard already patronized by Longfellows and Wadsworths. Indeed, it falls in the category of what we denominate "one-horse" affairs. It is small, limited in means, decidedly countrified in its aspects. Henry and Stephen go there for various reasons. It is near Portland. Henry's father is a trustee of the institution. Local pride is at stake. It has been but a year since Maine, sliced off from Massachusetts, became a state in its own right. The vast majority of students in Portland Academy naturally gravitate toward Bowdoin. The college, but twenty years old, is growing and its development becomes a matter of prime importance to the ambitious Maine burghers who see in it a possible rival to the more classic and mellowed halls of Cambridge. Henry and Stephen, therefore, are caught up in a sentimental urge which is bulwarked by various economic considerations. Being so young— Stephen is but two years older than Henry—the boys follow the precedent of other freshmen and remain at home during their first year. Such studies as are assigned them are pursued in Portland and they are assimilated to such good purpose that the boys run neck and neck with those students who are properly installed in Brunswick. Therefore when they do go to Bowdoin for residence they are qualified to enter the sophomore class. It is possible that Zilpah has done her share toward the inculcation of pedagogical knowledge, if not directly, certainly by persuasive measures. It is in the autumn of 1822 that Henry and Stephen go to Brunswick and install themselves in the house of the Rev. Mr. Titcomb in the village, a house, by the way, where Harriet Beecher Stowe is to write *Uncle Tom's Cabin* many years later. It is a cold house, sparse in furnishings, carpetless, and the boys must make their home in a bleak room unadorned except for bombazine window curtains and a set of card racks painted by their younger sister. Coming from the comparative luxury of the Longfellow home in Portland and being away from their parents for the first time both Henry and Stephen must have experienced the bewildered nostalgia of homesickness. After all, they came from a home that boasted the largest front room in Portland. The fierce New England winter comes down upon their new quarters and even the blazing wood fire in the open fireplace does not warm the room sufficiently. Zilpah is concerned over her departed children and writes: "I am sorry to find that your room is cold. I fear learning will not flourish, nor your ideas properly expand, in a frosty atmosphere, and I fear the Muses will not visit you, and that I shall have no poetic effusion presented on New Year's day." We begin to get a picture of a small village house, bleak in the late autumn and cowering amidst heavy snow-drifts in the winter. The windows are frozen white with frost. The crimson fire lolls bright tongues from the andirons but outside of a small semi-circle the room

is chilly. The bombazine curtains blow in the wind
which forces its way through the window frames. The
boys hover close to the fireplace during the long evenings. Henry is striving as well as his frost-nipped
fingers will permit to put together that "poetic effusion" which the newspaper carriers will present to their
patrons on the first of the year.

And now what about this college to which the boys
walk every morning, their heels crunching the ice-
crusted snow? As has been said, it is a "one-horse"
affair. It is simple and frugal, exerting such civilizing
powers as it may. Education in New England has not
as yet reached that state where the psychological factors
are taken into consideration. In 1802 there was only
one collegiate building at Brunswick. Five or six years
later Maine hall was erected. The process of augmen-
tation went on slowly and by Henry's time the institution may not have been imposing but it was at least
respectable from the viewpoint of a year-old State. It
was a college, not an academy. The new State of
Maine was behind it and, handicapped though it was
by insufficient funds, it nevertheless managed to secure
a corps of instructors who at least had the semblance
of college professors. They were adequate to their
time. Saying so much one says little, for professorial
adequacy in America during the first two decades of
the nineteenth century was rather deplorable. The
spectacle of Bowdoin in 1822, therefore, is not particularly thrilling. There were the few modest buildings, the gutted walls of Maine Hall which had been
destroyed by fire a year earlier, the small, unheated
chapel where the students shivered during religious
exercises, the barren, sandy campus with its scant herb-
age and its row of balm-of-gilead trees along the front,
the forest—not a particularly picturesque forest—sur-

rounding the entire institution, the few small buildings —one of them a blacksmith shop—on the road opposite, the rumbling lumber mills across the Androscoggin, and the sluices down which the turbid water raced with huge logs. Through the halls of the college tramped generations of boys who were to play important parts in the upbuilding of the state and country. Potential writers, lawyers, public figures, even (in Henry's time) a future President, found here those points of mental vantage from which to spring toward more impressive things. It was all rural, of course, and decidedly parochial. The training was shot through and through with religious impulses; regular habits were enforced, and a gravity of demeanor undoubtedly approved. The professors peregrinated from room to room, for recitations were held in the private quarters of the undergraduates for the most part, and dispensed an inefficient classical curriculum. There was little in the way of light amusements in the winter. Two societies flourished, the Athenæan and Peucinian, and their fall exhibitions were the most notable literary occasions of the college year.

The fall and spring seasons permitted outdoor diversions of various sorts. There were blueberries to gather under the pines where it was so pleasant to recline with a textbook and strive to concentrate on studies. There was always the Androscoggin where one could watch the logs tumbling along with the current, logs that were to form the beams of mansions merely conceived in fancy as yet. There were trout to catch in the shaded forest streams, bat-fowling in the long summer twilights, and pigeon and squirrel hunting among the tall trees during the day. Henry took but small part in these hunting diversions. They were more in the line of his martial-minded elder

73

brother, Stephen. Henry was engrossed in his teachers and studies for already the relentless bee of literature was buzzing in his bonnet. Fond pictures of preëminence in letters were dimly flashing at him among the tall pines but he was yet to actually put forward the idea to his father. The youth sat before his instructors and waited.

Who were these teachers and what had they to offer Henry? The Rev. William Allen, a Harvard graduate who had been president of Dartmouth College for a short time, was at the head of this Maine institution. He appears to have been a somewhat harsh figure. Years later, Dr. David Shepley, in a paper on the class of 1825 at Bowdoin, had this to say of him: "He may have been a little too unbending, have passed a student without recognition, or undesirably mistaken a name or person. His hymn book was one of those mistakes of which no good account can be given." Dr. Shepley goes on to affirm that President Allen was a scholar and a gentleman, but it is to be suspected that he was looking through the magic sentimental glasses of the past. With that blind kindliness that smothered the actuality of so many pictures of American life and men at that time he carefully looked for the best and rigorously ignored half the aspects which might shatter his fond portrayal. Rev. Mr. Allen seems to have been the well-known type of narrow-minded, ultrareligious pundit who existed in educational establishments at the beginning of the nineteenth century. Assisting him were such forgotten men as John Abbott, the professor of languages; Parker Cleaveland, who filled the chair of mathematics and natural history and who became a sort of Bowdoin institution through fifty-three years of teaching at the college; Rev. William Jenks, the professor of Oriental and English lan-

guages; and Samuel P. Newman, who taught Greek
and Latin until 1824 when he was succeeded by Alpheus S. Packard.   Of all these teachers Professor
Cleaveland appears to have been the most brilliant for
he wrote a work on mineralogy which won the praise
of Humboldt, Sir Humphrey Davy, Baron Cuvier and
other European authorities.   Cleaveland gave illustrated addresses in the towns of the state in addition
to his regular work at Bowdoin and he was wont to
travel with a yoke of oxen drawing the wagon upon
which he piled his apparatus.   It is a pleasant picture,
this of the pedagogue tramping through the snow behind his cloven-hoofed team and so bringing educational light to the Maine communities.   It would be
easy to grow sentimental about these forgotten and
shadowy men and assert that training under them was
a rare and precious gift.   However, there is no reason
to believe that this was so.   It is true that various commentators on Henry's college years have intimated as
much, but all these commentators have been kindly and
naïve souls who bent every effort toward revealing
shining perfections in Henry that were certainly not
there.   He was never a great scholar.   He was never
an authority on anything.   He was intelligent, active-
minded, but meagerly endowed with that profundity
and intuitiveness which mark great scholars.   And his
instructors, dogged in the pursuit of knowledge as we
may admit them to have been, suffered under distinct
limitations not the least of which were their religious
biases.

At Bowdoin Henry was in a peculiar position which,
perhaps, he did not realize.   The old Calvinistic tradition was still powerful at the college and Henry, it
will be remembered, came from a family who leaned
toward early Unitarianism.   Channing's important

75

sermon on Unitarianism had been preached in 1819 and what the late Barrett Wendell called "the religious and philosophic buoyancy of the New England Renaissance" was already gathering speed. It was to develop a new type of mind in New England as the edges of religious dogma grew less stark and cutting. The hard sharp outlines were to be dimmed. The old Puritanical fortresses were crumbling. Just what Henry's acutest reactions were to the spiritual emanations of Brunswick during his college days are problematical but we do know that he was among the minority so far as religious observances were concerned. Writing in 1824 to George W. Wells, a friend, he states: "I presume he [another friend noted as P——,] has frequently mentioned to you our little Unitarian Society at Bowdoin. I wish something could be done for us; we are as small as a grain of mustard-seed! There are but six members now, in college, and our library is limited to a hundred or two volumes. I wish you would exert your influence in our behalf. And I want you to purchase twenty-five or thirty copies of a little work called *Objections to Unitarian Christianity Considered*. I want to distribute one or two of them in this section of the globe." And again, in another letter to the same friend, he notes: " . . . I am confident that human systems have done much to deaden the true spirit of devotion and to render religion merely speculative." He was right about this although it does not appear that he ever took any dynamic stand in regard to his convictions. Henry, therefore, is antagonistic to certain phases of religious expression at Bowdoin even to the degree of propaganda. He is deliberate and kindly about it, however, and never harsh and passionate. His home training had alienated him from the majority of students who attended the college but it is evident that this alienation (which Samuel Longfellow called fastidiousness on Henry's part) was a mixture of innate snobbishness (we must remember that as a small boy he was unable to attend public school) and self-immersion. We may judge that he was not conscious of any snobbishness and would have been highly hurt to have the charge leveled against him. "He was known and recognized generally as one of the 'well-to-do' men in the college," remarks George Lowell Austin in one of the earliest books on Henry. This explains his position in part as any impoverished college student will testify.

It is in this small college with its barren and unsightly common that Henry is to pass four years and it is here that his first ambitious poetical efforts are to be composed. There is some necessity therefore to understand these surroundings and how they must have impinged on the consciousness of the intelligent, self-ambitious boy. We may see him walking sedately across the bare campus with his books under his arm, one or two chosen friends about him, pausing where old Uncle Trench is trundling his barrow of root-beer and gingerbread, plain and sugared, to make a small purchase. He is well dressed, reticent, quite the young master of himself. He speaks rather slowly and he emanates, possibly, an aura of that aristocracy which is to hover about him all his life. He is the son of a trustee and he bears himself as such. The young man is likable none the less as many of his classmates were to affirm.

III

Henry's years at Bowdoin were singularly uneventful. We catch the usual glimpses of the thoughtful, poetically minded, somewhat sedentary undergraduate pursuing his studies with concentrated gusto. Although he appears always to have been well prepared for his recitations—his chief difficulties being in the higher mathematics—he was a general reader as well. Therefore such letters of his as are extant and available carry the atmosphere of the library. Of course he turns to poetry, first of all. He writes to his mother in April, 1823: " . . . I have this evening been reading a few pages in Gray's Odes. I am very much pleased with them. The 'Progress of Poesy' and the 'Ode on Eton College' are admirable. And many passages of 'The Bard,' though, I confess, quite obscure to me, seem to partake in a great degree of the sublime. *Obscurity* is the great objection which many urge against Gray. They do not consider that it contributes in the highest degree to sublimity; and he certainly aimed at sublimity in these Odes. Every one admires his 'Elegy,' and if they do not like his Odes, they must attribute it to their own want of taste." Here we have a sixteen-year-old boy carrying on solemnly about "sublimity" and "obscurity." It would not do to call this precociousness, for Henry was not precocious. He was merely naturally bright and farther advanced in his general education than most boys are to-day. What he had to say about Gray, for instance, had been said before. His mother's reply to his letter is pertinent, for it seems to dimly foreshadow the attitude which Henry himself is to take toward poetry. She wrote: "Obscurity, you think, is favorable to the sublime. (Henry's loose comments may be twisted to this intimation although he did not say so directly.) It may be so, but I am much better pleased with those pieces which touch the feelings and improve the heart than with those which excite the imagination only and raise perhaps an indistinct admiration,—that is, an admiration of we know not exactly what." How clearly we can see the future work of Henry adumbrated in that phrase about "pieces which touch the feelings and improve the heart." It was the nearest that he ever got to authentic poetry. It is well to remember the influence of Zilpah when we consider the earliest manifestations of Henry, and even in his later phases it is evident that her attitude toward life colored in some measure his own.

Henry continued to write to his mother and to his father (who passed two of the son's college years in Washington as a member of the House of Representatives) and the placid days sped by with their seemingly unending chain of recitations, new books, exhibitions, casual meanderings through the woods, and, finally, the scribbling of poetry. He read Heckwelder's *Account of the History, Manners, and Customs of the Indian Natives of Pennsylvania and the Neighboring States,* for instance, and this resulted in his appearing as King Philip in a dialogue with a schoolmate, James W. Bradbury, who took the rôle of Miles Standish. "He maintained," wrote Bradbury, "that the continent was given by the Great Spirit to the Indians, and that the English were wrongful intruders." Somewhere, it is to be presumed, the spirit of Samuel Wadsworth who fell in the Sudbury fight must have listened to this bit of dialectic with a tolerant smile. And somewhere else the spirits of two unborn books,—if imagination may conceive of such impossibilities—*Hiawatha* and *The Courtship of Miles Standish,* started up from the nothingness of an unconscious urge. Indeed, the seeds of all his future attempts are already planted in the mind of Henry in so far as they are concerned with America. The boy

79

who wrote *The Battle of Lovell's Pond* is the miniature of the man who wrote *The Courtship of Miles Standish.* From first to last the sentimentalist reigned triumphant.

As the college terms progress Henry dips into philosophy. He tries Locke and finds him "neither remarkably hard nor uninteresting." It throws a certain light on his character to discover that he began the philosopher with the determination to like him "at any rate." We have the excellent schoolboy here. He finds out deliberately what is good for him and attacks it assiduously. This sanguinity of temperament is communicated to all his daily adjustments, to all his thoughts. He would like to be in Washington during the winter, for instance, but knows that such a desire is vain. "It would be more pleasant to get a peep at Southern people and draw a breath of Southern air, than to be always freezing in the North," he remarks a trifle wistfully. Dominating this weakness, he goes on resolutely, "but I have very resolutely concluded to enjoy myself heartily wherever I am." There is a bit of the old Puritanical timbre here. It is implicit in a scorn of adverse surroundings, or, if not a scorn, at least a willingness to adjust himself to the life about him. There is adjustment, too, in his remark, "I find it most profitable to form such plans as are least liable to failure." From one point of view this declaration is a distinct exhibition of an undue cautiousness in the long adventure of living. Henry will never venture all for the sake of a flaming ideal. The perilous and rocky highways of the world are not for his feet. Although certain of his manifestations are tinged with the Puritanical indomitability to adversities of circumstance the greater part of his nature has fallen away from any starkness of attitude.

The same cautiousnesss is shown in his consideration
of physical exercise, for instance. Henry, not particularly enamored of games (he was probably very bad
at them) took his exercise in walking. But one cannot
walk with any degree of comfort through a New England winter. Frozen ears and nipped toes are apt to
be the price for the constitutional so gained. The
deep and drifted snows obliterate the paths, anyway.
Of course, there is wood-chopping but Henry describes
that as "irksome." Therefore he casts about him for
some means of keeping his slight and dapper form in
trim that will yet be not too onerous. His imagina-
tiveness hits upon an unexpected strategy. He marks
out an image on his closet door about his own size and
whenever he feels the need of exercise he hauls off
his jacket, and, to use his own language, "considering
this image in a posture of defense, make . . . motions
as though in actual combat." The spectacle of Henry
shadow-boxing at his closet door with his long brown
locks fluttering in the frosty air must have been highly
diverting. "This is a very classick amusement," he
remarks to his father. But even "classick" amusements have their dangers and he goes on to state that
his "only doubt with regard to its utility is, whether it
may not be too violent." Such a remark from a boy
of sixteen is, to say the least, astonishing.

Not all of these college years are taken up with
reading, with the study of Mr. Locke and discussions
on such important questions as "whether the soul always thinks," with Exhibitions and the difficulties of
writing good dialogues, with perusal of political despatches in the *New York Statesman*—about as uninteresting to Henry "as so many columns of the trades-
man's advertisements . . . " or with singing classes.
There are vacation periods, the majority of which are

passed at home in Portland where Henry enters whole-heartedly into the social gayeties of his particular circle. Being, to a certain degree, at least, financially independent, the young man does not have to take up teaching in small country towns. He can go home and idealize the young ladies of Portland, for besides being young, Henry is quite susceptible to the rustle of silk. It is, however, an innocent susceptibility. "You were ever," wrote one of his youthful friends to him, "an admirer of the sex; but they seemed to you something enshrined and holy,—to be gazed at and talked with, and nothing further." Henry's sensitive and naïve nature undoubtedly made a romantic mooncalf of him.

One memorable vacation (that of 1824) is marked by Henry's first trip to Boston. He is seventeen years old when he first sees the so-called Hub in whose immediate proximity so many years of his long life are to be passed. He leaves Portland in the accommodation stage and passes a stormy night in Portsmouth, where, with a classmate, he walks about the streets a little but can see nothing because of the darkness. In the morning the rain has washed away most of the snow and the sleigh-runners drag along to Newburyport where wheels are put on the coach. Late that evening he reaches the "Literary Emporium" (the curious name frequently given Boston at that time), and puts up at the Exchange Coffee House. His visit is entirely delightful. He sees Charleston and the Navy Yard, Breed's Hill, the Athenæum, the State House, Stewart's painting room, Dogget's Repository. He even goes to Cambridge but has little to say about the town. It is not yet time for him to sense the ghosts of the future. It is twelve years too soon. But he is taken to a "splendid ball" given by Miss Emily Marshall and there he revels in a social function that

must have made the tamer pastimes of Portland seem
countrified indeed. He even dances with Miss Eusta-
phiève, the daughter of the Russian consul, and finds
her a true daughter of Terpsichore, "exceedingly
graceful and elegant." She also plays beautifully upon
the pianoforte. There is even a Jubilee in honor of
"the Bard of Avon" where an "elegant" pageant is
represented, the Tragick Muse appearing in a car
drawn by fiends and the Muse of Comedy drawn by
satyrs. Poor Henry's fluttering heart! It takes him
some time to get calmed and settled down to his studies
again when he returns to Portland.

IV

There is a great deal to be said about college friendships and no comment on Henry's student years, however cursory, would be adequate without due notice of
the various young men of the class of forty-four (only
thirty-eight graduated) wherein Henry found himself
for several years. He lived with these youths, sat in
their midst day after day, discussed with them the
problems of life and letters, experienced the "feel" of
New England with them. Whether or not any one
of them left a mark on Henry's nature is uncertain,
but we may guess that it was slight at best. Henry
was too much himself. He was too well aware of
his station, too deliberate in his adjustment toward the
semi-juvenile prospects of existence. He was a well-
to-do boy from the seaboard town and a proportion
of his immediate coevals were country lads whose wild-
est ambition was the law office or the pulpit. If
Henry possessed any particularly close friendships it
is difficult to nose them out now. He had companions,
yes, but no companions of the soul in the deeper mean-

ing of that phrase. Yet he was friendly, disposed toward intercourse when it was genteel, popular to a
degree and light-hearted, albeit humorless. Friendship
between college youths, it is to be suspected, did not
run deep during the early years of the Republic. The
new citizens were too reticent, too self-conscious, too
dammed up and inhibited by the very quality of their
training to attain that easy, unrestrained, affectionate
intercourse that marked, for example, the English college youth. Therefore we find few Davids and Jona-
thans.

Yet there was apt material from which Henry might
have found the closest bosom companions. Of course,
a proportion of the class of 1825 was altogether outside
his scheme of living and under no consideration would
Henry have attached himself to them. He was a prig
in certain ways, but a prig of the excusable sort. Behind him was a religious and moral training which
could be dashed back to whenever the looser ends of
living became too obnoxiously close. These looser
ends of living could not have been particularly dark but
we must remember that Henry was particularly white.
After all, Bowdoin was a small place, a world in miniature, and its major sins were tardiness, indifference to
studies, gambling and a feeble religious iconoclasm. If
the hydra-headed monster, sex, raised its head we do
not hear of it. Henry confined himself to a group that
was innocent of such escapades and flaws of New England training. There was his brother, Stephen, for
instance. Stephen was two years older than Henry
but he does not seem to have dominated the younger
brother as we would naturally infer. Stephen's case,
after all, was tragic. He was misplaced in life, for
all his desires centered on a military career. He, to
more purpose than Henry, had sat at the feet of Gen-

eral Peleg Wadsworth and listened to those martial
tales of the past, tales wherein the Longfellows and
the Wadsworths had played heroic parts, and from his
earliest childhood he had drawn plans of fortifications,
created mimic battles and assaulted imaginary outposts.
There were drums in his blood and bayonets in his
sparkling eyes. He loved to hunt and fish; in his
nature flared up for the last time in the history of the
Longfellow family the old pioneer and warrior impulses. But Stephen sacrificed himself to the desire of
his father and forced his reluctant feet into more sedentary ways. The long dull prospect of ordinary existence in a Maine law office loomed before him and to
it he eventually went, became a partner in the firm
to which he was unsuited by taste and temperament,
and was lost forever in the minor peccadilloes of the
courtroom. Such a youth could have had but small
interest in the quiet scholarly pursuits of his younger
brother.

The rest of Henry's class settles down under the
long gaze of time and certain figures rise to the top
for examination. They are important only in so far as
they are a comment on the time for, until his European
trip, Henry was molded less by his contemporaries than
by the paternal generation from which he sprang.
During the sophomore year the cream of these youths
betray unmistakable inclinations. Bradbury, Cilley,
Benson and Little are to be future statesmen. Dean
is the budding metaphysician. Weld and Mason lean
toward careers as naturalists. Henry, Hawthorne,
Cheever and Pierce give promise in belles lettres. The
future poet is to be Frederick Mellen. Now what becomes of some of these youths? Dean dies just before
graduation day. Josiah L. Little lives to fill many
civil and political offices. The same is true of James

W. Bradbury, for the profession of law catches him up as it does such a large proportion of this class. Jonathan Cilley is more interesting. He is described as possessing unquestionable genius. But he indulges in habits which, while not vicious, were too expensive for the times. He, too, is seized upon by the law, that profession which was *the* thing, apparently, in early New England, and eventually he goes to Congress. In one of his Congressional speeches he offended the editor of *The New York Courier and Exchange*. He is therefore challenged to a duel by the irate editor but Cilley declines on the ground that the challenger is not a gentleman. This sounds more like an old-fashioned supercilious Southerner than a graduate of a Maine "one-horse" college. A member of Congress (from Kentucky, of course) takes up the challenge and the two men meet with rifles. Cilley is shot dead. It would be interesting to know just how intimate Henry was with Cilley at Bowdoin. We may guess that they were not too close, for Henry was not addicted to expensive habits. Still Cilley was a gentleman and that must have appealed to the young man from Portland. Josiah L. Little was Cilley's particular "chum."

It is not, however, in this race of lawyers, this unending chain of solicitors and legislators, that we may expect to find the seeds of Henry's particular future. True enough he belongs to this breed, a breed, by the way, which is the most important in any new commonwealth where a code of lawful living is still in process of formulation; but even so he is rapidly putting distance between it and himself, a distance that must be gauged mentally and not by physical proximity. Henry is not cut out to be a lawyer and he knows it. He is to say as much in most explicit

S. E. VIEW OF PORTLAND IN 1832, TAKEN FROM FORT PEBBLE ON PURPOODUCK POINT

From a sketch by J. K. Vinton

Nathaniel Hawthorne.

language before his college years are completed. The sacrificial instinct is not as strong in him as it is in his brother. Now, not possessing the temperament of the lawyer but rather leaning toward self-expression in belles lettres Henry would seem to have more in common with such undergraduates as George B. Cheever, John S. C. Abbott and, last but not least, Nathaniel C. Hathorne, a young man who has still to put the "w" into his name. Cheever was undoubtedly a friend to Henry. He belonged to the coterie. From his earliest years this youth had studied Edmund Burke. He was an assiduous visitor to the college library and it is of him that the somewhat perturbed librarian once remarked, "It is fifty dollars' damage to the library every time a theme is assigned to Cheever. He searches every book on every shelf." Cheever continued to be a conscientious person after his graduation. He was a preacher, an author, an advocate of temperance, "the Gideon of the anti-slavery campaign." With him, we may be sure, Henry spent many hours in converse. John S. C. Abbott was also a friend. This future historian, the man who was to write the most popular life of Napoleon during his times, was a scholarly individual from the first. In both of these youths the germs of a high and platitudinous morality were implanted. The work of neither one of them amounts to anything to-day but during Henry's youth they must have seemed sparkling and promising flowers of New England culture.

And there was Nathaniel Hawthorne.

If Henry represented all that was *comme il faut* in the Bowdoin of his time, Hawthorne, the day-school boy from Salem, represented the reverse of the medal. He was the hermit, the solitary, the neglecter of studies, the indifferent, the independent. With his two friends, Horatio Bridge and Franklin Pierce, who was to become one of the most colorless Presidents of the United States, he ambled about Brunswick, cutting classes, writing a few verses, meditating on the scenes about him to such purpose as to force them into his first romance, the suppressed *Fanshawe*. Henry, perhaps much to his own loss, does not seem to have come into very close contact with Hawthorne, although they sat in the same classroom for a time—Henry, of course, in a front seat and Nathaniel farther back. The reasons are obvious. Nathaniel was not a good boy as good boys were understood at that time. Henry was. The President is forced to write to Mrs. Elizabeth C. Hathorne requesting her coöperation with the officers of Bowdoin in "the attempt to induce your son to observe the laws of this institution." Nathaniel has been fined fifty cents for playing cards for money. "Perhaps he might not have gamed," goes on the President in his most oily manner, "were it not for the influence of a student whom we have dismissed from college." Nathaniel is indignant over this attempt to clear his character by the intimation of a weak nature. "I was fully as willing to play as the person he suspects of having enticed me, and would have been influenced by no one," he writes to one of his sisters. "I have a great mind to commence playing again, merely to show him that I scorn to be seduced by another into anything wrong." Nathaniel wants the virtues of his own wickednesses, such as they are. Now what could Henry have to do with such a student as this? It is clear that he could not understand Hawthorne and it is equally clear that Hawthorne made no attempts at particular intimacy. Years later he was to address Henry as "Dear Sir" and end the note, "Your obedient servant."

CHAPTER TWO

In *Fanshawe* Hawthorne set down a picture of Bowdoin so clear and so revelatory of the types of students there that it may be quoted in the nature of a summing up. "From the exterior," he wrote, "of the collegians, an accurate observer might pretty safely judge how long they had been inmates of those classic halls. The brown cheeks and the rustic dress of some would inform him that they had but recently left the plow to labor in a not less toilsome field. The grave look, and the intermingling of garments of a more classic cut, would distinguish those who had begun to acquire the polish of their new residence; and the air of superiority, the paler cheek, the less robust form, the spectacles of green, and the dress in general of threadbare black, would designate the highest class, who were understood to have acquired nearly all the science their Alma Mater could bestow, and to be on the point of assuming their stations in the world. There were, it is true, exceptions to this general description. A few young men had found their way hither from the distant seaports; and these were the models of fashion to their rustic companions, over whom they asserted a superiority in exterior accomplishments, which the fresh, though unpolished, intellect of the sons of the forest denied them in their literary competitions. A third class, differing widely from both the former, consisted of a few young descendants of the aborigines, to whom an impracticable philanthropy was endeavoring to impart the benefits of civilization.

"If this institution did not offer all the advantages of elder and prouder seminaries, its deficiencies were compensated to its students by the inculcation of regular habits, and of a deep and awful sense of religion, which seldom deserted them in their course through life. The mild and gentle rule was more destructive to vice than a sterner sway; and, though youth is never without its follies, they have seldom been more harmless than they were here. The students, indeed, ignorant of their own bliss, sometimes wished to hasten the time of their entrance on the business of life; but they found, in after-years, that many of their happiest remembrances, many of the scenes which they would with least reluctance live over again, referred to the seat of their early studies."

This is, perhaps, a somewhat colored survey of the fellow students of Henry at Bowdoin. Hawthorne, a young man when he wrote it, lived to look back on those years with some misgiving, for he saw in them years of shame and depression when he was unable to ride the wave as victoriously as some of his contemporaries. Henry, however (one of "the models of fashion"), found in his college days a period of charm and advance. There were enough kindred souls to make companionship a pleasant matter, especially for a youth who did not need companions as sustaining props. Sufficient unto himself in that he could lose himself in scholastic pursuits he faced the daily tide of living with placidity. It was all a matter of small things, correct lessons, walks that did not exhaust him too much, scribbling, reading, debating, singing, and a fixed determination to like the things that he should like. His companions, therefore, were no more than the moving background of his days, some of them, like the trees and flowers, being pleasant aspects. It was not in him to study human nature and attempt to resolve the phenomena of individualities any more than it was to vicariously experience the throes of this young giant, New England, and so be caught up in an epic nationalism. He was blandly ambitious but he was possessed of no dæmon.

v

"I am very glad that I am not to be a physician," Henry wrote to his father during his junior year, "that there are quite enough in the world without me. And now, as somehow or other this subject has been introduced, I am curious to know what you do intend to make of me,—whether I am to study a profession or not; and if so, what profession. I hope your ideas upon this subject will agree with mine, for I have a particular and strong prejudice for one course of life, to which you, I fear, will not agree. It will not be worth while for me to mention what this is, until I become more acquainted with your own wishes."

Naïve Henry! As though he did not know what his father intended to make of him. The young man is shadow-boxing again, this time not with an image drawn upon his closet door but with the obvious intention of his father. He is sparring for an opening, somewhat nervously watching for an opportunity to drive in the desire that lies closest to his heart and hoping against hope that his father will be pleasantly stunned with it. But Stephen Longfellow, immersed in the politics of Washington, is not as malleable as all that. There is a delay in his answer and Henry's timid hope probably is somewhat wan by the time it comes. It is to the point, however. The answer is law, as Henry undoubtedly knew. What did the sons of established New England sires become when they reached the years of discretion? Lawyers, of course. The era had passed when they became deacons and preachers, for material desires had become accelerated with the commercial growth of the community. There were both profit and social distinction in law. It was a profession with a future. It led to the judges' bench, to the State House, to Washington. Here was a country growing so rapidly that it required an unending array of lawmakers, trail-breakers, executives. Stephen Longfellow, therefore, exhibits no hesitation in his answer although he softens his letter by enclosing a bit of cypress from the tomb of George Washington. "See!" the faded bit of bloom from the first President's sepulcher seems to say, "I am from the last resting-place of a legislator, of a lawmaker and leader. The law office opens upon such fair prospects." But Henry, too well bred and in awe of his father to quibble strongly, writes: "But in thinking to make a lawyer of me, I fear you thought more partially than justly. I do not, for my own part, imagine that such a coat would suit me. I hardly think Nature designed me for the bar, or the pulpit, or the dissecting room. I am altogether in favor of the farmer's life. Do keep the farmer's boots for me!"

This is probably written by a young man with a lump in his throat. Of course he does not want to be a farmer. If squaring off at an image is too strenuous exercise what would plowing be, especially in a land where the fields have more than their due share of stones? Henry merely grasps at the idea of farming to give himself time to break the news concerning his real determination and desire. Perhaps his father mentioned farming as an alternative or else Henry remembered that certain of his forebears had been farmers. Is not old General Wadsworth even now installed on his thousand acres at Hiram? None of these forebears had been what Henry desires to be and he is probably somewhat at a loss to express himself in a sufficiently emphatic manner to his father. It all comes out in a flood of language by December, however. "For my part," writes Henry, "I have already hinted to you what would best please me. I want to spend one year at Cambridge for the purpose of reading history, and of becoming familiar with the best authors in polite literature; whilst at the same time I can be acquiring a knowledge of the Italian language, without an acquaintance with which I shall be shut out from one of the most beautiful departments of letters. The French I mean to understand pretty thoroughly before I leave college. After leaving Cambridge, I would attach myself to some literary periodical publication, by which I could maintain myself and still enjoy the advantages of reading. Now, I do not think that there is anything visionary or chimerical in my plan thus far. The fact is—and I will not disguise it in the least, for I think I ought not—the fact is, I most eagerly aspire after future eminence in literature; my whole soul burns most ardently for it, and every earthly thought centers in it. There may be something visionary in *this*, but I flatter myself that I have prudence enough to keep my enthusiasm from defeating its own object by too great haste. Surely, there never was a better opportunity offered for the exertion of literary talent in our own country than is now offered."

What does Stephen Longfellow think of this letter? Does he believe that any young man can support himself in any degree of comfort by attaching himself to some "literary periodical publication"? Of course not. Does he believe that Henry is both visionary and chimerical? Of course he does. Does he take any particular stock in Henry's deliberate self-analysis in so far as the youth flatters himself that his prudence (what-

ever that may be in the great perilous passion of letters)
will keep his enthusiasm from defeating its object by
too great haste? Of course he doesn't. And what does
Henry mean by this, anyway? Is he not approaching
literature as though it were law, a mere matter of study?
The seventeen-year-old boy vows that he possesses
enough prudence to keep him from the enthusiastic
madnesses of letters, that he will develop himself
slowly, and so logically achieve that eminence in letters that is his heart's desire. The theory is good at
any rate but it is too cold-blooded. There is no élan
in Henry's desire. Even those words "my whole soul
burns most ardently" sound stilted and composed. In
a further letter we discover that Henry is less concerned
with his calling than with the possible eminence it may
bring him, for he writes, "Of divinity, medicine and
law, I should choose the last. Whatever I do study
ought to be engaged in with all my soul—for I *will be
eminent* in something." And now mark Stephen Longfellow's answer. "A literary life," he enunciates, and
the whole of the old New England seems to be speaking
with him, "to one who has the means of support, must
be very pleasant. But there is not wealth enough in this
country to afford encouragement and patronage to
merely literary men." Literature, it will be observed,
is no longer regarded as an actual offense. It is now in
the category of an avocation, a hobby, a genteel pastime
for those sufficiently endowed with this world's goods
to play at it. Writers are still "merely" literary men.
Henry therefore must content himself with the prospect of law and, perhaps, a year's study at Cambridge,
for his father is not too hard with him. If the young
man wants to go to Harvard for a year there is no
reason why he shouldn't. It can do him no harm and
might, indeed, add a bit of tone to him. Henry clutches

at the idea of a year at Cambridge, because, at the
moment, it seems to be the last straw pointing toward
a literary career.

It will be noted that Henry has declared that "there
never was a better opportunity offered for the exertion
of literary talent in our own country than is now
offered." A brief examination of the American scene
is necessary at this point. What is it, what achievements has it produced, and what opportunities does it
offer? In the first place, we are faced with a new
country that is just recovering from two wars, the
American Revolution and the War of 1812. It is true
that vast strides have been made in a materialistic way
but it is equally true that a nation in process of formation can afford little leisure for literature. An old biographer once remarked, "It takes a great deal of history
to make a little literature." Well, America was quite
busy making history in 1825. It was consolidating its
position as a free state, so to speak. Henry was not
aware of a literary tide running high and it is to be
doubted that he experienced any prophetic intuition of
what was to come. He saw about him a land of rude
and emphatic construction, a harsh conglomeration of
varying instincts that included the literary or esthetic
urge hardly at all. For two centuries the settlers and
their children had been outposts of reconnoissance
groups on the Atlantic seaboard, flung there by the
liberal hand of destiny as gathering points for adventurous wayfaring into the vast interiors. In this very
New England that bore Henry a fanatic urge had dominated at the beginning. What are the vivid pictures
that reveal this urge? We see Endicott and Standish
beating down the Maypole at Merrymount and dubbing
the spot "Dagon." We see a servant who smiled in
church being threatened with expulsion from the Col-

ony. We see a woman who blamed an elder going about with a cleft stick on her tongue. We see a saint praying so hard that he bled at the nose. We see Hathorne at Salem and hear the hysteric wailing of the witches. We see Jonathan Edwards pounding the pulpit and shouting, "The God that holds you over the pit of hell, much as one holds a spider or some loathsome insect over the fire, abhors you, and is dreadfully provoked; He looks upon you as worthy of nothing else but to be cast into the fire." It is from this dark and fanatic bedrock that the thin shoots of early New England letters rise. The starkness and cruelty is mitigated by the years but the spirit still hovers in the air, in the *cul-de-sacs* of the Colony, amongst the oldest families. We must never forget that Henry, that his contemporaries, Bryant, Hawthorne, Emerson, Holmes, Lowell, directly descended from the Puritan breed. Back of their gestures stood the dark-caped shapes.

And now what are these thin shoots of letters that rise from this dark bedrock? They begin with such somber efforts as William Bradford's chronicle, Increase Mather's *Illustrious Providences*, Cotton Mather's *Magnalia Christi*, and Jonathan Edwards' *The Freedom of the Will*. There is *The Bay Psalm Book*, Michael Wigglesworth's *Day of Doom* (described by Coit Taylor as "a sulphurous poem, which attributes to the Divine Being a character the most execrable and loathsome to be met with, perhaps, in any literature, Christian or Pagan"), and the works of Mrs. Anne Bradstreet. With the Revolutionary era comes a widening of impulses. The literature is still moral but it is not so religious. New England stretches out and the other colonies contribute to its book shelves. There is Benjamin Franklin's *Autobiography*, for instance. There is also John Wool-

man's *Journal* and the religious writings of Mather
Byles of Boston. Judge Brackenridge bursts into
verse about Bunker Hill and Joel Barlow delivers himself of an epic, *The Columbian*, that time has mercifully forgotten. The Revolutionary ballads, *Bold
Hawthorne*, *The Fate of Burgoyne*, *Wyoming Mas-
sacre*, *Yankee Doodle*, and others, have their moments.
Three mediocre poets, who are yet individualities,
arise: John Trumbull, Timothy Dwight and Philip
Freneau. They still have their interest for whoso desires to dredge through their dreary pages.

And now the time changes and we reach figures who
are the immediate predecessors of Henry, some of them
living to be older contemporaries. There is Charles
Brockden Brown, Washington Irving, James Fenimore
Cooper in prose, and William Cullen Bryant and J.
G. Percival in poetry. These are the foremost figures.
Lesser luminaries, John Neal, John Pierpont, Gulian
C. Verplanck, have their audiences and their fame. We
know that Henry is under the immediate influence of
Bryant as a poet and that Irving is his favorite prose
writer. It is also certain that he met Neal in Portland,
for Neal is one of the bright lights of the Maine town.
In spite of these men American literature is not actually
born. The few beggarly periodicals that exist have a
lean time of it and most of the publishing houses are
reprinting the works of English authors and, in most
cases, not asking permission to do so. American literature is to be born in Henry's youthful contemporaries.
And, curiously enough, it is to be born with the renewed
commercial activities of New England. And now
where are they? Poe may have been writing but he
had published nothing as yet, his first verses appearing
in 1829. Motley was a schoolboy at Dorchester. Prescott was reading and meditating his histories. Whittier

was on his father's farm near Haverhill, Mass., writing occasional verses for local newspapers and making shoes. Emerson was a young parson in Boston, yet to come forward as an author. Dr. Palfrey was discoursing upon the Old Testament at the Theological School of Cambridge. Holmes was on the point of entering Harvard College. Hawthorne was a classmate of Henry's at Bowdoin as we have seen. N. P. Willis, also a Portland boy and born in the same year as Henry, was yet to achieve distinction. Thoreau was eight years old and Lowell was but six. It is patent that there was an urge in the air but it is difficult to conceive how Henry, buried in his country college, could feel it and respond to its invisible summons. He came to a realization of his desires at the proper time, however. His insufficient background was a disability of momentous consequences to him for it flung him straight against the colored tapestry of European letters. He was yet to find this brighter scene, though, for there was none of it at Bowdoin.

VI

John Owen, a former schoolmate of Henry's at the Portland Academy, entered Bowdoin in the class of 1827. He is unimportant as an individual but he left a pen-picture of Henry at the inception of his career that is not without interest and certain revelatory indications. "I shall never forget one of the visits which I paid my old school friend just after the opening of my sophomore year," he declared in his recollection. "It was in the month of October, and on a Sabbath evening. [The year was 1824.] After some hours spent over my books, I called at his room late in the evening. I found him in an old armchair, with a copy of Shakespeare—an English copy, if I remember rightly—lying on his lap, and over that a sheet of paper, on which he had been writing, in a clear, legible and neat hand, which he has always preserved, some inspiration of the moment. The object of my visit was twofold: first, to obtain some information with regard to one of the instructors; and secondly, to renew our friendship. He received me most cordially, and at once told me he was jotting down some verses. He went over again, in pleasant talk, the experience of the ballad on 'Lovewell's [sic] Fight'; and I suggested that perhaps poesy was not his forte.

" 'Let me read you something,' he remarked, without directly responding to my playful jest. And he began with the lines,—

"When first in ancient time, from Jubal's tongue
The tuneful anthem filled the morning air,
To sacred hymnings and elysian song
His music-breathing shell the minstrel woke.
Devotion breathed aloud from every chord:
The voice of praise was heard in every tone,
And prayer and thanks to him, the Eternal One,
To him, that with bright inspiration touched
The high and gifted lyre of heavenly song,
And warmed the soul with new vitality.

" 'You see, I have a cold,' he added, 'and could not go to devotional exercises. But I must do something in keeping with the day.'

"I replied that I was but a poor judge of the quality of verse, and that, if he called what he had read to me *poetry*, I would assume that it was. But I could not refrain from adding that it was much too grand to be popular. He read me more of the poem, and then laid it aside unfinished. Towards the Christmas holidays he showed me the poem completed, published in one of the periodicals of the time. He had sent it to the editor of *The United States Literary Gazette*, and, in return, had been credited with a year's subscription."

Henry had been to Boston by the time this poem was composed (his first to be published in any periodical outside of the Portland newspaper) and it is presumable that the "Literary Emporium" had accelerated his poetic inclinations. And, as usual, these inclinations followed the easiest course, that of imitation of a living poet then in the public eye, and did not strike out for themselves. No one can stagger through *Thanksgiving*, the name of this first poem, without noting the close resemblance to the early work of William Cullen Bryant. Even the closing lines:

> Let him that in the summer day of youth
> Keeps pure the holy fount of youthful feeling,
> And him that in the nightfall of his years
> Lies down in his last sleep, and shuts in peace
> His dim, pale eyes on life's short wayfaring,
> Praise Him that rules the destiny of man,

are an uninspired echo of the solemn ending of *Thanatopsis*. But the editor of *The United States Literary Gazette* (he rejoiced in the name of Theophilus Parsons and later attained some eminence in Massachusetts jurisprudence) liked it. In fact he liked it so well that he urged further work from the fledgling poet of Bowdoin and during Henry's last two seasons at college no less than eighteen pieces from his pen found their way into the columns of this short-lived publication. There were also three prose articles written in the *Sketch Book* vein of Irving and appearing under the general title of *The Lay Monastery*. Besides this concentration on the Boston publication Henry kept up a scattered onslaught on the *Portland Advertiser,* a dozen or more of his verses adding tone to that small parochial sheet. And we must not forget the *American Monthly Magazine* of Philadelphia which took two poems, and, perhaps, some unsigned prose. Henry, in after years, acknowledged only seven pieces out of this bulk of work, and they were seven too many. There is little that can be said about this juvenilia except the obvious deduction that it exhibited Henry's inclinations. Now and then in some of the later pieces in *The United States Literary Gazette* there may be found a felicitous line or phrase, but as a whole this work is the work of a boy, imitative, over-didactic, and essentially uninteresting. It is, perhaps, unfair to insist on too much promise in juvenile productions, but we must remember that Henry was a college youth and in his last years at an institution that was supposedly advanced and not of primary rank. Therefore when we look through these efforts, these "Thanksgivings," these "Autumn Nightfalls," these "Italian Sceneries" and "Venetian Gondoliers," by a youth who has never seen Italian landscapes or the canals of Venice, we expect some faint and rosy hint prognosticating future achievement, a vague prophecy of dawn in this western wilderness of pines and heavy snows. We do not find it. We do not discern an iota of genius in this young man who is so scholarly, so ambitious, whose "whole soul burns most ardently" for future eminence in letters. There is not a particle of personal passion to be found. The creative instinct is shallow. After all, the urge could not have been too ardent, for in the years that are to follow, the most impressionable years of a poet's life—those between twenty and thirty, Henry does not write a single original poem. The truth of the matter is that he has not been "called." He is not among those chosen. He is a literary figure, yes, but he is not an inspired poet in the true sense of the term. Certainly the weak and gentle urge does not spring from his native pines, from the curious life of Portland, or the rusticity of Bowdoin College. Here in his first boyish attempts he is writing about Italian scenery and Venetian gondoliers and Savoy. His mind is already flying away to that Europe which is to afford him the peculiar stimulus that develops him into the powerful and necessary figure in American letters which he is to become. But this is in the future. For the present he is the ambitious youth to whom his father writes, "I think you publish your productions too soon after they are written . . . without allowing time for reflection and examination. If you reëxamine them you will find some defects which would have been corrected if you had adopted the course I recommend. I hope you will not be wounded by these observations. They proceed from the kindest feelings." The times also are to blame, for, as yet, American letters are lisping in infant syllables.

VII

These formative years at Bowdoin draw toward their close and Henry, burning most ardently for eminence in letters, continues to apply himself to his studies and those sporadic poetical endeavors through which his mildly blazing ardor reveals itself. The idea of a year's reading at Cambridge, already agreed to by his father, impinges most pleasantly upon his consciousness, and practical-minded as he is to be all his life, the young man casts up the expenses of such a venture. The government of Harvard College, he discovers, is quite willing to receive graduates from other educational institutions at all lectures and permit them the use of the library. A fair calculation of expenses for the year, besides Henry, will be about $184. There is a charge of one dollar per quarter for use of the library. Room rent varies from thirty to fifty dollars a year and board runs from two to three dollars per week. Assuredly this is reasonable considering the mental profit to be gained from such an undertaking. Henry, of course, sees in this departure from Portland to the more scholarly precincts of Cambridge a step toward that literary life so close to his heart. At least it puts off the unappetizing law office for a year.

The idea of an escape through his rural Alma Mater apparently does not enter his head at this time. Bowdoin is in bad shape. Although a petition for $3,000 annually for three years has been made the Maine legislature, thoroughly New Englandized so far as the outlay of money is concerned, will not consent to it. What does it matter if the infant institution desires such ambitious adjuncts as a new chapel and a professor of modern languages? "They manage things there *so slick*," observes one of the State Solons, "that the college saves annually three thousand dollars." It is Henry's understanding that the college has but $80 after the receipts and expenditures are balanced. So the young man, as his senior year travels along toward the momentous Commencement, turns eagerly toward Cambridge, his mind flashing with images of the fair town he has seen so briefly during his single and exciting visit.

He attends two lectures, each an hour long, during the day: one on Anatomy by Dr. Wells and the other on Chemistry by Professor Cleaveland. He decides that he does not want a copy of Rousseau's works after all. Perhaps Rousseau is too starkly honest to suit him. But he does desire a quire of paper and a bunch of quills. He also writes home for the large French grammar that "is covered with blue paper and gnawed a little by mice." Foreign languages lure him from the beginning. The supply of logs in his wood closet is low and he requests three dollars "to buy a cord of that necessary article," for it is March and the winter still huddles about Brunswick, and Henry, presumably, huddles about the fireplace. Besides, he has something special to read. In April he is pleasantly excited by receiving a three volume set of Chatterton's works in payment for his effusions in *The United States Literary Gazette*. He leaps into the three large octavo tomes with gusto. The May examinations are passed successfully and he goes to Fryeburg with Commodore Preble's son, there to take part in the Commemoration of the Battle of Lovell's Pond, his particular offering being an Ode sung to the tune of *Bruce's Address*, a poem which is a trifle better than his juvenile efforts but still inconsiderable. Henry is never good at the occasional poem. June comes and the various parts for Commencement are assigned, Henry finding himself fourth in a class of thirty-eight. How he reaches so high a ranking is a mystery to him although it is difficult to see why. Throughout his college years he has been the student always, and, besides that, he belongs to the cream of the college undergraduates. The appointments for the Commencement exercises are bestowed and Josiah Little gets the first oration, James Bradbury the second and Henry the third. Frederick Mellen is assigned the poem.

Why does not Henry receive the poem? Professor Alpheus Packard explains why. He declares, "Of his standing as a scholar in college one may judge from the assignment to him at Commencement of an English

BOWDOIN COLLEGE IN 1822

FANEUIL HALL, BOSTON, IN THE EARLY 1830s
  From an old print

GRADUATION SILHOUETTE OF LONGFELLOW, 1825

Oration, when fewer parts of that rank were given than of late years. His was the first claim to the poem; but as the poem had no definite rank, it was thought due to him that he should receive an appointment which placed his scholarship beyond question." So Henry casts about him for a subject upon which to expend his oratorical gifts. His eyes fall upon those three imposing tomes bound in full calf. Thomas Chatterton! Has he not read all about the unfortunate English poet in Rees's Cyclopedia? Has he not perused "a dolorous prose ditty" upon Chatterton in Knox's *Essays?* Henry sits down with his quire of paper and his bunch of quills and distills the essence of Thomas Chatterton into a seven minute oration. It is finished and though he is a bit dubious as to whether it will answer he decides that it must do. His father is not dubious at all about it. He *knows* it won't do. So he writes to his son, "To the man of genius, the poet, the scholar, the life and writings of Chatterton would be an interesting subject; but so few of your audience have ever heard of his name that I fear you will not be able to make the subject interesting to them. If you doubt, it is not too late to make another choice." At the eleventh hour, therefore, Henry concocts a new oration, this time upon *Our Native Writers.* Here, one would think, is something unusual, a prophet crying out in the Maine wilderness; but alas, *Our Native Writers* is compact with generalities. There is nothing specific in it except the colossal optimism of the young man wr'ting.

The whirl of Commencement comes in September. It is before the age of photography and "class pictures" are attended to by silhouette artists. Henry's features are approximated by the shears and black paper. Young Nathaniel Hawthorne positively refuses to have his profile cut, but the rest of the graduates are more amen-

able. The youths about to make their more or less ambitious onslaughts upon the world gather for the exercises with such friends and relatives as may choose to
be present. There are solemn speeches, music, the
poem, the presentation of diplomas. And there is
Henry, standing up very slim and carefully dressed,
declaring in a clear voice: "Of the many causes which
have hitherto retarded the growth of polite literature
in our country, I have not time to say much. The
greatest, which now exists, is doubtless the want of that
exclusive attention, which eminence in any profession
so imperiously demands. Ours is an age and a country
of great minds, though perhaps not of great endeavors.
Poetry with us has never yet been anything but a pastime. The fault, however, is not so much that of our
writers as of the prevalent modes of thinking which
characterize our country and our times. We are a
plain people, that have had nothing to do with the
mere pleasures and luxuries of life; and hence there
has sprung up within us a quicksightedness to the fail-
ings of literary men, and an aversion to everything
that is not practical, operative, and thoroughgoing. But
if we would ever have a national literature, our native
writers must be patronized. Whatever there may be
in letters, over which time shall have no power, must
be 'born of great endeavors,' and those endeavors are
the offspring of liberal patronage. Putting off, then,
what Shakespeare calls 'the visage of the times,'—we
must become hearty well-wishers to our native authors:
—and with them there must be a deep and thorough
conviction of the glory of their calling—an utter aban-
donment of everything else,—and a noble self-devotion
to the cause of literature. We have indeed much to
hope from these things,—for our hearts are already

growing warm towards literary adventurers, and a generous spirit has gone abroad in our land, which shall
liberalize and enlighten."

VIII

There is excitement in the Wadsworth house, for
Stephen Longfellow, fresh from the meeting of the
Board of Trustees at Bowdoin, brings momentous news.
It has been voted to establish a professorship of modern
languages at the college in spite of the lack of state aid,
and the thousand dollars, donated for this purpose
some time before by Madame Bowdoin, will be applied
toward the upkeep of this unprecedented addition to
the faculty.   What does this mean to Henry, the young
graduate, the nineteen-year-old littérateur who has
probably been outlining his campaign of reading at
Cambridge?   It means everything, as Stephen Longfellow goes on to explain.   Benjamin Orr, one of the
trustees of Bowdoin, is a great lover of Horace.   Henry
remembers his translation of an Ode of Horace for the
senior examination at which Benjamin Orr had been
an examiner and decides that application to studies is
a most excellent virtue.   For Benjamin Orr, impressed
by the youth's proficiency, has put forward an informal
proposal that Henry visit Europe to fit himself for
this newly created chair of modern languages, with the
understanding that he will be appointed professor on
his return, and the trustees have provisionally approved
it.   This, of course, settles Henry's future.   Cambridge, Harvard College, the Library, all blow up into
thin mist.   Here is something tangible, an escape from
the law office, an immersion in congenial duties, a possible leisure for the creation of prose and poetry.   Then

there is the wide vista of Europe in the immediate future. London, Paris, Rome! The Grand Tour! It is unbelievable.

Henry's head seethes with thoughts of the future and the potentialities of the opportunity so miraculously extended to him. It would be pleasant to start forth at once on this long pilgrimage but it is autumn and the season is not favorable to an ocean voyage. Steamships are yet to be invented and there are no passenger boats. It is still the era of sailing packets, and the spring is the proper time to be tossed about for a month on the gray-green waves of the Atlantic. Therefore Henry must occupy himself as best he may for eight impatient months. He must control himself, although he is already so deliberate as to need small warning. There are several things he can do and, of course, the thing that slips quickest into his mind is writing. But writing, according to the thought of the time, is not actually *doing* anything. It is an avocation, a hobby, a pleasant side issue. Therefore that appearances may be maintained Henry goes into his father's law office, after all; but how differently from the way in which he expected to go if nothing intervened during that prospective year at Cambridge to save him from the ominous career about which he was too well bred and filial to quibble. Now it was law that was the avocation, the hobby. He was merely reading Blackstone to pass the time; but it is to be suspected that his father regarded it as some sort of preparation, however tentative, for any eventualities of a professional career in a small college. Certainly there was (as there still is) a vast difference between the income of a professor and that of a lawyer.

So the winter passes and Henry dips into the musty Commentaries with the other cubs, his brother Stephen,

Patrick H. Greenleaf, George W. Pierce, and Frederick
Mellen, the Bowdoin class poet. Adjoining the law
office, which is in the lower northeastern room of the
Wadsworth house, is a closet about six feet square
known as "the little room." This room becomes
Henry's "cyclone cellar." He escapes to it from the
humdrum of technical legalities. There he scribbles
away at his creative efforts. It is to be suspected that
the desire to write was more imperative than the necessity to actually say something, for Henry's literary
endeavors do not appear to be instigated by burning
issues. Together with his co-law students he evolves
a series of papers which appear in the *Portland Advertiser* under an imposing woodcut. They are based on
his usual prose model, Irving. These essays together
with some half dozen poems mark his activities during
this impatiently lived winter. He goes very little into
society and abstains from most of the town's gayeties.
By the end of March the rigors of the New England
winter abate and Henry begins his preparations for
the long voyage. It is necessary to realize here what
this meant to the young man. Such trips were not
customary undertakings in 1826. Indeed, it was an
exceptional adventure; Europe was much farther away
from America than it is now. It was the unknown land
where all the culture of the earth was concentrated, and
it was a rare venture for a youth to set out alone on a
three years' pilgrimage.

Henry, starting out like a New World Columbus to
discover Europe, leaves Portland at the close of April
when the young spring shoots are out on the trees, and
makes his first stop at Boston. There he hears the great
Dr. Channing preach and passes part of an evening
with him. He dines with George Ticknor, youthfully
unconscious that he is to succeed this professor at Har-

vard, and Ticknor, good-hearted to ambitious young men, gives him letters to Washington Irving, Robert Southey and the German scholar, Eichhorn, and advises him to study at Göttingen. He sees in the young man an ambition to be fostered and he realizes only too well the necessity of raising the average of college professors in this new land. Henry also visits Dr. Charles Lowell of the West Church, Boston, the father of James Russell Lowell, and John Thornton Kirkland, then president of Harvard College. This slender young Longfellow, it need hardly be explained, is decidedly *persona grata* in the best and most scholarly homes that the "Literary Emporium" has to offer, for is he not the son of a well-known lawyer and public servant and the grandson of a Revolutionary general? He is therefore armed to the teeth with letters of introduction and plied with all sorts of good advice, for he is the sort of emissary to be desired. In short, Henry is sent on his way with all the weapons his country can give him.

From Boston he takes the stage to Northampton, riding past the Red Horse Tavern at Sudbury which is to be the scene of the *Tales of a Wayside Inn.* The pleasantly cultivated fields of Massachusetts sweep by, so different from the more primitive aspects of Maine. At Northampton he visits at Round Hill, the school of Joseph G. Coggswell and Mr. Bancroft. Both of these gentlemen provide him with more letters of introduction and repeat the advice of George Ticknor—that he establish a year's residence at Göttingen. He finds his college friend, George Pierce, there and the two young men, we may be sure, spent the evening making ardent plans for the future. Perhaps Pierce reveals to Henry the interesting information that he is a suitor for Anne Longfellow's hand. The Berkshires are tra-

versed and Albany is the next stop. Then Henry proceeds down the Hudson, past the rearing Palisades, to
New York, from which port he is to take ship. He is
compelled to wait some time for the packet to sail, and
part of this period is occupied with a short trip to Philadelphia. During this visit he comes upon the pleasant
enclosure of the Pennsylvania Hospital and the picture
remains in his mind, for years later he uses it as the
scene for the last meeting of Evangeline and Gabriel.
It is impossible to estimate his impressions of New
York and Philadelphia, but fired as he is with the prospect of Europe, it is conceivable that he walked through
them as through mirages, his whole being concentrated
on the far-away realities of the Old World.

So we reach May 15, 1826. It is shortly before ten
o'clock in the morning and the packet *Cadmus*, Captain
Allen commanding, is waiting down the bay for the
steamboat *Nautilus* which is carrying twenty passengers, only two of them women, who are to make the
transatlantic voyage. Henry watches the city recede
and turns his eyes to the rolling wastes of water before
him. The white-sailed ships tug at their moorings,
the sun shines, and Europe beckons. The young man
has already written his last letter to the affectionate and
somewhat perturbed family in Portland. He echoes
its concluding words as he gazes for the last time in
three years at America.

"Love to all! Farewell!"

CHAPTER THREE
Pilgrim of Tongues

HAVRE DE GRACE!

It is four o'clock in the afternoon and the date is June 14, 1826. The little packet, *Cadmus*, bearing freight and a score of passengers, most of them Frenchmen, pokes her way through the harbor, sliding by the fishing boats with their crimson sails and dark rakish masts, and the larger vessels from European ports. There is a hum in the air as the sun slopes westward from the French town leaving behind it the long shadows on the waters that suck about the wooden piers. Henry stands by the rail and watches this strange world approach him. He is about to set his feet on ancient soil, on soil darkened with the blood and dreams of a thousand years. What is this Old World which is now impinging upon his mind and nature with its countless colors and customs, its immemorial traditions, its crumbling palaces and cathedrals, its rivers of romance, and its endless array of battlefields? What is this France going to do to him, this France now ruled over by a weak-willed Charles X, this astonishing country that has so speedily forgotten the eagles and trumpets of the Emperor? Henry does not know and it is to be suspected that he does not care. He is not here to be translated into another being. He is here to pursue philological studies which shall equip him for the modest post of professor in a small college in a small town. He has come to sit down at this rich feast and pick from it such dainties as he sees fit. And he has come inhibited with the heritage of a Puritanical past, a young man with no vices and with small patience for those less fortunate beings who are cursed with vices. Yet he brings an urbanity that garments him with the semblance of maturity. In other words, he does not know what it is all about but he is willing to learn. It is this willingness to learn that is one of Henry's prime virtues. His mind may be quite drastically shaped by his heritage but at least it is more open than the mind of many another contemporary.

He has been a month on the ocean and that month now seems to him a blank. It has been eventless. No gales assailed the gallant little *Cadmus* and the sea, smooth as a mill pond, might have been crossed in a yawl. The French passengers, with the artful aid of gesticulation, have carried on an apparently uninterrupted conversation of thirty days' duration, and Henry is exhausted with it. It has left him incoherent and alone with his own thoughts. Henry, obviously, is a bashful youth, but once his feet are on terra firma again his boyish spirits bubble up. He laughs uproariously at everything he sees. The *gens d'armes* with fierce whiskers and curling beards, the women with their wooden shoes full of feet and straw, men in paper hats and tight pantaloons that seem about to split with every step, Normandy dames with tall pyramidal caps of muslin reaching up two feet into the air, all these curious phenomena seem altogether too ridiculous. Henry nearly bursts his sides with mirth. He cannot comprehend streets only a rod wide and lined with six-story houses with "a grand display from every upper window, of blankets and bedclothes, old shirts and old sheets, flapping in the wind." Has he not come from a country where congestion as yet is unknown? He laughs to see a Frenchman tuck his napkin under his chin. This is not done in the best Portland society. He laughs at the French *table d'hôte*. He laughs at a seven-foot dragoon who reminds him of Paddy Carey. "If Ned only knew the one-hundredth part of the laughable things which I have seen during one day's

residence in Havre," he writes to his brother Stephen
—Ned being young Mr. Preble back home—"he would
lament long and loudly that he had not come to France
with me." It is a funny, funny country. His first impression of France appears to have been that it was an
old, dilapidated circus.

Havre de Grace, however, is but a point of contact.
Henry's objective, of course, is Paris, and, after a day's
delay because of passport difficulties, he rolls out of the
seaport in a heavy old-fashioned diligence. It is a
curious and cumbersome machine, resembling the bodies
of three coaches placed upon one carriage, with a cabriolet on top for outside passengers. On the panels of
each door are painted the fleur-de-lis of France, and
upon each side of the coach there is emblazoned in
golden characters, *"Exploitation Générale des Messa-
geries Royales des Diligences pour le Havre, Rouen,
et Paris."* Five horses draw this huge vehicle and they
are directed by a comical little postillion garmented in a
short jacket of purple velvet with a red collar, tight
breeches of yellow leather and a huge pair of wooden
boots adorned with long rattling spurs. In this state
Henry travels to Paris, sitting on top, of course, that he
may the better observe the country. Along the dusty
highway they rumble, passing groups of peasants, asses
lurching beneath heavy burdens, shepherds sitting by
the road, girls in clattering wooden shoes leading cows,
and dingy villages where the folk run out to see the
wooden monster stagger by. There are pauses at infrequent intervals before cabarets where the passengers
climb down and hustle into the place of refreshment
"à boire et à manger." Then there are times when the
incline of the highway is so steep that the five horses
cannot manage it without the passengers emerging and
walking beside the diligence. Henry, sitting outside

with "a gay subaltern" and "a nut-brown village beauty
of sixteen," takes it all in with eager eyes, ever on the
qui vive for ridiculous aspects and relishing them accordingly.

This journey is broken by a night spent in Rouen and
here, for the first time, Henry begins to sense the old
world as something quite different from a lark.　He
goes to the Cathedral.　It is the hour of vespers and
some time after he is to set down his impressions. "The
religious twilight of the place, the lamps that burned
on the distant altar, the kneeling crowd, the tinkling
bell, and the chant of the evening service that rolled
along the vaulted roof in broken and repeated echoes,
filled me with new and intense emotions.　When I
gazed on the stupendous architecture of the church, the
huge columns that the eye followed up till they were
lost in the gathering dusk of the arches above, the long
shadowy aisles, the statues of saints and martyrs that
stood in every recess, the figures of armed knights upon
the tombs, the uncertain light that stole through the
painted windows of each little chapel, and the form of
the cowled and solitary monk, kneeling at the shrine
of his favorite saint, or passing between the lofty columns of the church,—all I had read of, but had not
seen,—I was transported back to the Dark Ages, and
felt as I can never feel again."

The sense of the past is creeping upon Henry and
instinctively he reaches out for it as something that is
most satisfying and salutary to his soul.　This Europe,
he begins to perceive, is a land wherein the imagination may stretch its wings.　He does not realize that if
that imagination be limited in creative power Europe
offers all sorts of props, for he is not self-critical of
his assimilations.　All the sceneries of the sentimental
but thinly intellectual writer are here.　The depth and

profundity of life may suggest themselves but if the brain is unwilling or unable to dig deeply into the dark soil for its nourishment and by that labor upturn the hidden treasures of Time there is a plenitude of sur-face aspects and sensations that will do. So Henry rumbles southward through France watching the country slip by in all its fresh and breezy greenness, observing the towns and tiny villages, laughing at the spectacle of a spawning life that is wholly alien to him, talking to casual acquaintances, and drawing ever nearer to his goal—the never-sleeping city by the Seine. He is one of the first emissaries from the Republic. Irving has preceded him but Irving is an urbane New Yorker and pretty much of a cosmopolite. Henry comes fresh from the more primitive section of New England and he comes with a long heritage and a blood that dates from the *Mayflower*. He is young, presum-ably malleable, filled with incoherent ambitions about writing. At the same time he is precise, a bit stodgy for a youth, spiritually thin-lipped, so to speak. His train-ing has not been without its expected results. What is to happen to this young man who has been flung so fortunately upon the Old World at a time when Ameri-can letters are just beginning to gasp with a faint life? We shall not know for three years, not, in fact, until Henry's long pilgrimage is done and he is safely in-stalled in Brunswick, Maine, and prepared to inculcate foreign languages into the minds of the backwoods boys who come so trustingly to Bowdoin College.

It is on a Sunday evening in June (the 19th, to be exact) that the diligence rumbles into Paris and Henry climbs down to be surrounded by the crackling activity of the French capitol.

The Paris of 1826 is a hive of feverish movement. It is the sort of city that any creatively inclined young man would find entirely adequate as a field of action for his desires and ambitions. He is apt to find there anything that he desires to find. Since 1814 France has been a constitutional monarchy modeled rather closely on the government of England. The thunder of the Empire having died away an era of peace has intervened, first under Louis XVIII, who died in 1824, and now under the ultra-religious Charles X, who is attempting with the aid of his ministers—notably Villèle—to stem the tide of liberalism and advance the temporal power of the Roman Catholic Church in Europe. Charles X, once the luxurious-minded Comte d'Artois, has turned religious and France experiences the spectacle of a ruler at heart a man of pleasure, a sport and a dandy, aiding and abetting the pro-Catholic movement that is spreading over the Old World. Already the instinctive liberalism which followed hard upon the downfall of the First Empire, a liberalism that manifested itself in the first tentative flowerings of Romanticism, in the work, for instance, of Guizot, Villemain, Cousin, Thiers, Mignet, Hugo and De Vigny, is beset by the attacks of the clericals and the advocates of the *ancien régime* who seek to turn back the wheels of history. Guizot is forbidden to lecture; Chateaubriand is dismissed from office; the press is gagged; the Jesuits climb into the seats of power. Paris is therefore a field of political and religious conflict when Henry, the young man from the pine woods of Maine, dismounts from the diligence and looks about him with the wide-eyed curiosity of youth.

Paris, at this time, is a city of some seven hundred

thousand people. Its city boundaries and thirty-two gates do not reach to the fortifications. It is therefore evident that it is a congested city. The main arteries are few in number and cursed with a black mud which oozes up through the uneven pavements. The houses are of yellow stone, streaked with smoke and dust, and the residences of the rich are to be found in narrow lanes of lofty and close-packed dwellings in which the lower classes and artizans live. An intense activity maintains except in those more distant purlieus, or where the gardens are, Monceau, Grenelle, or the Faubourg St. Germain. It is to these lungs of the city or to the Boulevards that the visitor must go for his pleasure. The Italian boulevards are the oldest and most frequented and there, on warm summer evenings, one may stroll beneath the lofty interlacing trees and observe the folk of quality rattling by in their equipages or stopping to taste ice cream while the footpaths are a fluctuating mass of nondescripts, musicians singing and playing the harp, jugglers, fiddlers, blind and lame beggars, men with monkeys, vendors of toothpicks, Turks in baggy breeches, and Frenchmen with curling whiskers, round straw hats, long-skirted coats and tight trousers of nankeen. The fever of trade clashes with the fever of pleasure. Twenty-five theaters fling open their lighted doors (one of them, the Théâtre Française, being tyrannized over by the aging Talma) and an endless array of cafés, restaurants and public balls exist in spite of the hovering gloom of clericalism induced by the King. The mind, too, is fed by this pulsating city, for are there not the salons to be frequented where feasts of reason are spread for the edification of the visitor? There are the gatherings of Madame de Broglie, Madame de Sainte-Aulaire, and Madame de Girardin. In the Faubourg St. Germain are the houses

of the Duchesse de Duras, the Comtesse de Boigne and
the Princesse de la Trémoille. Royalist salons flourish
also, in the Faubourg St. Honoré, and in the Chaussée
d'Antan the great bankers, Lafitte and Rothschild, and
important manufacturers such as Ternaux and Perier
open their houses. Even as always in the history of
civilization the rich are buying their way into the holy
temples of culture. Then there are the more literary
salons such as the Arsenal where Nodier receives Victor
Hugo and Alfred de Vigny. And at the Abbaye-aux-
Bois the graceful Madame Récamier still rules although
her hair is turning white, and to her comes Chateaubriand to read his *Mémoires d'Outre-Tombé*. In
the Quartier Latin a real Bohemia exists where youths,
hungry for fame, lead a Murger-like existence and
argue loudly about the *flamboyants* and the virtues of
young Eugene Delacroix.   This blooming Paris,
through whose streets "Young France" marches singing the songs of Béranger, is a city of novelties, of
daring, of experiments and cabals and cliques and quar-
rels and political and esthetic machinations. Gayety
rubs shoulders with gloom. Somewhere the discomfited Bonapartists hide while the Bourbons endure their
brief triumph (for Charles X is to lose his throne in
four more years) and strive with all the political acumen in their power to superimpose the *ancien régime*
upon a country that had once washed that defunct state
away with rivers of blood.

Henry, then, is in Europe (and, particularly, France)
at an historic moment. His sojourn parallels a tremendous mental upheaval that is as much retrograde, at
least intellectually, as anything else. England, fed up
with the sentimental atheism of Shelley, the pagan
sensitivity of Keats, and the Satanic outcastness of Byron, is returning to simpler and more obvious paths of

faith. It is shortly to produce the entire gallery of Victorian figures. France, as just outlined, is in full reaction against the negative exaggerations of the French Revolution by the inclination toward a positive faith. In Germany the aristocratic paganism of Goethe is being submerged in a flood of treacly romantico-patriotic nonsense, plainly the result of suddenly waking up after the years of Napoleonic domination and discovering that the Fatherland is an integral nation, after all. The pendulum of history swings backward as well as forward. A body of men, a new intelligentsia, is coming to the fore. The minds of these men are soaked in a half-sentimental, half-esthetic medievalism. It is because of this that the taste for historical and architectural study has grown so rapidly in certain Parisian circles. Henry, therefore, in spite of certain liberalistic tendencies of the day, finds much to color his soft sentimental nature. The Old World *has* a literature and an historic background which his native New World does not possess, and for him it is not the insidious logic of Shelley and Voltaire. It is rather the toplofty romanticism of Victor Hugo and the sentimentality of Jean-Paul Richter. It is eventually to be Lord Tennyson. If Henry had been an authentic genius it would have been much better for him to have stayed in Maine minus those standards that are evolved by backgrounds and to have worked out his own destiny and developed an autochthonous achievement. But he is not an authentic genius. Minus Europe he would have gone on writing the futilities of his youth or mercifully smothered them in his father's law office. He must lean heavily on something if he is to say anything and Europe presents him with all sorts of elegant and sentimental props. The other and more dark phases of European life he may blandly ignore and he does.

It is enough for him to select from this maelstrom of color and conflicting urges. His mind soaks up so much and no more.

III

In 1872 Henry James wrote, "It's a complex fate, being an American and one of the responsibilities it entails is fighting against a superstitious valuation of Europe." This was equally true in 1826 but in a different measure. When Henry hopped down from the diligence he entered upon a phase of living about which he possessed no definite notions. Although his native land was under the intellectual domination of England it had not, as yet, suffered (or been blessed with) the vast influx of European culture that was to come in the succeeding decades and which our Henry was to aid and abet with all the skill at his command. Some faint hint that there was such a thing as Spanish ballads may have permeated the Atlantic seaboard, and there were doubtless a few folk who could read French and would nibble gingerly at French letters. For the most part, however, America was an illiterate stretch of territory just becoming somewhat self-consciously aware of the fact. Soon there would be a hasty rush for culture. The get-rich-quick instincts of the American enamored of gentility would be translated into get-culture-quick instincts. Henry, being no prophet nor inspired seer, knew nothing of this. In the back of his mind it is possible that various inchoate dreams of literary eminence hovered but they were misty and gaseous with generalities. He did know, though, that he must learn certain languages, French, Spanish, Italian and German, if he was to be a professor of modern languages at Bowdoin. And acutely aware that his time as well as his purse was limited he set about it immediately, a diligence not extraordinary in a young man who had no wild oats to sow in Europe and who possessed no more than a perfunctory bowing acquaintance with the vices.

Henry, dismounting from the Norman diligence, turns his trunks over to the customs official and is at once declared innocent of smuggling in any contraband goods. He then jumps into a cabriolet and is driven across the river to the Faubourg St. Germain where at 49, Rue Monsieur le Prince, the amiable Madame Potet awaits him. He is now set for a time. All that he has to do is to present his various letters of introduction, secure his teachers, study intensively and imbibe the atmosphere. "Madame Potet," he confides to his father, "is one of the best women in the world." Henry is one of seven in this *ménage*, all of them American youths busily engaged in studies. These young men pay thirty-six dollars a month for board and room. The house is admirably situated for a student, being within five minutes' walk of public lectures on all subjects and but a few steps from the Luxembourg Gardens and the Pantheon. Henry is satisfied except for the comradeship of the American youths. He imagines, and quite rightly, that the temptation to indulge in his native tongue may stem the tide of his French. He casts up his expenses and discovers that he can live on six hundred dollars a year, which, apparently, is the allowance that has been made him by his father. "Perhaps you may think this too large an allowance," he remarks plaintively in a letter to the Honorable Stephen. "I am certainly very desirous of living as economically as I can, and at the same time respectably and genteelly." Gentility is always a point of honor with Henry.

Most of his letters of introduction disappear into a void, for the greater portion of the personages to whom they are addressed are at their country residences. Henry decides that venturing upon Paris in the summer time has its disadvantages. He meets the Storrow family, however, and finds there a place that reminds him of home. The great Lafayette responds to him from Lagrange. "My dear Sir,—With much pleasure I have Heard of your Arrival in Paris and Hope we may Have at Lagrange our Share of your European tour. I leave here Sunday Morning on a visit Half-way to town, where I shall of Course attend the Anniversary dinner. There, if you dont come Before, I expect the pleasure to see You, after which time you are sure to find us at this place. Be pleased to present my affectionate Regards to your father when you write to portland and Believe me—Most Sincerely Yours,—Lafayette."

Later Henry meets the old general on the street and is astonished to note that no particular attention is paid to him. After all, Paris is full of ancient heroes. They are as multitudinous as the *gens d'armes*. One or two young men, among them his cousin, Eben Storer, fill up the vague need for comradeship that Henry feels and the time passes quietly enough. He goes to the Louvre but the masterpieces there are so many blanks as far as he is concerned, his solitary comment being that one of the Venuses resembles a Portland belle. This is a rather racy statement for Henry. Pictures, indeed, seem to carry no appeal to this young man and all through his life he is quite indifferent to art except for a gentle pleasure in sculpture. Then there are the theaters. He goes to the Variétés and sees Apollo in a red hat and striped pantaloons and Vulcan in a flame-colored coat. He makes a trip to Montmorency where he visits the Hermitage of Rousseau and sits upon the rock where Jean Jacques composed *La Nouvelle Heloise*. The immediate object of Henry's trip is to find new quarters, for he is speedily tiring of the seven young Americans and the twang of his native speech. This change comes soon enough but not before Henry has had opportunity to wander about Paris a bit and familiarize himself with the topography. He doesn't see much. He makes no friends. He enters not at all into that rich and effervescing life that is so animatedly conducted in Paris. The reason for this hermit-like existence is revealed later in the year.

In the meantime Henry, more and more conscious that if he is to conquer the French language he must confine himself to French conversation, searches about for new quarters. A friendly young Gaul, one of Henry's ocean acquaintances, recommends Auteuil on the outskirts of the Bois de Boulogne. It is an escape from the stifling heat of Paris as well as a haven from the American tongue. So Henry goes to Auteuil in August after six rather disappointing weeks in the metropolis. A nostalgia for home seizes upon him when he sees Auteuil. ". . . After all," he writes home, "a French village, in its best estate, can be little to the taste of Brother Jonathan. There is so little about it—except, indeed, its quiet and tranquillity—to remind one that he is out of town; no cornfields garnished with yellow pumpkins; no green trees and orchards by the roadside; no slab-fences; no well-poles; no painted cottages with huge barns and out-houses, ornamented in front with monstrous piles of wood for winter firing; nothing, in fine, to bring to the mind of an American a remembrance of the beautiful villages of his native land." Boyhood memories of Hiram and Gorham are obviously flashing before him. How America pours into Henry's mind now that he is away from it, and, after he has returned to America, we shall see that Europe pours back into his mind in the same way.

Nostalgias are always symptoms of incipient sentimentalism for it is the easiest thing in the world to grow maudlin over the absent aspect. Auteuil, therefore, impinges on Henry's consciousness as a cluster of paved streets, dark and narrow alleys, dingy stone houses and eternal blind walls. The young man is getting terribly homesick. The house to which Henry has been sent by his French friend is a *maison de santé,* a shelter for invalids and hypochondriacs, and perhaps this is as good a place as any for the homesick youth. For a month Henry inhabits Dr. Dentdelion's establishment and it is plain to see that he is not there for long without distinctly picking up and enjoying better spirits. He takes long walks in the Bois de Boulogne. He enters into the rural sports of Auteuil, going to all the *fêtes champêtres.* The fairs lure him and he hurries forth to the rustic weddings. Best of all Henry hears the purest of French in his village retreat, for among the guests is an old gentleman who was of the household of Louis XVI and a Madame de Sailly, daughter of the advocate Berryer who defended Maréchal Ney when he was impeached for treason. Henry's linguistic accomplishments develop.

By the early autumn he is back in Paris again and unpleasantly aware of the difficult job he has before him. If he had known, before leaving home how hard a task he had embarked upon he would have shrunk from the venture. The reason for his abnegation of the lighter side of Parisian life is fully circumscribed in a letter to his father. "There are allurements enough around me, it is true," he writes, "but I do not feel myself at liberty to indulge in them; and there is splendor enough, but it is a splendor in which I have no share. No! The truth is, that the heavy responsibilities which I have taken upon myself, the disappointments I have met with—in not finding my advantages so great as I had fancied them, and in finding my progress comparatively slow—together with the continual solicitude about the final result of my studies, and the fear that you will be displeased with my expenses, are hanging with a terrible weight upon me." This is an extremely important admission on Henry's part. He has discovered that Paris is not as easily surmounted as Portland or Brunswick. He is beginning to be aware of his own shortcomings and how extensive they are, in fact, what a raw youth he is, after all, and how far away his cultural goal is. Added to this, is the continual prick of meager finances. Henry now is not laughing uproariously at everything he sees. It is doubtful if the bewhiskered *gens d'armes* could raise a smile on his solemn young face.

This melancholy into which he has fallen is lifted for a brief spell by the joys of a walking trip along the banks of the Loire from Orleans to Tours. He receives a powerful impression from the ancient walls of Orleans for he is always stirred by reminders of the past. It is on the fifth of October (the month that is to be his favorite throughout his life and which he is to extol time and again) that he sets out. The jaunt is pleasing but uneventful. He meets a pretty girl and ventures to accost her, explaining that he has a flute in his knapsack and inquiring whether she would like to dance to it. The poor girl doesn't know what a flute is. He passes various châteaux and sees their turrets shining in the sun. The spires of little churches rise out of the green plain. Cottages glimmer through the trees. The river dimples and sparkles. He meets a sailor who had fought at the siege of Rochelle and Henry asks him if he knew Lord Nelson. The acquisitive tar turns this to account by begging a few sous "to drink the Com-

modore's health." Diane de Poitiers' château, Chen-
onçeau, rises by the Cher before his charmed eyes. At
the Boule d'Or in Tours he muses upon Catherine de
Medicis and Francis I. It is all rather idyllic and pleasing and it must have raised Henry's spirits accordingly.

Toward the end of October he is installed in 5, Rue
Racine, and taking his meals out at restaurants and
tables d'hôte, these last having ceased to be food for
wonder and laughter. His father writes to him pointing out the necessity for an accurate knowledge of
French and Spanish and intimating that he considers
German more important than Italian. About the same
time his mother writes to him, saying, "It is true, Henry,
your parents have great confidence in your upright-
ness, and in that purity of mind which will instantly
take alarm on coming into contact with anything vicious or unworthy. *We* have confidence; but *you* must
be careful and watchful." Henry, on his six francs
a day, is not going very far on the primrose path even
if the desire to so travel should enter his head. His
watchfulness is aided by his poverty. The winter progresses and Henry occupies himself with lectures and
studies, with the theater and occasional appearances at
the Opéra, with lessons in Italian (in spite of his
father's advice) from Ferranti, the music teacher of
his cousin Eben Storer. He also goes a bit more into
society for by this time he has scraped together a few
French acquaintances. Instead of being lighter-minded
Henry suffers the old nostalgia. It still tugs at him,
and he finds the Parisian winter gloomy, chill and
damp. "It is not cold—not the clear cold of our New
England winter, which braces a man into good health,
and while it pinches his nose puts him into a buoyant
humor." New England is beginning to take on a
roseate tinge in his memory. However, his social ad-

ventures add interest to his life in this "graveyard" of a winter Paris where "whole hosts of pale, ghost-like beings, with overshoes shaped like coffins (by reason that French people wear square-toed shoes) are apt to put me in a doleful way." He goes to the house of one Guillet, an acquaintance of Lafayette and a politician who had been Interpreting Secretary of Foreign Affairs under Napoleon. There he meets Sir Sidney Smith and no less a personage than Mr. Cooper, the American novelist. Then there is Mr. Warden, a former United States consul, who introduces Henry to the *Institut* where the young man catches glimpses of Cuvier, Laplace, Legendre and Gay-Lussac. But Eben Storer is soon to leave Paris and Henry's social ventures are not sufficient to hold him in the city. He will wait for the carnival and then he will post off for Italy. After all, the straight-laced young man feels nothing but "thorough disgust for French manners and customs." Here his father intervenes and points out again that Spanish is more important than Italian. Is not all South America Spanish? Pierre Irving, the nephew of Washington Irving, and David Berdan arrive from Spain in the nick of time to emphasize the joys of that country. So Henry, rather pushed into it but assured that traveling is perfectly safe in Spain, sets forth for that southern country, going by way of Bordeaux.

France, therefore, proves a poor introduction to Europe on the whole, although we may guess that any foreign country would so suffer as far as Henry's mind is concerned. The young man has been lonely a great part of the time; he has met nobody of any particular interest; it is possible that he has been snubbed in some quarters; he has suffered the pangs of home-sickness; and the ominous encroachments of religious

Courtesy of George P. Putnam, Inc.

Washington Irving

Sunnyside Dec: 15th 1851

My Book   and Friend

FACSIMILE OF A PEN DRAWING BY MR. LONGFELLOW
GÖTTINGEN 1829

bigotry have amazed and disgusted him. Except
for the brief visit to Auteuil and the pleasant walking trip along the Loire the months have passed in
the hard drudgery of imbibing the essentials of foreign languages and attending lectures which, for the
most part, must have been totally incomprehensible to
him. There is no evidence of any poetical inclinations.
Indeed, Henry seems to have quite forgotten that his
whole soul burned most ardently for future eminence
in letters. The truth seems to be that he has discovered
himself to be a rather naïve young man with a tremendous quantity of learning still before him. Not being
addicted to any vices—unless wine-drinking in moder-
ation may be called a vice—he has no outlet for his
chaotic feelings. France has disappointed him. He
looks forward to Spain with the greater relish.

IV

Washington Irving, then immersed in his *Life of
Columbus*, noted in his diary under the date of March
8, 1827, "Mr. Longfellow arrived safely and cheerily
the day before yesterday, having met with no robbers."
Henry, therefore, reached Madrid on the sixth of
March.

The change from France to Spain was one calculated
to buoy up the flagging spirits of a young man who
saw in Paris nothing but a den of iniquity curiously
colored by a medieval religious intolerance. Spain, to
Henry, was shot through with the appealing hues of
romance. He was to look back on these months with
an almost ecstatic joy in contemplation, for the residence in Spain was unquestionably the highwater mark
of his European tour in so far as his romantic assimilations and pleasures were concerned. Although he

was to return to Europe three times during his more mature years he never ventured to Spain again. The charmed spell of his youthful months there was too idyllic, too perfect in itself to be ever broken by the more analytic investigations of the grown man. He was content to sequester Spain in the fragrant circle of poetic recollection and to invoke its spirit in gentle and pleasing rhyme.

> How much of my young heart, O Spain,
>   Went out to thee in days of yore!
> With dreams romantic filled my brain,
> And summoned back to life again
>   The Paladins of Charlemagne,
>   The Cid Campeador!

There were various reasons for this idealization of a war-ravaged and poverty-stricken land, which, in 1827, was noted principally for dirt and superstition. First of all, it was immediately suggestive of that boldly colored antiquity always so near Henry's heart. It was compact with historical names and associations. It was farther removed from the modern sphere of living than France. Washington Irving, the idol of Henry's boyhood, was there. The companionships the young man found were more agreeable than the casual contacts of Paris. The intellectual tempo was not so disturbingly taut. The rigors of an uncomfortable and rainy winter were left behind. The cities and villages were full of what might be called romantic innuendoes. There were banditti in the hills. There were Burgos and Valladolid and Toledo and Seville and Cordova and Granada. The country was traversed by gigantic ghosts, by the Cid, the Paladins, King Philip, Torquemada, and the dark hordes of vanished Moors where the Alhambra reared its bulk by the Darro.

CHAPTER THREE

Henry bestows eight months of his life on Spain. First of all he pays his respects to Washington Irving. He finds him "one of those men who put you at ease with them in a moment. He makes no ceremony whatever with one, and, of course, is a very fine man in society, all mirth and good humor. He has a most beautiful countenance, and at the same time a very intellectual one, but he has some halting and hesitating in his conversation, and says very pleasant, agreeable things, in a husky, weak, peculiar voice. He has a dark complexion, dark hair, whiskers already a little gray." The American circle in Madrid is extremely limited. Besides Irving and his brother Peter, there are Alexander Everett, the American minister, and his family, Mr. Rich, the American consul, a Mr. Smith, secretary to Everett, and Lieutenant Alexander Slidell. Henry establishes himself in the bosom of a Spanish family, "an elderly gentleman and lady, with their daughter, a young lady about eighteen, who has already become quite a sister to me." The young man, it may be noted, has an inveterate habit of making sisters of all the young ladies (that is, the attractive ones) who enter the immediate vista of his travels. Indeed, Henry is pretty much of a ladies' man, of the type that drinks tea with gusto, converses agreeably and flutters about politely. To be succinct, he is a carpet knight. He probably played his ubiquitous flute to edify the fair señorita of Madrid.

The six months which Henry passes in northern Spain with Madrid as his place of residence are marked by an unceasing current of good will and application on his part. He finds a Spanish instructor and discovers that the acquisition of this foreign tongue is easier than he supposed. There are various side trips, to Segovia and the Escorial, for example, and the multitudinous glimpses of the daily Spanish life which are soaked through and through with charm for him. It is true that the *bête noire* of a good Unitarian, the Roman Catholic Church, controls the minds of these simple Spanish folk, but even this may be forgiven in the face of so much that is agreeable and appealing to the poetic fancy. The generous pride in birth and the elaborate dignity maintained in social etiquette please the young man and the tinge of sadness which he senses as a Spanish characteristic touches his sentimental nature. Even the bull-fight, barbarous as it is, he finds "spirit-stirring." Though he may wander from Madrid to the surrounding villages and indulge in the country pleasures available at fêtes and small inns it is rather to his pleasant boarding quarters that he always returns for the chief delights of his residence in northern Spain. Here, we may be sure, is the prime source of his happy days. There are continual references to it in his letters. "I am in one of the kindest families possible. The whole house is goodness, from the mistress down to the domestick; and the daughter— a young lady of 'sweet sixteen,' with the romantic name of Florence—supplies the place of a sister much better than I had thought could be possible." And again, this time in a letter to his mother, "But the society which I have at home pleases me most. The daughter of the old lady with whom I am residing is one of the sweetest-tempered little girls that I have ever met with." No wonder Henry saw Spain through the rosy hues of romance in after years. The bright eyes of Florence undoubtedly had much to do with it. We may imagine that Henry felt some reluctance at departing from this comfortable ménage in September, but the south of Spain was yet to be seen and Henry always put duty before pleasure. Therefore, when the summer heats had abated (and one should note that Henry is always a trifle lady-like about his health), he set off, Italy being the vague goal, across La Mancha to Cordova and Seville.

"You cannot imagine with what fear and trembling one travels at the present day in Spain," he notes in the long journal-like letters which presumably alternately enthrall and thrill the family back in Portland. "The whole country is overrun with robbers." However, Henry passes safely through these hordes of banditti, possibly because of the "poor-gentleman" look which he ascribes to himself. By the thirteenth day of his journey he reaches Seville and is quite disappointed with the aspects of the city. There is no Florence there to be a sister to him, for one thing. And then: "The streets are extremely narrow; the houses are low." He is sick, weary and out of spirits, that mistiness of mind that is always so near the surface of his reactions toward life again blotting out the cheerfulness which has carried him so gallantly through six months of Madrid. This mistiness of mood is suspect; it does not seem to run very deep. Rather is it a youthful moodiness, an adolescent urge to be "poetical" whenever possible. We shall see that within a few days he is to be raised to the highest pitch of emotional excitement by the spectacle of the Alhambra. He visits the Cathedral at Seville and the Giralda but wastes little time in describing them. "Farewell to Seville!" he declaims. "I left it without regret and took the steamboat for San Lucar at daybreak." Cadiz appeals to him more but this was possibly because he fell in with pleasant companions, among them being a certain Mr. Maynard of Gibraltar who had "a thousand things to talk of concerning Portland in the 'olden time.'" The nostalgia for home continues to reveal itself in the young traveler. It is in his company that Henry canters to Gibraltar, making the two days' journey on horseback. From the British fortress (where the spectacle of Scotch troops in kilts awakened wonder in the young man) he takes boat to Malaga, meeting at this latter port the consul, George Barrel, who had been a midshipman on board the same vessel with Henry Wadsworth. Across the Mediterranean lies Tripoli and Henry's thoughts must have turned to the young uncle who lost his life there in the fire-ship twenty-three years before. From Malaga Henry sets out with a Mr. Ruden of New York for a visit to Granada.

"I was in Granada but five days," he writes. "But in those five I lived almost a century. No portion of my life has been so much like a dream. It was a season of most singular excitement to me. How much I wanted in those happy moments some early bosom friend to share these feelings with me! . . . How many solitary moments a traveler has! There is some truth in Madame de Staël's remark, that 'of all the *pleasures* of life, traveling is the *saddest!*" Henry is very shortly to find a bosom friend but he is not aware of it at the moment. For the present he must liberate his surcharged feelings by way of letters. It is, of course, the Alhambra that raises the young man to such a pitch of excitement. He is to recover some of this incoherent rhapsody of the spirit in *Outre Mer* when he writes: "Is this a reality and not a dream? Am I indeed in Granada? Am I indeed within the walls of that earthly paradise of the Moorish kings? How my spirit is stirred within me! How my heart is lifted up! How my thoughts are rapt away in the visions of other days!

"*Ave Maria purissima!* It is midnight. The bell has tolled the hour from the watch-tower of the Al-

hambra; and the silent street echoes only to the watchman's cry, *Ave Maria purissima!* I am alone in my
chamber,—sleepless, spellbound by the genius of the
place,—entranced by the beauty of the starlit night.
As I gaze from my window, a sudden radiance brightens
in the east. It is the moon rising behind the
Alhambra."

And so Henry goes on, babbling incoherently. It is
hardly to be doubted that the impressive bulk of the
old Moorish stronghold awakened again most vigorously within him those inchoate desires toward idealistic self-realization that had animated him in a weaker
degree during his college years. ". . . In these high
revelations, thou hast taught me more,—thou hast
taught me to feel that I, too, weak, humble, and unknown, feeble of purpose and irresolute of good, have
something to accomplish upon earth,—like the falling
leaf, like the passing wind, like the drop of rain."
Just what he is to accomplish is still rather hazy but
Henry knows that it must be good, at any rate. It
will not do to sneer at all this tension of spirit that
relieves itself in stilted outpourings for Henry is a
romantic sentimentalist basing his intellectual achievement, such as it is, upon a strong bedrock of didacticism,
and what he has to say is undoubtedly sincere. The
spectacle of the young man "carrying on" before the
Alhambra is, after all, a welcome relief from the usual
taciturn New England type of his day, a type more
likely to gaze solemnly and speechlessly than to give
vent to any feelings. Henry's last days in Spain are
days of high emotional exaltation and it is easy to
understand why the country occupied such a large place
in his heart through all the following years. It is
the land of his young idealism. Not so many years
before Childe Harold had seen the Colosseum by

moonlight and drawn its antique majesty into his soul and now Henry, Childe Henry, if you will—for he, too, is on a pilgrimage—stands before the Alhambra by moonlight and is shaken by its majesty into an emotionalism that is more incoherent than reasonable but yet authentic enough. It proves that Henry possesses a sensitive and receptive nature.

The fires die down as Henry turns from Spain and sets his face toward Italy. He had dreamt of Italy all his life. He had written poems about it and studied some Italian while at college. He had desired to go immediately to Italy from France but had been diverted by his father's advice, advice which, we may be sure, he is glad to have followed. He had hardly expected to be so pleased by Spain, for the let-down of France had put him in a dubious frame of mind. But his anticipations of Italy have always been golden. The voyage from Malaga to Marseilles is stormy, a blustering northwester blowing the vessel toward Corsica once and away from the coast when it neared Toulon. At Marseilles Henry falls into pleasant company, not the least being one George Washington Greene of Greenwich, Rhode Island, a grandson of the old Revolutionary general. Together with this youth, who is the unexpected bosom companion of his Italian wanderings, and several young naval officers, Henry sets off along the coast to Nice. He is at the door of Italy and about to emerge on the third installment of his pilgrimage. He has been a year and a half in Europe.

v

Henry does not like Italy as well as he does Spain. Indeed, it is almost a second France to him. This is assuredly a disillusionment but it would be unwise to consider it too weightily in any estimation of Henry's reactions to his European tour and the benefits that accrued to him from it. Everything that he saw was new. Set against his native background of Maine there was not a European city that was not a miraculous spectacle to him. It is therefore in degree that he likes and scorns various scenes on the continent. He may not have been happy in Paris but he certainly would rather have seen Paris than remained in Portland. Companionship, it is evident, has much to do with his reactions to a place although this would not seem to be borne out by his attitude toward Rome, which, on the whole, he disliked, though the sympathetic Greene was with him. Before he goes to Rome, however, he passes a month in Florence, going there by way of Mentone, Oneglia, Savona and Genoa, a brief pause being made at the last-named city. The Strada Nuova, he decides, is the most beautiful street he has ever seen. He ventures into the Palazzo Rosso and the Durazzo and inspects the paintings, those which hit his fancy being a Magdalene by Titian and a Cleopatra by Guido. He reaches Pisa on the twenty-ninth of December and on the first day of the new year, 1828, he starts across country for Florence, noting the "beautiful peasant girls" with a glowing and appreciative eye. Reaching Florence he takes quarters in a house looking upon the Piazza Novella. Boccaccio, he remembers, placed the opening scene of the Decameron in the church of Santa Maria on the Piazza Novella. He visits the Pitti Palace, as all good tourists do, and greatly admires the Venus of Canova. Indeed, he asserts that it is the rival of the Venus de' Medici, pointing out that it is adorned with drapery while the other is not. "What beauty, what elegance, what modesty!" he exclaims, rising to a New England climax. Nevertheless, Henry is not installed in Florence primarily to inspect Venuses, marble or otherwise, and he dips into the Italian language, discovering it to be more grammatical but harsher accented here than elsewhere. He decides that he will not stay too long in Florence though the society is pleasing enough, but that he will push on to Rome, for, after all, young Mr. Greene, poetically-minded and congenial to Henry, is installed in the city of the seven hills.

"There is very excellent society in Florence," remarks the young man, "chiefly composed of French and English." He sends a letter of introduction to the Princess Charlotte, daughter of Joseph Bonaparte, and receives an invitation to call on her. Arriving he discovers a small but select company including the Countess de Survilliers, wife of Joseph Bonaparte, "a fine, sensible old lady," the Duchess of Istria, "a beautiful Frenchwoman," and the son of Marshal Soult. For the first time in his life he hears an *improvisatore* and the cleverness of the man overwhelms him. Henry apparently makes an excellent impression on this Bonapartist circle, for the next day finds him at dinner with the Countess de Survilliers and to cheer him up a bit the Princess Charlotte plays "Yankee Doodle" on the piano! There is also in Florence at this time a fabulously rich Russian count named Demidoff who gives balls three times a week and to one of them Henry is taken by the American consul. "The Count," writes Henry to his father, "has a private company of French comedians attached to his suite, to lend a hand in clearing away the rubbish of his million a year." Observing the animated nature of the scene revolving about Demidoff, who is old and chair-ridden, Henry exclaims, "I must confess that I

hardly understand the old Count's philosophy. I
should not think he could be happy with so much
revelry about him." But even these diversions do not
make Italy the expected land of pleasure for Henry.
He is just as anxious to go to Germany as he is to
see Rome and Naples. "I must confess it," he writes,
"I am traveling through Italy without any enthusiasm,
and with just curiosity enough to keep me awake. I
feel no excitement,—nothing of that romantic feeling
which everybody else has, or pretends to have. The
fact is, I am homesick for Spain. I want to go back
there again. The recollection of it completely ruins
Italy for me. Next to going home, let me go to
Spain!" Henry is still permeated with the effect of
the Alhambra, the kindliness of Washington Irving,
the comradeship of Alexander Slidell, and, perhaps,
a certain pair of dark sparkling eyes belonging to a little
Spanish "sister."

Early in February and hardly anticipatory of any
surprises or pleasures, he goes to Rome by way of
Siena. His friend, Greene, meets him and takes him to
the Persiani family where Henry is made welcome
and lodged. Life begins to pick up a bit here for
Henry is careful to note that the Italian family includes "three young ladies, who have all been excellently educated and speak, besides their native tongue,
both English and French." It is also carnival time
and Rome begins to assume a more pleasing aspect.
"I shall make my residence in Italy something longer
than I had intended on leaving Florence," he remarks
after six weeks in the Holy City. Together with
Greene, who also lives with the Persiani family, he
proceeds with his linguistic studies, not seeing much
of the antiquities of the metropolis for a time, because
of his adjustment to the routine of a student's life.

In April the two friends make a trip to Naples and we have the spectacle of two dreaming young men in one of the most dream-like of places. One evening they return from a long afternoon among the relics of the Museo Borbonico and go to the flat roof of the house wherein they are staying, desiring to be alone together and to feel that life is all about them. The bay stretches before them and across it they see Ischia and Capri and Sorrento and over the housetops and vineyards the smoke of Vesuvius arises. Golden vapors crown Sorrento and they think of Tasso. Capri sleeps like a sea bird on the waters and they seem to hear the voice of Tacitus across the gulf of eighteen centuries. Not far off is the tomb of Virgil and near them is the spot consecrated by Sannazaro's ashes. Henry opens his heart to Greene and an intimate friendship is consolidated, to last the rest of their lives. Thirty-nine years later Greene is to write, "It was then that you unfolded to me your plans of life, and showed me from what 'deep cisterns' you had already learned to draw. From that day the office of literature took a new place in my thoughts."

The emotional impetus given Henry by Granada and the Alhambra is still active and the mind of the young man is a turmoil of aspirations and tentative literary ventures for the future. Though poetry would naturally come to mind as the instinctive method of circumscribing the high idealism implicit it seems rather to be prose that is occupying his thoughts. He is, perhaps, laying out the plan of a book which he is to submit to an American publisher within a few months of this trip to Naples, a plan that will be noted in its chronological order. In the meantime he returns to Rome where a disaster is to befall him.

Late in June he is comparing ancient and modern

Rome for the benefit of his brother, Stephen. His attitude toward contemporary Rome is revelatory of his dissatisfaction with both France and Italy. The young man simply cannot understand or accept any divergences from domestic morality. Dissoluteness in any form leaves him aggrieved, bewildered, and disgusted. And he is evidently incapable of making any allowances for the drastic differences in social milieus that, in some measure, palliate certain extraordinary relationships. "Whenever I go to the principal street of the city at the hour for promenade," he writes, "I see a lady of the highest *ton* (who has a rich young banker for her 'cecisbeo') driving in her carriage with her daughter, her husband and her lover! However, there are many families, of manners and morals as uncorrupted as ours. Though in morality, as in geography, a great deal depends upon difference of longitude; and in Europe playing cards and dancing and going to the theater on Sunday night are thought very innocent amusements. Nobody here has the least suspicion of its being immoral, any more than we have of any immorality of eating dinner on Sunday." We may imagine the young man's eyes flashing with indignation as he observes what he considers the debaucheries of Rome. He is troubled, too, by the superstitions of the church, but having dwelt so long in Roman Catholic countries these have rather ceased to stir him to reproach.

Midsummer comes and still Henry lingers in the Holy City in spite of its sins. There are various reasons for this, the most important, perhaps, being the miscarriage of certain letters, among them a letter of credit to Germany. This unfortunate delay in correspondence which keeps him in Rome is indirectly the cause of the disaster which befalls him. Toward the beginning of July he contracts a cold which grows so violent as to end in a high and dangerous fever. For a time he lies helpless in the home of the Persiani family, nursed by the eldest daughter, who administers medicine to him with one hand while she holds off the Italian doctor desirous of bleeding the patient for a fourth time. Henry is quite sure that he owes his life to this daughter. The resiliency of youth responds to treatment and presently Henry, able to get about though "completely shattered," goes to the village of Arricia, there to recuperate. He passes a month in this small haven, his good constitution and temperate habits speeding him on the road to health. The time is passed quietly, reading Italian poetry, conversing with George Cooke of Virginia, "an artist, an enthusiast, and a fellow of infinite jest," strolling in the Chigi villa, and rambling about the wooded environs of the village where he throws stones into the Alban lake and discourses with the monks from the monastery. Greene appears to have vanished from the scene.

He returns to Rome where he lingers until December, and then, having settled his affairs accordingly, sets out northward through Italy for Germany. From Venice he posts a letter to Greene bewailing his loneliness at Christmas. Two days letter he writes to his father concerning a cruel shock which he has received in the parent's letter dated September fifteenth. "I unsealed your letter," he writes, "with the usual delightful feelings of hearing from home. But the tidings that the anticipated appointment at Bowdoin has been refused me were very unexpected and very jarring to my feelings; and the more so, because it was a situation which neither yourself nor I had solicited, but which had been gratuitously offered me upon certain conditions—which I have scrupulously fulfilled.

"I assure you, my dear father, I am very indignant

at this. They say I am too young! Were they not
aware of this three years ago? If I am not capable
of performing the duties of the office, they may be
very sure of my not accepting it. I know not in what
light they may look upon it, but for my own part, I
do not in the least regard it as a favor conferred upon
me. It is no sinecure; and if my services are an equivalent for my salary, there is no favor done me: if
they be not, I do not desire the situation. If they
think I would accept the place [an instructorship]
which they offer me, they are much mistaken in my
character. . . ." It is evident that Henry possesses
spirit and good judgment. The truth of the Brunswick mixup appears to be that the trustees, striving
as well as they may to make both ends meet on a
meager endowment, have reached the conclusion that
they cannot afford to add a full professor's salary to
their expenses. To obviate this outlay they suggest
Henry's acceptance of an instructorship. But Henry
will do nothing of the sort and there the matter rests
until he returns to Maine and fights it out with them.
This disappointment coming so rapidly after his illness
must have changed Henry into a dispirited youth for
the time being. Venice cheers him up a bit; its ageless
beauty impinges pleasantly enough on his consciousness.
The glimmering lamps, the palaces, the domes, the
spires, the gondolas darting along the canals, all these
things strike vividly on his impressionable nature. He
also notices that "the Venetian ladies are not handsome,
but they have a great deal of vivacity." One slight
misfortune befalls him. While he is busily sketching
the Bridge of Sighs "a wench of a chambermaid" emp-
ties a pitcher of water from a palace window directly
upon his head and Henry almost tumbles into the
canal.

VI

Henry arrives in Dresden late in January, 1829, his pockets crammed with letters of introduction, the gift of the good-hearted Washington Irving. The young man has paused at Verona, Padua, Trieste, Vienna and Prague on the way. At Trieste he writes home hoping that "something may be done more favorable in regard to my prospects touching the professorship at Bowdoin." The antique armor at Vienna recalls his martial-minded brother, Stephen. In Prague he notes that the Bohemian pine forests remind him of Brunswick and the Bohemian small-beer recalls old Uncle Trench's brew. Ensconced in Dresden he settles down to the study of German, but the many letters of introduction open too many doors to him. A social atmosphere catches him up and he is hurried to and fro. He goes to "Der Freischutz" one day, calls on Counselor Bottiger the next, passes an evening with Baron von Lowenstein on the third, and so it goes. There is Paganini to hear. "How the world goes mad after a 'fiddler'!" he notes in his journal. There are beer houses wherein to observe the world, public gardens that afford pleasant places for strolls, and music everywhere, even at Gunter's where he lodges.

In spite of all this entertainment, in spite of the rich horde of books at the Public Library (he even finds a curious old book on the troubadour poetry of Spain there), in spite of certain literary projects fermenting in his mind, he is not happy. The uncertainty of his professorship at Bowdoin is weighing upon him. He is growing homesick for Portland. After all, these new friends do not smack of America, as Irving did in Spain, or Greene in Italy. There is no intimate touch, however kindly disposed these jolly Germans

are. It is this loneliness of spirit and this nostalgia
for America, possibly, that call forth the prospectus
of an unwritten book, a work that he is never to write.
He queries Carey and Lea, the Philadelphia publishers,
about a series of sketches and tales of New England
life. This is a rather curious thing to happen to a
young man who has passed two years in Europe, but
it is quite in accordance with the peculiarly sentimental
functioning of Henry's mind. There is still no thought
of poetry but there is undeniably a lump in his throat
when he thinks of Maine. It results in a prospectus
which reads:

"1. New England Scenery: description of Sebago Pond;
rafting logs; tavern scene; a tale connected with the 'Images.'

"2. A New England Village: county squire; the parson;
the little deacon; the farm-house kitchen.

"3. Husking frolic: song and tales; fellow who plays the
fife for dance; tale of the Quoddy Indians; description of
Sacobezon, their chief.

"4. Thanksgiving Day: its merry-making, and tales (also
of the Indians).

"7. Description of the White Mountains: tale of the
Bloody Hand.

"10. Reception of Lafayette in a country village.

"13. Down East: the missionary of Acadie."

Something of this may have been in his mind when
he experienced his first great thrill before the Alhambra. He may have confided in Greene, also. One
thing is certain, and that is that these scattered notes
and hints of a possible book of essays and short tales,
a sort of Maine *Sketch Book* à la Irving, are the result
of an accumulation of wistful thoughts of home, throw-
backs of memory uncolored by the European scenes
through which he is passing. He has, as yet, not become un-Americanized; a faithful and devout ideal-

ization of the raw and new land of his birth has been quickened by his absence from it. And yet this is but a passing phase, a manifestation that does not go very deep; for we shall see that but little comes of it.

Downhearted and dissatisfied with Dresden and aware that his friend, Preble, is now at Göttingen Henry bethinks himself of the advice of George Ticknor and Joseph Coggswell and transfers himself to the University town. By the time his twenty-second birthday comes he is settled in and quite satisfied with Göttingen. It is a small city with none of the dash and plethora of amusements that Dresden boasts and therefore it possesses its advantages for the student. Entrenched behind his rampart of books and overjoyed at the proximity of Preble Henry applies himself most industriously to his studies. It is, for the most part, a sedentary period although such a statement sounds like an attempt to paint the lily white. After all, Henry is not much more than a sedentary all through his life. It is during this time that we catch a glimpse of Henry's own reactions toward that poetical career which he had meditated as a youth. It is quite succinct. "My poetic career is finished," he writes to his sister Elizabeth. "Since I left America I have hardly put two lines together . . . and no soft poetic ray has irradiated my heart since the Goths and Vandals crossed the Rubicon of the front entry, and turned the *sanctum sanctorum* of the 'Little Room' into a china closet." It is true that Henry has attempted some few translations and that he is to do many more in the immediate years that follow but his creative instinct, never very strong, seems now silenced for all time. Such literary ambitions as he does have lean very strongly toward prose. This is surely not the attitude of the born poet.

In April he takes a vacation from his studies and
lectures traveling to England for a few weeks, but the
impressions of that country are few and slight. By
May 15 he is back in Göttingen at the old grind again
and writing to his mother, "It is to-day three years
since I left America. It seems more like an interlude
in the drama of life, than a part of the play." Rather
is it a prologue to a drama that has yet to start and
which will not start for several years. Henry is merely
imbibing, unconsciously for the most part, an atmosphere the importance of which is hardly clear to him at
this time. "What shall I say of London?" he asks
in this same letter, "of my pilgrimages to Temple
Bar, Eastcheap, and Little Britain? Indeed, I know
not what to say. We will talk of these things hereafter." He carries away with him a more definite
impression of Holland through which he passed from
England. "The Dutch women," he writes, betraying
his usual curiosity in the aspects of the feminine sex,
"are not handsome, but they possess that beauty which
springs from health and a quiet, peaceful life."

His studies now occupy him very much. There is
no modern literary history but he attends Wendt on
Natural Law and Heeren on Ancient and Modern
History. This takes up three hours of his day and
a large portion of the remaining time is devoted to
the study of the German language under a professor.
There is some desultory English and Spanish reading,
too. He also admits to his father that he is writing a
book, "a kind of Sketch-Book of scenes in France,
Spain and Italy." This, certainly, is the beginnings
of *Outre Mer*. The American sketch book appears
to have dissipated into thin air very soon after the
prospectus for it was drawn up. "I have no longer
a very high estimate of my own talents," he remarks

rather gloomily. It is easy to see why. He has been close to various literary men and heard intimate converse regarding the functions of literature. It is not, after all, just putting pen to paper. Henry, indeed, seems to be getting a trifle sour for he goes on to hint, "I am persuaded of the charlatanism of literary men." Now what does he mean by this? Has he discovered that the author and his work are two distinct things, that the creator is often a disreputable being with a deal of skill at his command to make things seem fairer than they actually are? Or is he just sort of blubbery about the whole business? The latter seems nearer the truth for he affirms emphatically "For the rest, my fervent wish is to return home." Three years has been quite enough. The despair that visited him in Paris has settled on him again. Still, Henry would like to spend the summer in Göttingen and get through with this difficult German language which is probably twisting his brain into knots. But letters from home suddenly change his plans. On June 18th he is writing to his friend, Greene, from Paris: "I write you two lines—no more—merely to say good-by. I was obliged to leave Göttingen on account of letters from home requiring my return. My parents think I have been long enough absent; and, in addition to this, by my last letters I learn that one of my sisters is dangerously sick." Stephen Longfellow apparently has decided that Henry has been long enough in Europe and that it is time for him to return and fix up his difficulties with the Bowdoin board of trustees. The illness of Henry's sister coming at this time probably clinched the matter. So the young man hustles through Paris to London, spends a day in Oxford, another at Stratford, and on the first of July sails from Liverpool in the ship *Manchester* for New York. In Paris he

learned of the death of his sister, Elizabeth. It was
to her that he had written the sad news that his poetic
career was finished, and he had written this in a letter
congratulating her on her engagement to be married.

VII

The ship moves to the west. It follows the path of
the *Mayflower*. It follows the Puritans. It follows
the English ships of war. It follows the trading vessels. Which way does history move? Which way does
the dominating Time Spirit move?

Henry does not know. He does not care, for, homesick after more than three years of foreign faces, disturbed and agitated over the uncertainty of his professorial appointment, and grief-stricken at the unexpected
news of the death of his eldest sister, he is hastening
home to onerous duties that are essentially practical,
that have in them little of that high idealism which
carried the young man on a rising wave to Europe.
So we leave him for the moment, facing the banked
clouds of the west from his vantage point on the deck
of the *Manchester*, and seek the answer to the riddle
Life propounded Henry when it flung him eastward.
"I will pick you up at a delicate moment," said Life
to Henry, "at the moment when your adolescence
trembles on the brink of young manhood, and remove
you from the parochial limitations of your native land
and set you down for three long years in the midst
of the hum of Europe. I will show you the cities of
the world and the culture of the ages and you will
pick your way amongst these massive monuments of
the mind and orientate yourself to a vaster scheme,
to a potential internationalism which surmounts the
boundaries of nations." This is what Life said to

149

Henry but it is quite certain that the young man's ears were closed. He played his modest rôle unconsciously and its subtle nuances escaped him wholly.

It has already been intimated in these pages that Europe afforded Henry a background which set off a figure that, minus that rich back tapestry, would have been entirely lost. In other words, passionately as Henry was attached to America, and that is indubitably evident throughout the history of his days, he was congenitally incapable of drawing inspirational sustenance from his native rocks and springs. He desired to do so violently, and, indeed, imagined that he was doing so, but the mark of a European drift of culture is an indelible aspect of his best work. It is not so much in the actual theme (for the theme, more often than not, is no more than a scaffolding) as it is in the handling, in the esthetic and spiritual garmenting, that we observe this confirmed Europeanism. Henry, except for a didactic element that is the heritage of his Puritan forebears, *thinks and feels* like a citizen of the continent, especially like a sentimental German of the neo-Goethe period. It will probably be pointed out that there was no essential Americanism so far as literature was concerned during Henry's formative years and this is true enough; but, on the other hand, there were few of Henry's contemporaries who leaned as strongly on European culture as he did. One of the reasons for this is implicit in the fact that the greatest of Henry's contemporaries, Hawthorne, Emerson, Thoreau, Poe, leaned as much on themselves as they did on the esthetic divagations of the day. Henry, being so weak, so limited in essential creativeness, so lacking in the stuff of self, needed European culture as a prop if he was to be anything at all. Without it he would have gotten nowhere.

Because of this very weakness the young man developed into an important adjunct of American letters. He showed his countrymen the way from parochialism by showing them the literature of the Old World. He brought European culture to America at a time when America was a congeries of raw and semi-primitive settlements. He became a bridge, a connecting link between the actualities of the Old World and the potentialities of the New World. Of course, he was unaware of this and probably regarded himself as an able representative of American culture. He was; but American culture was but the reflection of European culture during his times. The idea of tearing a literature out of the lusty bowels of America was as far away as Walt Whitman when Henry was a young man. It was trickling into the air, perhaps, but it lacked any aspects of formation for its pioneer would have to be a brave man, a man as brave as the early Indian fighters. Henry was never mentally brave. His mental equipment, rather suave for his time, followed, as his life did, the easiest and most genteel course. It will not do to dismiss him because of this for he came during an age of rudeness and vulgarity and his gentility was an admirable leaven for the crude mass called America. It is, as yet, too early to ferret out the actual reasons for his enormous popularity. That will be considered in its proper place. Here we can but note a few scattered aspects of his Europeanization, always understanding, of course, that this translation of spirit was accomplished, at first, by unconscious assimilations on his part. Henry's first three years in Europe were tremendously important to him but he did not realize their importance. A nostalgia of the spirit constantly turned his eyes toward America but all the while the European scene was seeping into him. The seeds were being planted and he was not to be many years back in his native land before they began to sprout. It must be emphasized again, it was a lucky thing for him that they did sprout; otherwise he would have remained a small-town professor, gentle and innocuous, all his days.

CHAPTER FOUR
The Young Professor

FOUR years may be either an instant of time or an illimitable æon. It is long enough for the mastery of the sonnet form or the duration of the Civil War. The aspect of a nation may be changed or the heart of a man be lifted into unsuspected and astounding ways. Henry, standing by the Androscoggin and watching the logs race down the sluices, is emotional enough to know this. Having traveled so arduous a road toward his professorship, a road which has taken him through France, Spain, Italy and Germany in order that he may reach Brunswick, Maine, he is, perhaps, aware that he is not the same young man who left these native pine groves in order to prepare himself for the onerous duties of maturity. He is still very young, very callow, very sanguine, but now he knows that these evergreen trees are not quite the same as the Bois de Boulogne, that Brunswick is not Göttingen, that Portland is not Madrid and that Boston is neither Paris nor Rome. What cultural lesson is to be drawn from this knowledge is as yet undefined in Henry's mind. It is, possibly, a lucky thing for him that these marked differentiations exist, for Henry was never quite at ease in Europe. He was not fashioned to be a cosmopolite, and the European scene which alternately delighted and shocked him was never an integral part of him. It is already seeping into him to a certain extent, rounding those rough corners that a lack of tradition and standards had hewn so crudely when his nature was formed, polishing the urbane exterior that lended itself so readily to the charming and antique influences of the continent; but beneath all this, softened by an unconquerable gentleness of temperament, perhaps, is the granite bedrock of the Puritan. He has almost reveled in the nostalgia for home and now that he is here it will be instructive to see how Europe has shifted his values. At first the change is imperceptible, for the European onslaught resulted, first of all, in Henry's instinctively raising the strongest barrier he could against it. And this is his Puritan birthright. It will not do to assert that he is bigoted, for bigotry intimates a dynamic and militant attitude. The Puritan in Henry is quiescent but it is there all the same. It is manifest in a bland non-comprehension, in a one-sidedness of purpose that is congenital and incapable of being broadened. There is no reason to doubt that Henry considers himself a liberal and so far as the tendencies of his immediate environment go he is to be entered in that category. But the liberal of 1829 is not far from the Sunday school superintendent attitude toward life so far as the settled and defined consciousness of New England goes. It is exemplified in Henry's disgust with France. Yet Europe is still beating at Henry's barrier as it will continue to beat all his life.

Henry is now professor of modern languages at Bowdoin College. The differences between him and the Board of Trustees who naïvely purposed making him an instructor have been settled by the young man's flat refusal to accept so subsidiary an office and the Trustees' reconsideration of their position which culminates in an official notice reading:

In the Board of Trustees of Bowdoin College, September 1, 1829:
Mr. Henry W. Longfellow having declined to accept the office of Instructor in Modern Languages,
Voted, That we now proceed to the choice of a Professor of Modern Languages.

And Mr. H. W. was chosen.

Voted, That the salary of said professor be established at eight hundred dollars annually, until further order of the Board.

Voted, That H. W. Longfellow be appointed Librarian for one year, with a salary of one hundred dollars.

This is the first of Henry's many victories of personality. It is true that it is not a complete victory for the full salary of a professor at Bowdoin appears to have been a thousand dollars, but in so far as Henry is concerned it is decisive enough, for the young man achieves his coveted title. He is now, at twenty-two, a professor and the head of his department. For five and a half years he is to remain at Brunswick, creating a particular curriculum out of nothing, even to putting together the textbooks, establishing himself in a modest position among the New England intellectuals, and unconsciously preparing himself for the wider scenes of Cambridge. Henry's actual accomplishments during this half of a decade are meager and they give no promise of the position which he is to achieve eventually. He does some amateur editing, some translations, and writes a few essays, besides putting together the travel reminiscences which make up *Outre Mer.* There is no sign of a poet here unless it be discerned in an inveterate sentimentalism and an occasional rhapsodical running-on in the heightened passages of *Outre Mer.* To understand this period of gestation (which it presumably is) Henry must be observed as professor, man and author.

The young professor springs into instant popularity. In the first place he comes back to Brunswick with some brief—albeit local—reputation because of various juvenile verses which have already crept into some of the school readers and compilations of "ele-

gant" extracts of the day. He is the youngest member
of the faculty and naturally nearer the youths who sit
under him. He is also good-looking, addicted to ultra-
neatness in dress—a trait that is to grow into a near-foppishness during his early years in Cambridge—gentle in
demeanor, charming, always courteous in manner.
Indeed, there seems to be an incipient feminine streak
in him held in abeyance only by his consciousness of
his own dignity and the self-realization (ever with him)
that he is a professor. This engenders an aloofness
and dignity that, perhaps, are but enhanced attributes
of his youth. In spite of Henry's partial loss of
faith in his poetical inspiration (which, possibly, was
his New England commonsense coming to the surface)
there can be but little doubt that he approves of himself. He constantly sees himself as a faithful pilgrim
traveling on the high and difficult road of culture,
and, though this may create a sort of semi-conceit
in him, it also has more important reactions, not the
least of them being that conscientiousness that keeps
him at his French and Spanish studies during these years
as a professor and urges him into the adaptation of
textbooks for his unprecedented class at the college.

One of the prime reasons for his popularity with the
students is his lack of the old-fashioned type of discipline that maintains in the New England educational
establishments of this time. He is never a Ma'am
Fellows. Perhaps his experiences in Göttingen stand
him in good stead here and render possible a realization
that the professor is not necessarily the martinet. Instead of this he is nearer the gentle forgetful type of
professor although we may be sure he never oversteps
the border-line and becomes a comedy figure. He is too
young for that, too freshly interested in his work. The
faculty is, of course, the same old faculty who punishes

the slightest misdemeanors, but Henry is hardly a part of it. Instructed to "admonish" a student who has infringed some one of the multitudinous regulations Henry is circumvented by the bright youth's immediate positing of some point in French literature. A lively discussion follows and it is not until Henry has turned away that his disciplinary objective pops back into his mind. The unpleasant duty is discharged with "Ah! I was near forgetting. The faculty voted last night that I should admonish you for [naming the offense], and you will consider yourself admonished." His gentleness does not obviate a certain wit, as witness his bland remark to a student obviously coached while reciting: "Your recitation reminds me of the Spanish theater, where the prompter performs a more important part than the actor."

Together with his classes in modern languages he has other duties. He is librarian as well and spends an hour each day in the library where he finds opportunity to pursue various researches and acquaint himself with a huge number of books. Then too he takes over classes from brother professors at times, for Bowdoin is still miserably limited and the overworked faculty has more than it can handle. In a letter to George Washington Greene (now returned to America and installed in Narragansett) he gives a clear picture of a typical day. "I rise at six in the morning, and hear a French recitation of Sophomores immediately. At seven I breakfast, and am then master of my time until eleven, when I hear a Spanish lesson of Juniors. After that I take a lunch; and at twelve I go into the library, where I remain till one. I am then at leisure for the afternoon till five, when I have a French recitation of Juniors. At six, I take coffee; then walk and visit friends till nine; study till twelve, and sleep till six, when I begin the same round again. Such is the daily routine of my life. The intervals of college duty I fill up with my own studies. Last term I I was publishing textbooks for the use of my pupils, in whom I take a deep interest. This term I am writing a course of lectures on French, Spanish, and Italian literature. I shall commence lecturing to the two upper classes in a few days. You see, I lead a very sober, jog-trot kind of life. My circle of acquaintances is very limited. I am on very intimate terms with three families, and that is quite enough. I like intimate footings; I do not care for general society."

This paragraph is extremely revelatory for it gives a clear picture of the low horizon about Henry. His main outlet is through books; the cut-and-dried life of the college with its groups of farm boys and city lads can hardly offer him much. The drastic change from the European scene would seem to discontent him and yet there is no evidence that he is so troubled. He is still following that naïve philosophy of his, to like what he should like and to apply himself unremittingly to the immediate duties in hand. He certainly does so as a professor. Finding no adequate textbooks for his classes, to note but one aspect of his conscientiousness, he sets about to prepare several and they are printed by the modest press of Griffin in Brunswick. Three of these books—*Elements of French Grammar*, translated from the French of C. F. L'Homond, *Manuel de Proverbes Dramatiques*, and *Novelas Españolas*, both small volumes of edited selections—appear in 1830 and are immediately put into use by Henry's classes. The next two years are to see three additional books, *Syllabus de la Grammaire Italienne*, written in French by Henry, *Cours de Langue Française*, a volume of edited selections, and

Coplas de Manrique, containing some verse translations by the young professor.

These years, therefore, are a period of typical small college teaching unadorned by any flamboyant gestures or unmistakable promises. Henry is a painstaking young pundit not too engrossed in his own studies but still paying sufficient attention to them to keep his weak creative urge from entirely flickering out. If the fates are not with him the young man will grow into an undistinguished old man still explaining French and Spanish verbs to generations of youths, and, perhaps, composing a few mildly entertaining books. But the Fates *are* with Henry. They have nothing to do with the professor, perhaps, but the man and the author are to be stimulated and prepared for the niche which American development is rapidly building for them.

II

When we turn from the professor to the man we are immediately met with romance. Henry is to be an incurable romantic all his life and it is to color his days accordingly, to wrap his sorrows—and it will not do to underestimate them for he is to suffer several poignant and tragic shocks during his career—in a fine and almost impalpable mist, and to bring out the graver facets of even his joys. He is not Byronic in the real meaning of the word but he is naturally sentimental and of that sentimental order that experiences so easily the sadness implicit in all life. There is good reason to believe that such a type of being withstands the shocks of life with more aplomb than the cheerier temperament, for the supreme indifference of nature spreads over a wider area instead of sinking in too deeply. Because of this Henry is to show a certain elasticity in his recovery from the various tragedies which beset his years. His immediate reactions of anguish to the deplorable climactic waves of tragic interference are undiminished but his romantic and sentimental nature buoys him above a too destructive submersion. It has already been affirmed that Henry is sanguine of outlook and at a first glance the intimation that his romantic urges lean toward sadness would hardly seem to hold water. But this misty sentimental sadness is to grow on him with the years and to be accelerated by the cruel surprises which life has in store for him. For the present he is distrait with the fine shock of unexpected romance in the personality of Mary Storer Potter.

This young woman, a forgotten classmate of Henry's at the school of Bezaleel Cushman, is one of the débutantes of Portland, one, in fact, among several whom Henry finds decidedly diverting during the brief interim between his return from Europe and his installation at Brunswick. Her dark hair and deep blue eyes flash upon the impressionable young man while he is attending church, and so deeply is he smitten, that he follows her home without daring to speak to her. It is the Portland of 1829 and young men do not address young ladies except in the most socially approved manner. It is still an era of profound moral dicta and the subdued femininity is thoroughly bulwarked by convention, wholeheartedly chaperoned and unceasingly dominated. Henry, therefore, hurries home, puts on his best waistcoat, and induces his sister, presumably Anne, to accompany him to the Potter home. The entrée once made—and we are to imagine an extraordinarily polite young man habituated to European courtesies—the usual New England courtship ensues, with its walks about Munjoy's Hill, its devitalized dances at the vari-

ous homes of "the set," and mild tête-à-têtes in the
rose garden by the Wadsworth house. Henry has much
to tell Mary. He undoubtedly expands on Europe.
He certainly reveals all those longings so near his heart
concerning an eminent career. Mary listens. She
observes a handsome youth with sparkling eyes and a
high degree of self-command. He is the son of
Stephen Longfellow and he is about to become a professor—indeed, before this courtship runs its course
he *is* a professor hurrying back to Portland from Bowdoin to continue his love-making. All of this could be
rendered most charming by extension but the indicated picture implies the whole, and knowing Henry's
temperament as we do, his idealization of the feminine
sex, for example, it is unnecessary to treat it at length.
The Potters and Longfellows are neighbors and friends
and the course is supremely clear of any dangerous
rocks. Indeed, it is one of those fortunate affairs where
two young people in the same social strata meet with the
benignant approval of the elders. Mary is the second
daughter of a judge and Henry is the second son of a
prominent lawyer and legislator with certain prospects
of his own. The couple are accordingly married on
September 14, 1831, after the customary years of courtship. Mary is nineteen and Henry is twenty-four. The
young man does not burst into verse either before or
after this significant change in his life. It is to be
wondered what stimulus his somnolent poetical faculty,
such as it is, does need.

Mary is the daughter of her father and to approach
her nature at all adequately it is necessary to note him.
Judge Barrett Potter, born at Lebanon in 1777 and
graduating from Dartmouth College in 1796, is the
typical old-fashioned New England figure. From the
assiduous practice of law at Gorham he achieves a part-

nership with Salmon Chase at Portland, developing into a sound, round, bluff pillar of the community, a Judge of the Probate Court (which post he held for twenty-five years) and a decisive arbiter of his daughter's development. Judge Potter disbelieves in too much education for young women. It leads to such disastrous results. The daughter may grow either soft-witted or independent. Therefore he interdicts such accomplishments as Greek and Latin but encourages Mary in mathematics. The drawing of a calculus is more important to his daughter than the ability to read Livy. This type of mind is so curious that it would be amusing to investigate it further but Judge Potter does not warrant such consideration in so far as Henry's career is concerned.

Mary, who has been educated at Miss Cushman's school in Hingham, Massachusetts, is the product of her time through her father, who *is* the time. In other words, she is modest, intensely polite, quiet and instinctively subordinate to her male relations. Also, she probably enjoys calculating ellipses. Her books give an idea of her mind for they include such treasures as *Harry and Lucy*, by Mrs. Edgeworth, *Sabbath Recreations*, by Emily Taylor, *The Wreath, a Selection of Elegant Poems from the Best Authors* (from which she regales herself with Beattie's *Minstrel*, Blair's *Grave*, Gray's *Elegy* and Goldsmith's *Traveller*, besides shorter pieces by Campbell, Moore and Burns), *Poems and Essays* by Mrs. Bowdler, *Legacy for Young Ladies*, by Mrs. Barbauld (this includes discussions of beauty, fashion and botany), *Elements of History*, by Worcester, and *The Literary Gem*, which contains translations of Goethe, Richter and Korner, buttressed by their forgotten American imitators. Her literature is morally edifying, at any rate. A sort of faded

sweetness emanates from Mary. We see her, undeniably attractive in her precise way, as "good as
gold," tending to her household duties in the house
on Federal Street, Brunswick, to which Henry takes
her after the marriage. She copies out verses for her
husband, accompanies him on his limited visitations
about the town—to Parker Cleaveland's across the
way, for example—and diffuses a delicately charming
atmosphere that somehow suggests a whiff of lavender
from some old bureau drawer.

Henry is no longer rooming in the college and taking
his meals out. He is the head of a household and he
enters with urbane dignity into his new function. Being
so young a husband it is fairly certain that he under-
takes his new duties in life with the zeal of the youth
who likes what he should like. The seeds of *Excelsior* and *A Psalm of Life* are already implanted in
his nature. "He is a good little dear," remarks Mary
in a letter, "and I approve of everything (*almost* smoking) he does." He even attends Temperance Lectures
and meditates joining the Temperance Society, but for
some reason and certainly against the advice of Mary,
this falls through and Henry is blessedly preserved to
appreciate those bottles of wine that are to appear so
constantly on his table throughout his life. The wine,
the flamboyant waistcoats, and the obvious relish for
feminine society which add their brief exotic note to
his life from early manhood on assuredly are escapes
from the starker Puritanism of his training, faint gestures of a playfully disposed personality that might, if
his backbone had been genius instead of a moral propa-
gandism, have diverted him into more esthetic ways.
There is a feeble leaning toward the lighter aspects of
living here and a delight in the sensory surfaces of
things. But at Portland and particularly with the ultra-

domestic Mary by his side, there is meager incentive for the development of such an inclination. Instead of wine, therefore, he is to be noted meditating a vegetable diet. The idea of health is obsessing him. He even lectures Mary on corsets although it is certain that he does not advise her to do away with them entirely.

Life at Brunswick is almost cruelly circumscribed. Congenial companionship is decidedly limited and during the winter there are the elements with which to contend. Keeping warm, for instance, is a problem of prime importance. But there are warm days as well, days when Henry sitting in his study and listening to Mary's quill as it scratches away industriously (for Mary copies quotations from the poets into Henry's lectures) is rapt away in a dream and the dream, as we would expect, takes him back to the sunny joy of Spain. "I can almost fancy myself in Spain," he notes in his journal, "the morning is so soft and beautiful. The tessellated shadow of the honeysuckle lies motionless on my study floor, as if it were a figure in the carpet; and through the open window comes the fragrance of the wildbriar and the mock orange. The birds are caroling in the trees, and their shadows flit across the window as they dart to and fro in the sunshine; while the murmur of the bee, the cooing of the doves from the eaves, and the whirring of a little humming-bird that has its nest in the honeysuckle, send up a sound of joy to meet the rising sun." The still charm of the summer landscape in New England when every leaf seems in a delicate trance and when the shadow of a bird or the tiny booming of a bee breaks like a miracle on the intelligence is implicit in these sentences. There is even a thought here that might be developed into a symbol of Henry's life. He notes the shadow of the honeysuckle on the study floor appearing like a figure

FROM A PENCIL-SKETCH.

HENRY WADSWORTH LONGFELLOW
28 YEARS OLD

MARY POTTER LONGFELLOW
    The Poet's first wife
    From a portrait in the possession of Mrs. Higginson

in the carpet. It is Henry James (not to be born for eleven years from this time) who is to write that supremely controlled story, *The Figure in the Carpet*, wherein a man strives ineffectually to discover the secret of a great writer's genius, the interior spiritual pattern of his work, the "figure in the carpet," and why may not we take this shadow of the honeysuckle on Henry's study floor as the pattern of our young man's self-expression? This moveless shadow of sweetness, graceful in outline and without depth, is the figure in *his* carpet.

He has yet to begin the weaving although he is already unconsciously sorting out the various threads that are to go into it. For the present, he is no more than a young man, newly married, and knocking at the door of life. In spite of his youth he is wholly contained as a man, already mature in deliberation, indeed too much so to quite achieve the ends for which he longs. But his peculiar caste of mind bulwarks him against too poignant a realization of the shortcomings of his creative instinct, and, though he may be depressed at the formidable heights of literature and actually pass through a period of trepidation that silences him so far as poetry is concerned, he is on the whole happy enough. He plays his flute in the evening to the accompaniment of Professor Cleaveland's harpsichord, the same flute that he offered to play for the French maid by the banks of the Loire, and the stream of Time flows sedately along by the pine groves of the college buildings. The rigid Calvinism of Brunswick has been breached to a degree in that a Unitarian Church has been built there and part of Henry's activities as a man concenter in this religious edifice. He attends regularly and enters into church activities, singing for a time in the choir and even conducting the Bible class. New books trickle in to him and he is "as delighted with them as a child with a new drum." Indeed, books have now taken the place of that "pretty drum, with an eagle painted on it" which the six-year-old boy desired in 1814 when there was war and rumors of war at Portland.

III

Side by side with the professor and the man walks the writer. If Henry is an eminently safe professor and a wholly contained man he is no less a tentative and cautious writer with no desire to astonish or perplex his modest group of readers. The genesis of neither a Poe nor a Whitman is contained in this urbane young man. He has industriously applied himself to the production of textbooks for his classes and parallel with this "chore" work moves that slightly deeper urge which affords him his modest means of self-expression. It is natural to assume that Henry, now installed as an educator and somewhat his own master, will bethink himself regarding his boyhood ambition of achieving fame as a poet, but there is no evidence to show that he is strongly bitten by any such desire. There is no flame in him. The pedestrian note is accented so overwhelmingly as to break down any signposts that zealous disciples of the young man may choose to erect as indicative of a growing poet. Henry is simply *not* a growing poet and that is all there is to it. He is not troubled by the perilous and incomprehensible moods and passions that animate the poet's soul. It is true that he thinks about poetry occasionally and once, after an eight years' silence, he dips into it, writing a Phi Beta Kappa ode for a Bowdoin class, a poem which is later revised and read at Harvard, where the orator, Edward Everett, compares the handsome young man to a "flashing sickle." But this poem, a strictly occasional and academic piece of work, does not establish Henry's claim to the heritage of the poet. Indeed, the ode may be searched for in vain among his collected works. It has not even the curious urge of the juvenilia and the young man never retrieved it from the tentative wreckage of the past. No; Henry is not a poet. The most impressionable years of his life pass, years that include his European travels with all their unexpected vistas and his first marriage, and the young man does not burst into song. What kind of a talent is this that lets the years between twenty and thirty slip away without any accomplishment? To be succinct, it is a prose talent, a talent with impressions to give the world but no passions.

We catch Henry's own comments on his silence in a letter to his friend Greene. "I am proud to have your favorable opinion of those little poetic attempts of mine which date so many years back," he writes on June 27, 1830. "I had long ceased to attach any kind of value to them, and indeed, to think of them. Since my return I have written one piece of poetry, but have not published a line. You need not be alarmed on that score. I am all prudence now, since I can form a more accurate judgment of the merit of poetry. If I ever publish a volume, it will be many years first." Indeed, it is to be nine years before *Voices of the Night* appears. Henry goes on to state, ". . . I have such an engrossing interest in the studies of my profession that I write very seldom except in connection with those studies." Now there appears to be a rather subtle reason for Henry's silence in poetry. While he was yet a boy and the incoherent urge of song for the mere sake of song was upon him he possessed the crude scattered background of his native terrain and, such as it was, it afforded him the adolescent sustenance that made possible some few verses. He had no rigorous standards and did not know what wretched poetry he was turning out because the literary level of America was not high enough to dwarf his compositions and shrink them to their true size. If Henry had kept to this background and known no other he would never have become an eminent figure—that desire so close to his heart—because he did not possess enough richness in himself. He is no mine, but a fallow field waiting for innumerable plowshares. As a youth he was a "copy-cat" and sitting down before the models of Washington Irving in prose and William Cullen Bryant in poetry he managed to produce work that was rather pleasing for a boy of sixteen or seventeen in the America of 1825. His father was suspicious of the crudities implicit in this work and, perhaps, aware that the boy was being overpraised by the itinerant editors who got something for nothing out of their laudations. But it took the European trip to open Henry's eyes. There he discovered what a fledgling he was. He was growing older, of course, and maturity combined with travel and a closer knowledge of the great literatures of the world sufficed to awake in him a "more accurate judgment of the merit of poetry." This "more accurate judgment" shamed and silenced him because he had no flaming inward urge that drastically demanded expression. His emotions were either too sluggish or he was always, because of his training, too self-conscious to let himself go. Not even love could move him. It is a most excellent thing to be self-critical and to destroy one's puerile efforts but it is not good to be so self-critical as to silence one's self completely. Such discipline merely reveals an urge so feeble as to be dumb in the face of literature.

Henry, partially bereft of his background and seeth-
ing unconsciously from the pricks of his European
adventure, is floundering about and semi-satisfying
himself with modest prose ventures and translations.
The poetry implicit in him, that gentle universal vein
whose clipped wings lifted it but ever so slightly above
the vernacular of the semi-literate American public of
his time, still sleeps, but there are two streaks in Henry
that are to bring it out.   One is the result of America
and the other is the result of Europe.   America gives
him that didactic concern which is to read moral lessons
into the domesticities of existence and Europe is to
afford him the many colored background for his facile
stanzas.   He has yet to realize Europe as Europe, an
intellectual achievement that is, even to the last, but
incompletely attained.   Indeed, it is not until his second
European visit, already in the near future although unknown to the young man, that the old world background affords him sufficient sustenance for song.   He
has yet to pass through a spiritual Valley of the Shadow
that will in some measure rarefy his nature and give
him that slight impetus which changes prose into a
pleasant but limited poetry.   This, be it repeated, is in
the near future.   For the present he is without a decisive
urge and somewhat demoralized by an acute realization
of how good poetry may be and how limited he is to
perpetuate his moods.   Part of this realization is unconscious, perhaps, for Henry is not unduly self-ana-
lytic.   He cannot sit down and dissect himself with any
measure of success.   Instead of this he slides grace-
fully over the surface of life, painstakingly applying
himself to his duties and recapturing the glow of life
(as it appears to him) in the essays that go to make up
Outre Mer, that first book of prose which is to be
published in 1835.

Henry, therefore, is a prose writer during the four years at Bowdoin following his marriage to Mary Potter. Settled in their vine-covered cottage on Federal Street with the great elms before the door, the two young people lead a gently social life that is somewhat repressed by Henry's assiduous application to books. A single week's entries from his journals will show the sort of existence the young man leads.

November 29, 1832. Five o'clock in the morning. Commence the preparatory reading for an essay on the History of the Spanish Language; beginning with the *Origines de la Lengua Española* . . . por Don Gregorio Mayáns y Siscár. Finished the first volume. In the evening read four chapters of the first book of Livy.

30th. Rose at half-past five. Ran over the second volume of Mayáns; commenced the second book of Aldrete's *Origen y Principio de la Lengua Castellana.* Read five chapters in Livy, and the fourth and fifth acts of Ben Jonson's *Alchemist;* a fine comedy, though too broad,—the better suited to the prurient taste of his age, of which his noble genius should have been the castigator, not the pander.

December 1. Commenced a new introduction to my Phi Beta Kappa poem, to be delivered in Cambridge in August next. I am flattered that the committee of the Society should have thought of me as Poet. Finished Aldrete. He is altogether too diffuse for my taste. His work wants perspective; all objects seem of equal size, and he devotes as much time to points of minor consideration as to the most important. Cortes read to me Chapters XV.—XVII. of *Don Quixote.* It is a pleasure to hear it read by a Spaniard. One might believe that the Knight of the Rueful Countenance and his Squire were talking with us.

2d. Sunday. A bright sunshine after yesterday's snowstorm. Read Massillon's sermon, *Sur les Tentations des Grands;* one of Wieland's Psalms; Livy, three chapters.

3d. Revised and corrected a paper for "The Schoolmaster," entitled "Saturday Afternoon." Read Moratin's Comedy,

El Si de las Niñas, one of the best pieces of the modern
theater. In the evening, four chapters of Livy; among them
chapter XXIX. of Book first, containing the beautiful description of the destruction of Alba.

4th. Ran over a Dissertation on the best method of studying
the languages of the Bible, translated from the German by
Professor Stuart. Livy, four chapters.

Interlarding these labors—labors that show plainly
how intensively Henry is cultivating his mind by drop-
ping the seeds of foreign culture into it—are the various prose attempts. They begin before the young
man's marriage and continue to the end of his five and
a half years at Bowdoin. Alexander Everett, whose
friendship Henry had secured in Madrid, has been
appointed editor of the *North American Review,* the
most important quarterly in America, and this appointment affords the young professor an outlet for his
essays. In April, 1831, the first of them appears. It
is called the *Origin and Progress of the French Language,* and is just such an article as we would expect
from a young professor intensively concerned with
philological subjects. There is scholarship apparent
and accuracy. There is also dullness. Parallel with
these contributions to the *North American Review* are
the more personal sketches that appear in *The New
England Magazine,* an enterprise started in Boston in
1831 by Joseph T. Buckingham. It is in July of this
year that the opening installment of *The Schoolmaster* is printed. But before noting this series it will
be more consistent to enumerate the more scholarly
efforts called forth by the *North American Review.*
Especially is Henry's second contribution, *The De-
fence of Poetry*—it may be found in the January,
1832, issue of the quarterly—to be approached with
more than ordinary curiosity. Henry here delivers

himself of some sound nationalistic reasoning and posits a poetry which he rarely achieved in his own career. "With us," he announces, "the spirit of the age is clamorous for utility,—for visible, tangible utility,—for bare, brawny, muscular utility. We would be roused to action by the voice of the populace and the sounds of the crowded mart, and not 'lulled asleep in shady idleness with poets' pastimes.' We are swallowed up in schemes for gain, and engrossed with contrivances for bodily enjoyments as if this particle of dust were immortal,—as if the soul needed an aliment, and the mind no raiment." How can we account for these statements except by ascribing to Henry a brief perspective on the hurried growth of his own country occasioned by his observation of Europe? Fresh from the life of Spain and Italy and Germany he notices all the more clearly the American "schemes for gain" and the potential Age of Mechanical Invention already knocking at the door and "engrossed with contrivances for bodily enjoyment." The true American, however, will adjust himself to all this and draw from the "bare, brawny, muscular" scene an autochthonous poetry. Henry seems to realize this for he writes: "We wish our native poets would give a more national character to their writings. In order to effect this, they have only to write from their own feelings and impressions, from the influence of what they see around them, and not from any preconceived notions of what poetry ought to be, caught by reading many books, and imitating many models." This advice is excellent but does Henry follow it? No, he doesn't. ". . . Let us have no more skylarks and nightingales," he adds. "For us they warble only in books." All this is from the young man who is to be rudely chastised by Margaret Fuller for his imitative-ness, for the Pentecosts and bishops' caps and heather of his first book of verse.

This defense of poetry is the solitary essay contributed to the *North American Review* that is of more than perfunctory interest to the modern reader, although it is well to be imagined that the additional pieces in the quarterly interested and instructed the America of the 1830's. The very titles, *History of the Italian Languages and Dialects* (October, 1832), *Spanish Devotional and Moral Poetry* (April, 1833) and *Old English Romances* (October, 1833), show how concerned Henry is with the results of his travels. His mind is immersed with foreign letters and he has but scant time to fling a thought to the state of literature in America. Perhaps his statement should be revised a bit to infer that Henry's thoughts of the state of American literature circle about a conviction that the native intelligence requires an adequate comprehension of foreign culture. It is possible that some dim realization floats about in the back of his mind, a realization based on the premise that the American cannot wholly know America until he has known Europe. But if this is so it is too nebulous to be stated forthright. On the one hand we have Henry in a single essay urging a decided nationalism on native writers, and on the other hand we have him busily spreading the glad tidings that there is such a thing as European culture and European languages. The young man's nationalism springs from his instincts and his Europeanism springs from his influences. It is his influences that shape his more personal writings if we are to regard the series of papers called *The Schoolmaster* as in this category.

Six chapters of *The Schoolmaster* appear at irregular intervals in *The New England Magazine* from July,

1831, to February, 1833, and then they are discontinued, for Henry by this time is reworking this matter into *Outre Mer*. "I am a schoolmaster in the little village of Sharon," he declares in the first installment of this semi-fictional treatment of his European travels. "A son of New England, I have been educated in all her feelings and prejudices. To her maternal care I owe the little that is good within me; and upon her bosom I hope to repose hereafter when my worldly task is done, and my soul, like a rejoicing schoolboy, shall close its weary book, and burst forth from this earthly schoolhouse. My childhood was passed at my native village, in the usual amusements and occupations of that age; but, as I grew up, I became satiated with the monotony of my life. A restless spirit prompted me to visit foreign countries. I said, with the cosmopolite, 'the world is a kind of book in which he who has seen his own country only has read but one page.' Guided by this feeling, I became a traveler. I have traversed France on foot, smoked my pipe in a Flemish inn——." All this is a setting of the stage for the travel description that is to come in future installments. The second chapter is practically the same as *The Norman Diligence* in *Outre Mer*, and the third, *The Village of Auteuil*, contains the material now to be found in the chapter with that title in *Outre Mer*. Indeed, it is needless to plow through these six chapters, noting the differences between them and Henry's first book of prose. Much of this periodical matter is revised and rewritten and fully a half of it is canceled when the young man puts his book in shape. There is little to be said about it except that the influence of Irving's *Sketchbook* vein is much in evidence. These chapters are certainly fashioned from the material which engrossed Henry while he was studying in Göttingen.

Henry reached the age of twenty-six with no more
to his credit than these philological essays, these travel
sketches, a solitary poem, two forgotten stories and
several public addresses, one of them on Female Education. It is a modest showing but we must remember
that the young man is now retarded by "prudence"
and a fear of his own abilities. He will wait until he
has something really fine to say. Much has happened
to him. He has traveled extensively, he has been appointed an astonishingly young professor; he has
married; and he has cultivated a deliberate and kindly
exterior. He is "playing safe" with life and waiting
expectantly for opportunity to knock at his cottage door.
And opportunity, sometimes surprisingly well disposed,
is fluttering about Cambridge and casting fond eyes at
Brunswick, Maine, where the painstaking young man is
so immersed in his scholastic pursuits.

IV

Time moves sluggishly and the young professor,
having exhausted the potentialities of Brunswick,
having established his courses, having written his
philological essays, having seen the seasons wax and
wane about the small college, experiences the prick of
unrest. By 1832 he is writing to a friend: "On com-
mencing my professional duties, I was actuated by the
same feelings which seem now to influence you. I
sought retirement; and I am confident that I did wisely.
Next September completes three years that I have been
laboring on in this little solitude; and now I feel a
strong desire to tread a stage on which I can take longer
strides and speak to a larger audience." So he begins
to cast about him for means of escape. Brunswick
cramps him now although he is too urbane to feel the

175

pinch disagreeably. Still he would like to get away.
That "eminent career" is shining somewhere in the
distance before him and there seems to be but small
opportunity to develop it at Bowdoin. The college,
after all, is in bad condition. The Maine Legislature
refuses much-needed appropriations and the faculty
must struggle along as best it may. There even crops
up a dispute about the presidency of the institution, a
complicated matter that must be taken into the courts
and made a matter of tortuous litigation. Henry is
drawn slightly into this and it is not at all to his liking.
The young man intimates his desire for a change, query-
ing his friends discreetly enough. For two years he
casts about for a new sphere of action. Various possibilities present themselves and Henry tests them out.
Greene, for instance, suggests a professorship in New
York University and there is some correspondence
culminating in a visit to New York. It is on this visit
that Henry bears a letter of recommendation from
George Ticknor of Harvard, a letter that is like a peal
of trumpets. It gives a clear idea of what Henry's
elder contemporaries think of him. "Soon after he was
graduated at Brunswick," writes the amiable Cambridge
professor, "he became known to me by an interest quite
remarkable at his age—and still more so, perhaps, from
the circumstances in which he was placed—an interest,
I mean, in early Provençal literature, and in the literatures of Spain and Italy. He passed some time in
France, and still more in Italy and in Spain; and his
knowledge of the language and literature of each of
these countries has, for several years past, seemed to
me extraordinary. He writes and speaks Spanish with
a degree of fluency and exactness which I have known
in no American born of parents speaking English as
their vernacular. His knowledge of Spanish literature

is extensive and to be relied upon; and several publications he has made on the subject have been accompanied by poetical translations of much spirit and fidelity. Besides this, he is, for his years, an accomplished general scholar, particularly in modern literature, and full of activity and eagerness in the pursuit of knowledge. His address and manners are very prepossessing, his temper amiable, and his character without blemish from his earliest years." In spite of this letter nothing comes of the proposed professorship at New York. It is to the point, though, to remember this enthusiasm of Ticknor's for it is to bear fruit shortly and in the most pleasantly surprising manner for Henry.

Other prospects are considered. Mary writes to her sister-in-law in Portland: "Henry left us Friday noon in the mail for Boston, as George will tell you. I do not like the idea of his going to Northampton at all—although it would be a most beautiful place to reside in. Still I feel sure he would not like the care of a school, and such an extensive establishment as that is, too." This "extensive establishment" is Mr. Joseph Coggswell's school at Round Hill, that educator having decided to go to Raleigh. Henry, however, demands $1,600 a year and negotiations speedily flag. There are still other projects to consider, one of them being the founding of a school in Boston with Greene as partner and another a possible post at the far-away University of Virginia. The Boston idea is rapidly disposed of but the tentative negotiations with the Southern college continue for some time. At this time the Southern college is, perhaps, the most progressive institution in the country. It has, in some measure, liberalized itself from the pietistic punctilios of such Northern centers of learning as Harvard. "No news from Virginia," writes Henry to his fidus Achates, Greene, on April

26,1834. "Oh, vile pen, ink, and paper! I write this in agony." The young professor is discovering that it is easier to get into Brunswick than out of it. After all, the fact that one's father is a trustee of an institution is quite liable to render one somewhat ignorant regarding the difficulties of living. Life is not so simple when one must cleave one's own way without the pleasant assistance of friends. Henry, by now, is suffering from a dampened ardor and it begins to look as though Bowdoin is pretty much of an Old Man of the Sea who clings tenaciously to the as yet young and unbowed shoulders. It is at this juncture that the erratic goddess, Opportunity, travels from Cambridge to Brunswick in the form of a letter, having, presumably, received a nudge from George Ticknor. We may imagine the excitement in the Federal Street cottage, the enthusiasm of Henry and the trepidation of Mary, when the letter is opened and discovered to read:

"Dear Sir,—Professor Ticknor has given notice that it is his intention to resign his office of Smith Professor of Modern Languages in Harvard University, as soon as the Corporation shall have fixed upon a successor.

"The duty of nominating to that office devolves upon me; and after great deliberation and inquiry my determination is made to nominate you for that office under circumstances which render your appointment not doubtful,—provided I receive a previous assurance from you of your acceptance of it. To ascertain this is the object of the present letter.

"The salary will be fifteen hundred dollars a year. Residence in Cambridge will be required. The duties of the professorship will be of course those which are required from the occupant of a full professorship, and such as the Corporation and the Overseers may appoint. If a relation such as I suggest with this University be one acceptable to you, I shall be obliged by an early answer.

"Should it be your wish, previously to entering upon the duties of the office, to reside in Europe, at your own expense, a year or eighteen months for the purpose of a more perfect attainment of the German, Mr. Ticknor will retain his office till your return.

Very respectfully, I am
Yours, etc., etc.,
JOSIAH QUINCY."

This letter is dated December 1, 1834. Henry is twenty-seven years old. "Good fortune comes at last and I certainly shall not reject it," the young man writes to his father. To Greene he pours out his joy. "Great things have happened since I last wrote you. A few days ago—*this is confidential*—I received a note from Pres. Quincy of Harv. University informing me that Mr. Ticknor had signified his intention to resign his Prof as soon as a successor should be appointed, and that if I would give him assurance of accepting the situation he would nominate me, under circumstances that would render my election not doubtful. Some further correspondence has passed between us, and next week I am going to Cambridge to meet the gentlemen —satisfy myself upon some points which I wish to know—and the whole business will then be brought to a close. Now tell me—am I not a very lucky fellow? Do you not wish me joy of my good fortune? Is it not most cheering to have such a place offered one—without making an effort to obtain it? How different from that infernal New York business.

"Well, I pass a few days in Boston—and then I go to New York to publish my book, for which I am to be paid part in advance."

For the second time Henry has received a professorial appointment, "without making an effort to obtain it," which comes as an unexpected benefit, and for the second time it is to take him to Europe. The goddess, Opportunity, can sometimes be excessively generous. The young man goes to Cambridge and matters are settled in the most satisfactory manner, an arrangement being concluded whereby Henry is to visit Germany and the Scandinavian countries to perfect himself for his new post. It is while Henry is on this brief visit to the scene of his future life that his old school friend, John Owen, introduces him to Cornelius C. Felton, Professor of Greek at Harvard, and it is in Felton's rooms that the youthful Bowdoin educator meets an unknown Suffolk County attorney named Charles Sumner, a young man who is to share with Greene the intimate friendship of Henry's life. These are but flitting contacts, however, and Henry is soon back in Brunswick breaking up his household preparatory for the second European trip. By February he is sending lists of his books to Greene with prices attached and offering the lot at a deduction of twenty-five dollars. Everything is in confusion. Bells ring and moving men tramp through the house. The carpet is snatched from beneath Henry's feet in his study. Furniture is nailed in boxes and shipped back to Portland. There are letters to write and farewells to be made. There is the important matter of concluding negotiations with Harper and Brothers in New York relative to the publication of *Outre Mer* in a two volume edition. Already some of these chapters, rewritten from *The Schoolmaster* essays of *The New England Magazine*, have appeared in two paper-covered parts, elegant trifles that adorn more than one parlor table. By the last of March all this business is concluded and in April, 1835, Henry is again on the high seas, this time with a young wife and two young women friends of hers, certainly agreeable enough company for the impres-

sionable young man. He sets forth auspiciously, totally
unconscious of the tragic event in store for him.

v

England welcomes an agreeably tempered young
man who is about to embark upon a professorship in a
major American college, although it is doubtful if the
English intellectuals take any great stock in the educational potentialities of America. London is kind to
Henry. He breakfasts with Sir John Bowring. He
dines with the Lockharts, J. G. "always less scornful
than his beautiful features proclaimed him," according
to Abraham Hayward. He spends an evening at Mr.
Babbage's where he meets and converses with Miss Jane
Porter, Abraham Hayward, and the reigning beauties,
Mrs. Blackwood and Lady Seymour. There, too,
he meets Sydney, Lady Morgan, wife of the eminent
physician, Sir Charles Morgan, and author of the
Wild Irish Girl. At the house of Lady Dudley
Stuart, who is, among other things, the daughter of
Lucien Bonaparte, he hears Rubini and Grisi sing. He
runs across his fellow townsman who has developed
into a New York littérateur, Nathaniel Parker Willis,
and finds him hobnobbing with the Duchess of St.
Albans. It is regrettable that Henry does not accompany Willis about London more, for Willis is blessed
with an entrée to Lady Blessington's house and there
Henry might meet an ambitious young Jewish novelist
named Benjamin Disraeli. Henry certainly would be
interested in Disraeli's waistcoats, for by this time the
youthful professor is beginning to blossom out in sartorial splendor himself. For three weeks Henry flutters about London, dapper, gracious and armed to the
teeth with letters of introduction from influential folk

"back home." With him goes Mary, quiet, self-possessed, always looking for the didactic lining in the cloud, most properly subdued to the New England plane for women. The young professor is still floating along on that unvexed tide of slow development and appraisement that has been both his good fortune and his weakness since he was graduated from Bowdoin. Life has not bitten at him as yet. He is unhurt, sanguine, happily engaged in rearing his cloud-castle. It is true that he has been somewhat neglected by life if the truth be told, that life has offered a cool, impartial front and barely noticed this ambitious young man who has so far escaped the barbarities of existence. The gentle-minded bookman is living in a world of limitations, perhaps, but not of cruelties. So it is with a bland and confident front that he hurries about London, placing an edition of *Outre Mer* with Bentley (the book has already appeared in America), dashing in and out of bookshops, making delightful impressions to right and left as he attends teas and dinners. One of his many letters of introduction is to Thomas Carlyle (it is the gift of Emerson) and the Scotch writer visits the young man. "He has very unpolished manners and a broad Scottish accent," notes Mary, but she succumbs to his "fine language and beautiful thoughts." They take tea therefore with Carlyle and go to Chantrey's studio with him and Mrs. Carlyle, who is, according to the observant Mary, "a lovely woman, with very simple and pleasing manners." They see the Queen pass into the city escorted by the Horse Guards and Mary notes that "the Queen is very unpopular among the people." Two years later—in 1837—another Queen is to rule England and she is to come to the throne just when Henry is settling down to his labors at Cambridge. His first book of original poetry is to

appear two years after Victoria's coronation and his long
life is to run parallel to hers (although she is to outlive
him a score of years) and the spirit that is to dominate
her reign is to dominate his mind as well. And noting
these dates it is also of interest to discover that the
young Disraeli is to be elected to his first public office in
1837. This year, too,—to continue profitless parallels
—is to mark the removal of Alfred Tennyson from
Somersby to Epping and so nearer to London where he
is to enter somewhat sulkily into the semi-Bohemianism
of the metropolis. The actors in the great Victorian
drama are advancing from the wings and the long-
drawn sugary epic (an epic not without its astonishing
high moments) is about to begin.

Henry's three weeks in London pass swiftly, and on
the ninth of June he departs with his party by steamer
for Hamburg. Immediately setting out for Copenhagen and, eventually, Stockholm, where he is to pass
the midsummer months, he is soon immersed in Scandinavian scenery and customs, responding with alacrity
to the charm of a country which is always to be near
his heart, second only, perhaps, to Spain, that lost
Southern land of his boyhood dreams. At Lydkoping
he reads in the public square at midnight and listens to
the watchman crying from the church tower. He
passes through groves of pine and sees drooping fir trees
with rose-colored cones. White-haired children and
civil peasants hurry to open the frequent gates for
him. The little timber houses painted red flash by.
He sneezes and the good-natured Northerners cry,
"God bless you!" He finds the floors of the taverns
strewn with the fragrant tips of fir boughs. Stopping
in communities where there are no inns he puts up at
private houses, sleeping in rooms where the walls are
hung with rude Bible pictures, where the curdled milk

is dipped from the pan with heavy silver spoons, where he eats oaten cakes that are months old and bread with aniseed and coriander in it. Village churches dot the wayside and by each church are the graves where the dead sleep with their heads to the westward. Through the traveler's mind run thoughts of Odin and Thor, of Vikings and their beaked ships, of the fiery swords of the Northern Lights. It is near the end of June when he reaches Stockholm and presents various letters of introduction from that unceasing store which he carries, letters to Berzelius, to Liljogren, to Schroder. He is fortunate in meeting distinguished men and his way is made easier for him by the American minister, Hughes, and the former charge d'affaires, Appleton. The hand of friendship is extended by Arfwedson, who possesses an American wife, and Baron Stackelbach who has been Swedish minister at Washington. "They are unwearied in their attentions," Henry notes. The Puritan is still rampant in him, however, and he is scandalized to find clergymen smoking in the streets, drinking punch in the cafés, and playing cards on Sunday. Henry's eyebrows lift and his New England lips grow thin. The peasants, he decides, are "dull and lumpish," after all.

Settling in Stockholm he plunges into studies in Swedish, putting himself under the direction of Professor Lignel of the University of Upsala who is passing the summer in the capital. Mellin gives him lessons in Finnish. "The Swedish language," he writes, "is soft and musical, with an accent like the lowland Scotch. It is an easy language to read, but difficult to speak with correctness, owing to some grammatical peculiarities. Its literature swarms with translations. Cooper and Irving are well known, most of their works having been translated, and are read with delight. I

have also a Swedish copy of Slidell's *Year in Spain*.
Sweden has one great poet, and only one. That is
Tegner, Bishop of Wexio, who is still living. His
noblest work is *Frithiofs Saga*, a heroic poem, founded
on an old tradition." It is from *Frithiofs Saga* that
Henry is to imbibe some of the atmosphere that is
later to appear in *Evangeline*, for Henry is extremely receptive. His nature fills easily to the brim
with the books he reads and the land he sees and the
people with whom he talks and then pours over and
into the work upon which he is engaged at the moment.
It is this receptivity which is later to draw down the
verbal castigations of Margaret Fuller and Edgar Allan
Poe.

After a month or more of intensive study in Stockholm Henry makes a trip to Upsala where he wanders
about the University and observes with some degree of
astonishment the conditions that maintain there. The
professors, he discovers, receive their salary in corn
which is sold for them by an agent, their income therefore varying with the market price of the grain. For
private instruction they receive thirty-seven cents an
hour. In the library he pores over the famous Codex
Argenteus of the sixth century and in the cathedral he
stands before the ancient wooden image of the war-god,
Thor. He wanders through the botanical gardens and
thinks of Linnæus. The summer, however, is cold and
rainy and Henry returns to Stockholm, there to pack up
and start for Copenhagen. At Gothenburg he is de-
tained a week waiting for a steamboat and he passes
the time agreeably, meeting Olaf Wijk—to whom he
presents one of his ubiquitous letters of introduction—
and visiting the wild environs of the town. Reaching
Copenhagen he settles down again, scattering abroad
more letters of introduction, this time to Molbech,

Thomsen, Rafn, and Finn Magnussen. The Danish city pleases him. "It is a finely built city," he writes, "with spacious streets and handsome houses." However, there is something desolate about it and Henry's sensitive nature responds. Perhaps there is a faint prophetic sound of dark wings in the air above him. Anyway, he is briefly troubled. But there is much to keep him amused and his active mind busy, a library of four hundred thousand volumes, a crowd of literary men, lessons in Danish from one of the librarians, A. Bolling, the Museum of Northern Antiquities, and the Round Tower with its huge collection of Icelandic MSS. He becomes intimately acquainted with Professor Rafn, twelve years his senior and immeasurably his superior in scholarship, and Rafn asks him about the American Indians and their habits. For a moment the young man's mind is turned back to the aborigines of his native land. It is due to Rafn's instigation that Henry is nominated and made a member of the Royal Society of Northern Antiquities. He is in Copenhagen but six weeks approximately and these short periods of study must be borne in mind. No student can perfect himself in so limited a period and it therefore becomes apparent that Henry is taking his erudition at high speed. Two months at the most in Stockholm and less than that in Copenhagen are not going to make a Scandinavian authority out of this young man. He is blessed with a fatal facility but he is not exhaustive in his application.

By the first of October he is in Amsterdam, having relinquished the idea of passing the winter in Berlin. "The objects I had in view could be equally well accomplished in a pleasanter and cheaper place," he writes to his father. He has put Scandinavia behind him. There are probably unnoted reasons for this transference farther south, for Henry by this time must be apprised of the fact that Mary's condition is not all that it should be and that she is shortly to become a mother.

VI

On November 29, 1835, Mary dies at Rotterdam, her death being due to the premature birth of a child.

This unexpected blow strikes Henry like a thunderbolt. His warm comfortable scheme of living has been destroyed. For the first time he stands face to face with tragedy and he must endure it in a foreign land without friends or relatives by his side. The steps that lead up to this tragedy are few and may be disposed of speedily enough. For three weeks Mary has lain ill in Amsterdam, having given premature birth to her child on the night of her arrival, but the thought of fatal consequences does not seem to have visited Henry strongly. He occupies this enforced leisure in studying the Dutch language and in wandering about the bookstores and purchasing old tomes from the Jewish dealers. Mary recovers, indeed, seems quite restored and traveling is resumed by way of the Hague and Delft. On the night of their arrival at Rotterdam the frail wife has a relapse, suffering from extreme debility, low fever, and nervous headache. This occurs on October 23rd. On the 27th Mary grows worse, then seems to recover slowly and by November 11th she sits up. But within two days she is seized with a violent rheumatism and goes back to the bed from which she is never to rise. Still Henry feels no imminent tragedy or else he manages most successfully to conceal his forebodings. On November 26 he is writing to his father: "My own health is perfectly good. I pass most of my time in reading and writing, having one or two acquaintances here who supply me with books. The most agreeable and friendly man I have met here is an English clergyman, Dr. Bosworth, known in the literary world by an Anglo-Saxon grammar. He is now publishing a dictionary of the same language. Rotterdam is rather a pretty place. The houses are large, and many of them fine; and there are public walks on the banks of the river, though at this season the trees are bare and black." But two days later the inexorable truth is slowly impinging upon Henry's startled consciousness. Mary continues to sink and the young man writes: "I am much grieved to say that Mary is not so well to-day. She is very feeble, and the physicians tell me that her situation is dangerous. My anxiety is very great. She suffers no pain, and is perfectly calm, but does not regain her strength . . ." It is possible that Henry can hardly grasp this unexpected and cruel development. The next day Mary dies and there follow the heartbreaking duties of re-arranging one's life as a solitary individual again. Henry no longer has this quiet helpmate at his side. There is no one to keep his journal in order, to do his copying for him, to apprize the families back home as to various movements. This woman, who is no more than a shadow in Henry's long life, is, perhaps, the most affecting personage in it. Henry, suddenly broken by grief, attends to the few pathetic functions that follow this death. He carefully lays away the garments which he is to carry all the way back to America, to Cambridge from which haven he is to write to his dead wife's sister, Eliza: "By to-morrow's steamer I shall send you two trunks, containing the clothes which once belonged to your sister. What I have suffered in getting them ready to send to you, I cannot describe." We may imagine the young man in Rotterdam folding and laying away the quaint old-fashioned garments of Mary. It is sometimes the hardest part of death, this putting away for all time the inconsequential things, the garments, the books, the odd knick-knacks, for the spirit of the dead is in these things and it may never be removed from them. Henry must turn his face alone to Germany now, for he will still adhere to his plan of studying in Heidelberg, and he does so like a man stunned. For some men such a sudden death would mean a drastic tearing apart of the very scheme of life and a shifting into altogether new channels, but we must remember that Henry, from the very first, has always made the best of things as they are and adjusted himself accordingly. He may not be quite a Doctor Pangloss for he is not consistently cheerful, but he is deeply imbued with a religious fervor that carries him through the dark ways without too great a loss in spiritual strength. The grief that the young man experiences is real but it does not touch those dark levels of tragedy that mark great love affairs. Henry does not possess the passion to so forget himself. Rather does he strive to face life bravely and he does so, although part of his very strength is implicit in that receptivity that accepts and reacts so agreeably to the innumerable offerings of life. The young man will never tear a passion to tatters, kill himself, run amok, or forget his good manners. Instead of this he turns to Germany, there to continue his studies and prepare himself for the career which is still before him.

VII

The effect of Germany on Henry is incalculable. If the young man is to be regarded as a sort of American

Queen Victoria (and this is set down with no invidious implication other than to emphasize a total lack of moralistic analysis and an eminently "safe" observation of life) the Fatherland is no less to be considered in the aspect of a spiritual Prince Consort, a sentimental and blameless Albert, who stood at Henry's elbow whispering the sweet banalities of a semi-intellectual domesticity. It was, of course, the Germany that Henry's nature instinctively desired that entered upon the scene, a Germany of romantic loftinesses, innocent herd-girls, haunted castles, and loudly chanting idealists. Another Germany existed but Henry no more than the most popular German writers of the day seemed to see it. We must remember that the Germany of this year 1836 was, in the main, an unknown land among English-speaking peoples. The popular idea predicated a plodding race distinguished for sausages, beer and military drill, a race devoid of courtliness and personal refinements and notable in an intellectual sense only for its dry-as-dust philosophy. But this picture is vastly mistaken. Germany is a young land newly knit in a national consciousness. It is bringing to birth a literature that already is seeping into the furthest corners of the earth and which will shortly be almost universal in its application. Even at this early point of time foreign scholars and bookmen, reacting from the ebbing radicalism of the post-literature of the Revolutionary era, are tasting this new romantic vintage and reveling in it. Coleridge had steeped himself in it and Carlyle, enchanted with it, undoubtedly discoursed upon it to the young American visitor. This Germanic influence is to permeate Henry as, in degree, it is also to permeate young Hawthorne, his forgotten classmate. That solitary and reticent personage still buried in Salem is to respond delicately to the mysticism of

Fouque and the comparative subtlety of Tieck. Even
Emerson, the friend of Carlyle, is already inoculated
with this foreign influence, so much so that the Transcendental movement later is to solemnly enunciate
German philosophical principles at second hand.
Therefore when Henry—his sensitive nature debili-
tated by the unexpected sorrow that has befallen him
—slips into Germany he is most responsive to the urges
of the contemporary German attitude toward letters.
In the work of Uhland, Herder, Tieck, Müller, Salis,
and Goethe he is to find those responses to which his
nature will best react. Most important of all, he is
to discover the books of Johann Paul Friedrich Richter
(his dear Jean-Paul) and to find in them the misty
and sentimental philosophy of living which he is never
to outgrow. Richter, whose work is the exaggeration
and sentimentality of the "Sturm und Drang" inoculated with the granite-like idealism of Fichte and placed
in the old-fashioned scaffolding of the German Romance, gives Henry exactly what he desires. In this
immediate acceptance of the Germanic attitude Henry
is alienating himself from the American scene albeit he
is doing it most unconsciously.

Henry enters Germany by way of Dusseldorf, where,
stopping for half an hour, he wanders into a Roman
Catholic church and in the grave stillness of the ele-
vated Host he experiences a brief flash of peace. The
old Puritan in him must have slumbered at this time.
At Bonn he takes the time to call upon the aged August
Wilhelm Schlegel who appears to have unthawed for
the occasion and welcomed the mournful young pilgrim. He resumed his journey along the Rhine, pausing at Rolandseck where in the early morning mist he
sees the Drachenfels rising like a hooded monk. Co-
blenz is reached and in the twilight he stands upon the

191

esplanade of Ehrenbreitstein. On his way to Bingen he pauses to climb through falling snow to the ruined castle, Stolzenfels. At Salzig he crosses the river, visits the ruins of "the Brothers" and wanders down the defile to the Kloster where he rests under the walnut trees and listens to the bells pealing noon. Mayence is passed. He reaches Worms and visits the cathedral. At Mannheim he changes horses and by nightfall of this day is driving through the long Hauptstrasse to the Prinz Karl hotel. We may imagine that during these few days, in spite of the companionship of a friendly fellow-traveler, he moves like a man in a lethargy. Besides his traveling companion, grief is riding with him in the carriage. It is therefore to be expected that Germany is seen through the frail veils of sadness. Yet he can react to the immediate stimuli of the place wherein he may pause, whether it be a Roman Catholic church or the home of testy old Schlegel. The young man is bruised and bewildered by the grief that has befallen him and the sadness implicit in his nature is deepened for all time, but he is not destroyed by it. His temperament changes only in degree.

At Heidelberg he settles down in pleasant rooms in the house of Frau Himmelhahn, near the end of the Hauptstrasse towards the Karls Thor. From his window he can see the winding Neckar, as afterwards from his study in Cambridge he is to see the shining Charles. He is a lonely man now, no longer a sanguine youth, and it is from this winter in Heidelberg that we must date his maturity. But a few months before he had been an excited young man looking forward to a European trip which was to be crowned with a professorship at Harvard, and mingling happily enough in social gayeties. The same vista is before him but the colors have

changed. The gold is now gray. All is to come true
except the one desirable thing. The expected child
will not be in Cambridge and the quiet-eyed mother,
as "good as gold," will not be the chatelaine of the
new household. It is alone that Henry must go to
Cambridge as alone he went to Brunswick. He looks
back wistfully at those three happy weeks in London
where he took his young wife everywhere. He thinks
of Stockholm and Copenhagen with regret. There are
friends in Heidelberg but somehow they are not the
same. Mittermaier, the liberal leader and professor-
lawyer, is kind to him. He establishes friendly contacts with Gervinus, the young German scholar; with
Schlosser, the professor of Modern History; with
Reichlin-Meldegg, who is lecturing on Shakespeare
and Schiller; with the venerable Thibaut, who is holding forth on the Pandects; and with Paulus, the aged
theologian. Dr. Umbreit shows him the manuscripts
in the library, Luther's sermons, for example, and
part of his translation of the Bible. But these contacts are no more than scholastic contacts. He turns
elsewhere for that immediate sympathy which he desires
so much. Learning that William Cullen Bryant and
his family are in Heidelberg he calls upon them and
there follow frequent meetings and long walks about
the hills. The mild and thoughtful poet of *Thanatopsis* appeals to Henry. He is somehow touching
hands with home when he talks with him. It is at this
time, too, that he meets Sam Ward of New York and
enters upon that long and unceasing friendship that is
to prove so useful to him so far as the New York
periodicals are concerned. In the same house with
Henry dwell Professor Bertrand of the University
and a youthful Russian baron, van Ramm. The
Slav strikes a responsive chord in Henry and they

ramble about together after studies—for Henry is now studying hard—to Handshuhsheim, to Rohrbach with its ancient mill and gleaming waterfalls, and to the Königsstuhl tower on the mountain top. Together they read Herder and discuss life. Henry draws from his pocket his dear Jean-Paul's "Kampaner-Thal" and holds forth enthusiastically about the vast humanity of Richter. Some degree of equanimity returns to his pliant nature, but Christmas Eve hurls him down again with the news of another tragedy. His brother-in-law, George W. Pierce, the husband of Anne, is dead. "Oh, my dear George," he cries out in January to his friend, Greene, who is now in Florence, "what have I not suffered during the last three months! and I have no friend with me to cheer and console me. . . ." Cast down again he applies himself with increased ferocity to his studies.

He buries himself in old books. He works his way diligently through the ancient poetic lore of Germany. He translates the *Song of the Silent Land* by Salis. "You can well imagine that it requires a great effort for me to discipline my thoughts to regular study," he writes to his father. "I am doing, however, all that I can." After all, Heidelberg is beautiful and he responds to the charm of the scenery. There is a good library crammed with manuscripts wherein he may lose himself. The four hundred students are, in a degree, amusing and pleasant companions, although Henry is quick to note that "they smoke in the streets, and even in the lecture rooms." But the people are limited in their notions. ". . . One of the professors' wives said the other day that in America the ladies sit with their feet out of the window!" Still Henry can stand even this libel.

Spring comes and the almond trees blossom and with

spring comes the *wandertrieb*. The restless young man
must be off although at first this itching of the spirit
is placated only by short trips, a four days' excursion
to Frankfort along the Bergstrasse beneath the cherry
blossoms where he sees the annual fair and Goethe's
house and hears *Don Giovanni*, his favorite opera,
sung, or to the baths of Ems where he drinks Lauben-
heimer wine and relishes it. By April the nightingales
are singing about the old castle at Heidelberg and
crowds begin to fill the alleys of the gardens where
they sip tea and listen to the horn players. It is impossible to be too lonely now. He hears Handel's
Judas Maccabeus played by five hundred musicians
in the castle courtyard but it does not appeal to him.
He likes better to wander up the Philosophen Weg and
through the woods to the Engel Wiese where the for-
get-me-nots bloom. It is more pleasant to sup on
bread and milk at the Stiftsmühle while the cuckoos
sing than to travel into Mannheim to see *Nathan der
Weisse* acted by the seventy-year-old Esslaer. All
this while his restlessness grows upon him. It mounts
up until he can stand it no longer. He desires to go
home but he dreads the lonely ocean voyage. This
fear is like the urge of Fate for eventually he decides
upon Switzerland, traveling to that mountainous country through the Tyrol, and it is in Switzerland that
the first faint prophecies of a renewed life begin to
dawn upon him. Mary has been dead six months.

He leaves Heidelberg toward the end of June, going
first to Stuttgart where he hears Luther's hymn, *Ein
feste Burg*, sung, but tiring of the interminable sermon, he leaves the church and visits the sculptor Dan-
necker. He tries vainly to locate Uhland and then
pushes on to Augsburg where he first sees the snow-
crowned summits of the Tyrolean mountains. In

Munich he delights in the bronze monument to Ludwig
in the cathedral, the statues of the Glyptothek (for he
is ever to prefer sculpture to painting), Schnorr's
frescoes in the Royal Palace, and the English garden
of Count Rumford. He meets Grillparzer, the Vien-
nese poet, in the diligence to Salzburg and finds him
entertaining. Hurrying away from Salzburg because
the bells remind him of those ominous Holland chimes
he goes to Ischl. Here he fails to find George Ticknor,
who has been in Dresden, and therefore returns to
St. Gilgen where he passes a few days. By the sixth
of July he is on his way to Innsbruck, continually struck
by the poignant reminders of New England in the pines
and fir trees and wooden houses and fields of Indian
corn. At Innsbruck a trifle changes his course of procedure, for it has been his determination to go into
Italy. For some reason unascertained the police refuse
to *viser* his passport and after vain remonstrances Henry
must make up his mind to go immediately to Switzerland. Fate continues to guide him in the path that
she would have him go.

Therefore to Switzerland he goes, posting to Bre-
genz, crossing Lake Constance, visiting Zurich, and
passing over the Righi to Arth and the William Tell
country. He sees Andermatt, walks over the Furca
pass, studies the Rhone glacier, goes into ecstasies at
the waterfall in Handeck, drives up the Lauterbrünnen
Thal, and reaches the town of Thun. At Thun he
converses for a few moments with Nathan Appleton,
a Boston merchant, who is on his way to Interlaken
with his family. "Oh, what a solitary, lonely being
I am!" the young man confesses in his journal. "Why
do I travel? Every hour my heart aches." He goes
on to Berne and then Lauzanne. There he sees Gibbon's house. At Vevay he jumps into a cabriolet and

drives to Chillon where he is unimpressed by the châteaux. From Vevay he takes a steamboat to Geneva and arrives there after a dull day. He is "not a little disappointed in Lake Leman." Early the next morning he goes with French acquaintances to Voltaire's house at Ferney, but "as I have neither love nor veneration for this arch-scoffer, the visit has not afforded me much gratification." We may imagine the young man, still wrapped in the gloom of his sorrow, staring with an aggrieved and shocked eye at the home of the famous Frenchman. "Every friend seems to keep out of my path; and the world seems so lonely," he writes that night. He goes to Chamouni. He sees the heavy vapors rolling away from Mont Blanc. The roar of the avalanche is in his ears and a passage from the Apocalypse flashes into his mind. "I saw a great white throne and Him that sat thereon, before whose face the heavens and the earth fled away and found no place." Back in Geneva he finds friends at last. Thomas Motley, of Boston, is there with his family and attaching himself to this party Henry pushes on with them to Berne. From Berne they travel by way of Thun to Interlaken and there (arriving July 31) Henry finds the Appletons "still stationary, as if there were a charm about the place." The young man so followed by the furies of restlessness and sorrow has —although consciously he is unaware of it—reached the end of his spiritual flight. In the family party of Nathan Appleton is his nineteen-year-old daughter, Frances Elizabeth.

It is impossible to disentangle the threads of sheer romance and actuality which now compose the woof of Henry's life. There can be no doubt that Frances Elizabeth Appleton impinged with startling effect on Henry's impressionable nature. Whether or not the young man falls immediately in love with her or is merely sympathetically attracted is a problem that is arguable. By 1838 he is returning to the notes that he has already made for his romance of *Hyperion* and it is obvious that these notes were made some time before, perhaps but shortly after this happy meeting in 1836. The barely disguised narration in *Hyperion* of Henry's meeting with Frances Appleton is plain enough to all, for the book becomes to a large degree no more than a bold plea for her affections. If Henry up to this meeting at Interlaken has been a young Hamlet it is equally evident that now he has shifted somewhat from that lachrymose condition in which he traveled through the Tyrol and Switzerland. Time begins to "slip pleasantly away" as he wanders about with the Appleton family. "I now for the first time enjoy Switzerland" he notes naïvely enough in his journal under the date of August second. Mary has been dead about eight months and the resilient young man is beginning to recover from that grief which so obsessed him. "A day of true and quiet enjoyment," he notes, as he travels from Thun to Entelbuch on the way to Lucerne. "But this lake is so beautiful," he jots down when they reach Lucerne. How different this is from his lonely observation of Lake Lemon. Indeed, life is changing for him. He even makes up a rhyme on the exorbitance of the prices at the Hôtel du Corbeau in Zurich.

> Beware of the Raven of Zurich,
> 'Tis a bird of omen ill;
> A noisy and an unclean bird,
> With a very, very long bill.

We may be sure that all of this fairly peaceful re-action from grief is due to the companionship of Frances

'Appleton, that already the young man is beginning to visualize her as something nearer than a mere friend, although the thought, perhaps, is unadmitted to himself. It is in the back of his mind. It is particularly romantic. The lonely grief-stricken youth wandering over Europe is suddenly met by a charming and sympathetic personage who fills, in a measure, the void left by Mary's sudden passing. There is something absolutely Byronic in it. The fact that Mary has been dead but eight months does not invalidate the integrity of Henry's love for her, for his nature, be it repeated again, is not deep but shallow. Happiness and grief cast equal shadows over it. The young man responds almost immediately to his surroundings and he sees life through a bright Germanic mist of sentimentality. He is now to dream of Frances Appleton for seven years. At least, by 1838 she is to be intimately entangled in his literary schemes and his quick and fortunate reaction from a possible hypochondria has both its good and bad concomitants. This semi-idyl amidst the pleasant surroundings of Switzerland does not last long for by the 17th of August Henry, in response to an urgent letter, is on his way back to Heidelberg. There he prepares for his return (a roundabout one, to be sure) to America and bids farewell to his friends and acquaintances. "One nasty little professor," notes the indignant young man, "in a dirty *schlafrock* took the pipe out of his mouth and kissed me on the lips. I had a great mind to shake him by the ears."

To Baden-Baden he goes with Mrs. Bryant and her family and from Baden-Baden they drive to Strasburg through a heavy rainstorm. By the third of September he is in Paris again. "What a throng! What a confusion of sounds!" he notes. "How marvelous it is to me,—the great and good providence of God, that

holds in its hands all this varied world." He strolls
about the Boulevards, "breathing the pavement" of
the streets, amazed at this great living cataract of people.
He is tempted to wander back into the past and so he
seeks out the old house of Madame Potet where he
had lived as a youth. Everything is unchanged there.
He even seeks out the *maison de santé* at Auteuil and
he almost wishes to take up his abode there again,
"once more in a place where nine years ago I passed
some happy weeks,—no, not happy; I was not happy
then, I was too young and feverish,—never satisfied
with the present, and reaching out my hands to grasp
the future, as a child tries to grasp a star." It is a
man who is speaking now, a man who has looked upon
the face of death and seen the grayness of life. And
yet, in spite of this maturity, this maturity which comes
so late, for Henry is now twenty-nine years old, there
is an invincible naïveté implicit in his nature. His
youth has gone and he has to show for it several unimportant textbooks, a handful of juvenile verses, a
small book of translations and *Outre Mer*, a direct
imitation of Washington Irving. It is not much. It
hardly gives Henry the dignity which is already being
accorded him by his kindly and older friends. As for
the nature of the man, this second European trip has
given him much. It has impressed upon him, first of
all, the sense of the tragedy implicit in life. And
second it has flung open the gateways of contemporary
German letters to him. Then, too, there is the Scandinavian impulses that are to play their part in his
future. But, for the most part, it is a solemn and
somewhat bewildered young man who boards the vessel
at Havre on October eighth and turns his face toward
home and a new environment.

HARVARD UNIVERSITY, CAMBRIDGE, MASS.
From an early 19th century print

STATE STREET, BOSTON, IN THE EARLY 1830s
From an old print

" Under a spreading chestnut tree
The village smithy stands

H. M. S. 1840

CHAPTER FIVE

The Cambridge Victorian

CAMBRIDGE drowses in early summer sunlight and
the walks are shadow-dappled by the elm leaves.
The tall trees stand like sleepy sentinels. The young
man, proceeding along Brattle Street, pauses by the
oddly patterned fence and gazes across the lilac bushes
at the spacious old mansion painted in yellow and
white. The house fascinates him. It is seated far
back from the road and across its ample front stretch
large verandas. The roof is guarded by a balustrade.
This house is a footnote to history. Its white pilasters
speak of the troubled and extravagant past but calmly
now for its place in active time is done. The innumerable footsteps have died away. It stands by the roadside in silence facing the divagations of man with that
quiet indifference of old knowledge which is neither ac-
cusatory nor surprised. But to the young man who is so
amorous of sentimental imaginings it is active with
delicate troupes of ghosts who parade up and down
the walks and stroll across the green sward. The
pageantry of the past advances to meet Henry as he
opens the fence-gate and walks slowly up the path
to the front door where the heavy knocker hangs
waiting the touch of his hand, a touch which is to
mark the inception of a new lease of life for this old
house that has known the rustle and laughter of extravagant revels and the thunder of Continental boots.
The ghosts surge forward expectantly to greet this
youth in the brightly hued waistcoat and gloves which
appear to be a shade too light for the strictly virtuous.
Phantom ladies in mob-caps stretch pale hands across
the lilac bushes, and across the veranda thump be-
ruffled, bewigged, sworded and laced old bucks with

faces scarlet from strong rum. It is Time that is
gathering here to meet this young man. It is nearly a
hundred years of American social and military history,
of all that was fine and picturesque and sometime alien
in old New England which surrounds this massive and
antique edifice. The young man lifts his hand and
the knocker sounds sonorously through the silent halls.

Henry stands before the door, and behind him Cambridge, quiet, dreamlike, scholastic Cambridge, sleeps in
the early summer sun. There is a charmed silence
over this town so near Boston, a town that is little
more than a village and which exists as a fringe to
Harvard Square. It is an altogether proper setting for
the old house before whose door Henry stands listening
to the slow shuffle of feet that reluctantly approach. It
seems almost within the bounds of possibility that a
phantom in knee-breeches and pig-tailed wig will stand
framed there asking plaintively why his long rest has
been so loudly disturbed. But a mild serving man
opens the great door and bids the young man to enter.
Henry crosses the threshold and inquires for Mrs.
Craigie, and even as he speaks the tiny parlor door
is flung open and a tall figure crowned with a turban
stands there, her keen gray eyes inspecting the intruder
from the Present into this *cul-de-sac* of the Past. She,
for her part, is the evocation of a vanished era. The
dignity of her fallen estate is about her. Behind her
cluster the ghosts, peering over her shoulder at the
adventurous young man. Henry enquires for a room
in his deliberate way. "I lodge students no longer,"
replies the stately old lady, her eyes inspecting the
rosy face, the elaborate waistcoat and the neat boots.
"But I am not a student," explains Henry, "I am a
Professor in the University." Perhaps he draws himself up a bit stiffly as he describes himself. "A Pro-

fessor?" ejaculates Mrs. Craigie, her turban bobbing
dubiously as she looks in vain for any mark of clerical
severity—a white cravat or, at least, a pair of learned
spectacles. "Professor Longfellow," declares Henry,
with pardonable pride. A light dawns on Mrs. Craigie's
face and her eyes flicker toward the copy of *Outre
Mer* on the table. Her severity of demeanor is re-
laxed to a certain degree as she says, "Ah! That is
different. I will show you what there is."

Henry follows her up the handsome staircase, noting
its twisted balusters and low, broad steps. The door
closes behind him and he is merged in the soft gloom
and aroma of the ancient mansion. The sense of the
past, fragrant and frail like the thin odor of old musk,
numbs the bright young mind now preoccupied with a
disturbing albeit pleasant present. Mrs. Craigie flings
open the door to a room, a room that is a delight to
Henry's eyes and one in which he is sure he can pass
his leisure time most agreeably. "You cannot have
that room," remarks the chatelaine grimly, her gray
eyes snapping. Henry speechlessly follows her to
another door where the same remark is repeated. "You
cannot have that room." In this way the young man
is led over the entire house and shown all the rooms,
rooms delightful in themselves, adorned with ancient
wooden carvings and breathing an air of opulent respectability. It begins to look like a quaint sort of
Barmecide hospitality on Mrs. Craigie's part, perhaps
one of her grim jokes, for it is rumored that she—
breathe it softly!—reads Voltaire. The young man
begins to think that the bruited room to let is a fig-
ment of some friend's imagination. They come at
length to the southeast corner room in the second story
of the old house and again the door is flung open.
Henry stares wistfully and waits patiently for the to-

be-expected, "You cannot have that." But Mrs. Craigie changes her formula. Her voice drops and she whispers, "This was General Washington's chamber." Immediately Henry seems to see a tall booted figure standing by the window, gazing over the meadows toward the river—for this room is on the front of the house. He is so enchanted that he fails to hear Mrs. Craigie further remark and she must repeat it. Then it dawns upon him what she is saying. He may have this room providing the door leading into the back entry be locked on the outside. The ghosts smile significantly to one another and withdraw. The tall booted figure by the window merges into a mere shadow flung by the sun. He has reached the subdued station of old ghosts; he is to become part of a background.

Henry is now settled for the rest of his life. Though he may travel to Europe again he will come back here. It is here that he will bring his second wife, here that his children will be born and reared, here that his major works will be written, and here—at the long last—that his ultimate breath will be drawn. But all this can be no more than a matter of vague premonitions to the young man somewhat sobered by woe, who has ventured upon Cambridge and Harvard College to start his career anew. He has already been eight months in Cambridge orientating himself in the new milieu wherein he is to bourgeon so luxuriantly and which is to foster him so carefully. He agrees eminently with Cambridge and Cambridge agrees with him. In no other place could Henry have prospered so well, for he is in an oasis now and surrounded by loyal friends who will shower the most exorbitant praise upon him. It was in December, 1836, that Henry, arriving in Cambridge, installed himself in the house of Dr. Stearns, on Kirkland Street, and set about the task of preparing his first lectures and cementing his first friendships. Heretofore his intimacies had been confined to his dead brother-in-law, George Pierce, and his loyal comrade of the Italian months, George Washington Greene. Now he is to enlarge his circle, to take in—with curious acumen—those men who especially count in so far as his advancement is concerned. These friends are to be enumerated in their proper place. For the present the indication that they are now standing on Henry's doorstep, figuratively speaking, is enough.

The Craigie House becomes an integral part of Henry's life and it must be emphasized if we are to understand the environment wherein the young man develops. Henry lives entirely apart from his curious landlady and he is surrounded by a silence that is peopled with shadows. In the morning, after he has settled himself to the day's occupation, he can hear the faint slow tread of Mrs. Craigie as she descends to her late breakfast, her silken gown rustling through the halls. When he visits her little parlor to wish her good day the turbaned head, a few gray locks straggling from it, lifts from the open volume of Voltaire on her lap and the keen gray eyes inspect him with a semi-malicious curiosity. At night he can hear her playing her harpsichord, sitting alone while her wrinkled fingers wander along the yellow keys and draw from them a faded music, a music that to her, perhaps, resurrects those phantoms that never desert this house. Mrs. Craigie belongs to the Past. She lives in it almost wholly. Except for the curious mental vitality, the Voltairian touch that animates her lined features, she, too, is a ghost. And like ghosts she is eccentric to the last. She is a free-thinker, as any reader of Voltaire must be. She sees God in nature and wants no mediator to come between Him and her. Canker-worms attack the elms before the old mansion and she sits in the window with the worms crawling unmolested over her white turban. She will do nothing to protect the trees, saying, "Why, sir, they are our fellow worms; they have as good a right to live as we have." She has a passion for flowers and cats and dogs. She hates the Jews and when she is reminded that Jesus was a Jew replies, "I can't help it, ma'am." Even in death— to jump forward a few years—she is unique, calling Henry to her bedside and saying, "You'll never be married again; because you see how ugly an old woman looks in bed." There is something devastating about this aged woman, widow of the Apothecary-General of the American Army during the Revolution (if that was his title) and there is something vital and pleasing also. Henry is not quite alone with Mrs. Craigie and the ghosts that haunt the mansion, for in the next chamber to him young Habersham of Savannah plays upon his flute, departing, however, when the chill breezes of the northern winter sweep across the river. And there is the farmer and his wife who live in the back part of the house. This wife, a pious giantess named Miriam, provides Henry with his meals at such an exorbitant rate as to win for her the nickname of "Miriam the Profitess."

The house itself fascinates Henry and he explores its history. He finds both truth and legend. This ancient building, erected presumably about 1759 by one Colonel John Vassall (it may have been his father who built the place), was once the center of an inherited estate of between one and two hundred acres. On the eve of the Revolution Colonel Vassall, taking the side of the King, sailed for England, erasing from his family coat-of-arms the motto, "Semper pro republica, soepe pro rege." The house was confiscated by the Commonwealth and, after the Battle of Bunker Hill, the Marblehead Regiment was quartered under its roof, their muddy feet staining the sturdy floors. Then Washington, coming to Cambridge to take command of the American forces, established his headquarters here after a brief stay at the Wadsworth house. The General remained only nine months in the old mansion but it was long enough to create a series of apocryphal stories which may or may not be true. There are two stories concerned with the solemn-faced Washington laughing here. One of them has to do with an old woman who had been arrested in the American lines as a spy. She was brought before General Putnam and he thought the matter important enough to be broached to the Commander-in-Chief. The old woman, therefore, was brought to Washington's headquarters but, refusing to pass the gate, Putnam was compelled to pick her up bodily and carry her into the house. Washington, from the window, saw his bluff general striding up the pathway bearing an old lady who was kicking and squawking with an extraordinary vitality. Washington nearly burst the buttons off his uniform roaring at the spectacle. Greene is the hero of the second story, for, during a meeting of several of the generals at the old house, an alarm of a British demonstration from Boston set them all scrambling helter-skelter for their accoutrements. "My wig! Where is my wig?" shouted Greene. "Behind the looking-glass, General," responded Lee, and Greene, staring pop-eyed into the mirror, saw that his wig was on his head. Again Washington is reported to have laughed.

After Washington's departure the house fell into the brief possession of one Thomas Tracy of Newburyport, a fabulously rich fellow, and about his tenure more legends evolved. During Tracy's time the servants drank costly wines from carved pitchers. A hundred guests sat down to banquets, feeding upon the rarest delicacies and drinking the richest liquors. Tracy sent forth privateers to scour the seas and rape Spanish galleons of their riches, of fruits and spices, silks and satins. But Tracy's day ended. He failed; the banquets ceased; the privateers no longer sailed into Boston Bay; the servants, the costly wines, the carved pitchers dwindled and vanished. Then a Captain Joseph Lee, brother to Madame Tracy, became owner of the house, but history is fairly silent regarding him. The house that had known the laughter of Washington and the uproar of Thomas Tracy's Neronian feasts did not respond to the colorless personality of Captain Lee. After the Captain came Andrew Craigie, Apothecary-General to the Northern Provincial Army, who had amassed a fortune in that office, and the house took on new splendors. He it was who built a bridge over the Charles River connecting Cambridge and Boston. He even enlarged the house. But the doughty general appears to have been heavy and dull, and his fortune fled on the wings of the four winds, not, however, before he had an opportunity to give various banquets, at one of which appeared the peruked and powdered Talleyrand. Another of them is reported to have been graced by the Duke of Kent, father of Victoria. Craigie disappears in the mists of history, snuffed out by Time, and the house continued under the guidance of Mrs. Craigie. The surrounding acres had dwindled and disappeared with Craigie's wealth and his widow, brought low by disastrous shifts, turned to paying guests. Edward Everett and Jared Sparks are among the names of the young men who lived here.

It is to this mansion that Henry comes and it is here that he stays. The house is to know new life while he is here and it is to resound to blithe footsteps, for the friends of the young man are to come here, starting almost from the time that Henry first secures his quarters. Forty years of the literary history of New England are to know this building intimately, and important figures from all parts of Europe are to turn naturally toward this house. It is to be the Mecca for a countless horde. Henry settles back luxuriously in his new rooms and applies himself to the duties that devolve upon him. With the years of European travel in the back of his mind he comes to this dwelling that is filled with the curious and contradictory history of old New England. Life begins to spread out for the young man, who has not as yet entirely recovered from the cruel shock of fate experienced in alien Rotterdam so short a time before. It is true that a new figure is slowly evolving in his mind, a charming feminine figure which must have intermingled with the more scholastic precisions of his days and added a fillip of color to them. But it is hard work to which Henry must turn now, work that will cement the position which kind fortune has thrust so easily upon him. He sits in his study and gazes out the window at the dimpling river that is to be his dear comrade for the rest of his life.

II

Henry is the "Flashing Sickle" to certain of the young women of Cambridge. He titillates feminine bosoms—gently, of course. Coming, as he does, into a community based upon an essential staidness, he finds that he must live down his waistcoats and gloves, that he must vindicate the Europeanisms now perceptible in his character. Two trips abroad have cut him somewhat adrift from the safe anchor of colorless living. It is not that Henry has changed at heart, for he is still New England, but his surface values have brightened. He is immediately met with some criticism therefore, a criticism that centers most of all on his sartorial effects. "If you have any tendency to 'curl your hair and wear gloves' like Edgar in *Lear*, do it before you return," he warns Charles Sumner, his great new friend Sumner, when that liberal travels abroad. And in the first book that he is to write in the Craigie House, *Hyperion*, he makes his Baron say to the impossibly lachrymose Paul Flemming, "The ladies already begin to call you Wilhelm Meister, and they say that your gloves are a shade too light for a strictly virtuous man." And again, somewhat later, Sam Ward writes him, "I have for you an Endymion waistcoat better suited to your style than mine." This foppishness of Henry's maintains throughout the whole of his younger life, for in 1842 Charles Dickens notes: "McDowell the boot-maker, Beale the hosier, Laffin the trowsers-maker, and Blackmore the coat-cutter have all been at the point of death; but have slowly recovered. The medical gentlemen agreed that it was exhaustion, occasioned by early rising—to wait upon you at those unholy hours!" Henry's neatness, it appears, is an exaggerated neatness for New England, and it is one of the pleasant things to be recorded about him. Although it is somewhat of an obstacle he manages to surmount it, perhaps because of his excellent disposition and essential conservatism of innate personality, for he is not long in Cambridge before he is entering the august portals of Boston society to a high degree of acceptance and welcome. To his father he writes, "There is such a social spirit here that I seldom see a book by candle-light. Indeed, I pass half of my evenings, at least, in society,—it being almost impossible to avoid it."

There are the homes of the elder Otis and Prescott where he finds acquaintances of his father. George Ticknor after his return from Europe throws open his home on Park Street. The younger Prescott, now a member of the examining committee of his department, welcomes him. And there is Charles Amory whom he had met at Göttingen, ready to renew the old friendship and discourse on Germany and her virtues. He sees Dr. Palfrey frequently, Jared Sparks (already working on his life of Washington) every day, and plays whist with Andrews Norton (now retired from his professorship) at Shady Hill every week.

We may be sure that Henry likes society and does not strive very hard to keep away from it. There are so many pleasant homes open to him in Boston and Cambridge. Besides that, he has developed the social sense in London and Germany. He has observed a scene where conversation is being practiced more or less as a fine art. In the meantime there is also the college. If Henry "steps out" by night he strives with equal grace to "step in" by day, to fit himself into the faculty of Harvard University. The inclination to romanticize about the Harvard of Henry's early years, indeed of Henry's entire period as a professor there, 1836 to 1854, is tempting, but a rational observation of those years shows the college as a quiet stagnating place conducted by ultra-academic pundits. It is historically important, perhaps, to point out that in September, 1836—two months before Henry receives his formal appointment—the second centennial anniversary of the college had been celebrated with great éclat, and that it had been marked by the appearance of an old "grad" of the class of 1774. In spite of the illuminations, the recited odes, the speeches of Edward Everett and Joseph Story, and the formal address of President Josiah Quincy, it is doubtful that this old "grad" found any of the fever of his student days implicit in the college atmosphere. The world progresses but Harvard slumbers in a *cul-de-sac*. There is a scarcity of lectures and the recitations are cut-and-dried affairs of dull routine. The philosophical textbooks are prejudiced. Politics are treated gingerly. The great Daniel Webster is worshiped, of course, and the ultimate triumph of Whigdom is devoutly to be desired. The anti-slavery agitation, now growing into an ominous cloud on the horizon, is looked at somewhat askance, for it seems to predicate a revolutionary violence quite alien to the sleepy buildings in Cambridge. Timidly conservative the college dawdles along and the rushing Time-Spirit carrying flame and havoc is seen from afar through mildly curious eyes. These professors who as late as 1866 consider Agassiz a great man, although Darwin's *Origin of Species* had shot his ideas on original types to pieces years before, these students who black their own boots and sit solemnly in chapel every day, seem, in the light of future developments, like ostriches burrowing their heads into the sand. The Republic is rushing toward its first great catastrophe, but the ostriches, young and old, will not see it. Charles Sumner sees it and logically enough he becomes extremely unpopular and is to develop into a person suspected of all sorts of revolutionary madnesses. Indeed it is, perhaps, his close friendship with Sumner that is to play a part in

Henry's departure from the sleepy halls of Harvard
in 1854.

That sundered relationship is still far in the future,
however, for Henry, at this time, is adjusting himself
to the scene before him. And what does he find?
Well, first of all, he does not find a desert, as he did in
Bowdoin. The onerous duties of creating a department out of nothing do not loom before him, for
Harvard has had a department of modern languages
for many years and its direction has but recently been
dropped by a man of liberalistic tendencies, George
Ticknor. Henry's duty therefore is to fit in and continue a curriculum that is already fortified. Francis
Sales is instructor of French and English, a brilliant
man, an appointee of Ticknor's, a man with a powdered
head and an old-fashioned "Haw! Haw! By George!"
Pietro Bachi instructs in Italian, Spanish and Portu-
guese; Francis M. J. Surault handles the French
classes; and Hermann Bokum teaches German. It is
Henry's job to oversee the department, to keep the
instructors in order, and to lecture. But he does more
than this. No recitation room being available in the
cramped quarters of the college, he conducts a class
in German in a sort of parlor called the "corporation
room." Here, surrounded by pictures, he sits while
his students lounge about a mahogany table meant for
the use of the trustees at their dinners.

Henry is never a pundit and the youths who sit
under him soon become aware of the fact. He begins
by reading familiar ballads and then requests his students to read them back to him. In this way they soon
commit them to memory without meaning to. There is
a minimum of dull grammar taught and therefore a
certain freshness about his methods, which thoroughly

delights his undergraduates. But this German class is only an aspect of these busy days wherein Henry roams from class to class, checking up on the instructors and virtually conducting their classes for them. Besides this, he lectures on authors and literatures, painstakingly preparing these lectures in the quiet study of the Craigie House while Mrs. Craigie sits in her little parlor turning the pages of Voltaire or Diderot. There is nothing of the schoolmaster about this young man, no dry bursts of technical wisdom, none of the usual professorial displays. He is human and because he is so anecdotes spring up about him, his jaunty walk is joked about, and various quips at his expense are bandied to and fro by the students. But it is all kindly, for the youths are proud of this poet who is teaching them. They bask in his reflected glory, so to speak, and his peculiarities of manners and dress are accepted, in spite of the jokes, as the man is accepted—a good fellow, a wise friend, a man congenitally disposed toward kindliness.

He is quite apart from his fellow professors, a distinct figure, a flash of color in a dull atmosphere. The gentle bonhomie of his nature, the European twist, as it were, marks him from the solemn college president, Josiah Quincy, LL.D., from the Dane professor of law, Simon Greenleaf, LL.D., from the Boylston professor of rhetoric and oratory, Edward Tyrrel Channing, LL.D., from the Rumford professor of the physical and mathematical sciences as applied to the useful arts, Daniel Treadwell, from the Hersey professor of physics, John Ware, M.D. The very names sound ominous. These men are undoubtedly eminent to their time, for Harvard stands high as a college but there is a portentous solemnity about them, an aura of grave unsmiling New England delving seriously into the mysteries of physics and law. Here, at least, Henry's youth is manifest. He is liberalistic in tendency if we set him beside these men who still follow the old methods of teaching and frown upon such a departure as elective courses. Henry does not merely profess learning, he practices it. The enthusiasm of foreign languages, foreign romance, foreign color, foreign letters, colors his mind and temperament. And being so young a professor among so old a group, an exception like Felton, for instance, brings with it certain advantages. It materially assists his reputation. It carries him into the best of the society about him, and his charming deportment establishes him after he gets there. He knows how to please, how to say the courtly or kindly thing, how to charm women, and how to stop short of flattery. He is sensitive to a high degree, and this makes him "easy," for it forewarns him of the feelings of others and he is accordingly gentle with them and anxious to discover excuses for their lapses.

III

It is not long before Henry is a founder and member of the Five of Clubs. To understand the young man's early years at Cambridge and the apparent ease with which he swims into public notice one must pay due attention to this quintet. Every young man (student or professor) going to college naturally shakes down within a short time to that particular group which displays kindred inclinations and tastes. Henry is no exception to the rule. Although he may dip into the festivities of Boston, making frequent appearances at dinners and *converzationes*, he realizes well enough that his milieu is Cambridge and that there he will find those cronies who are pertinent to his development.

He does not have to seek very far for them. The young men are just around the corner, walking through the halls of Harvard College, and no sooner is Henry settled than he turns the corner, meets them with an expansive gesture and is heartily received by them. His reputation has preceded him and they suspect his general timbre. Henry always possesses the power of grappling his friends to him with hoops of steel. There are no defalcations, and the only departures are through the doors of death. When he steps into the Cambridge scene he settles for a time on Kirkland Street, a fact that has already been mentioned, and beneath him "lives and laughs Cornelius, whose surname is Felton." Felton therefore is the first of those doughty champions who are to wield such wordy warfare for the poet during those years when he is most in need of praise and encouragement. Felton is a curious and admirable man, a Greek scholar set down in the wilderness, a man who parallels in some ways Henry's own career. His birth-year is the same as Henry's, 1807. His native town is West Newbury, that Massachusetts community from which the first of the American Longfellows sprang. It is true that his boyhood has been one of poverty, a poverty probably induced by that fatal embargo which proved so ruinous to maritime New England during the War of 1812, while Henry's boyhood has been passed in comparative comfort, but these very differences afford opportunity for fond reminiscence and comparison. Felton's later history is the history of the usual scholar. There is the entrance to Harvard in 1823, the inevitable A.B. in 1827, two years at the Livingston Country High School for Boys in Geneseo, N. Y., and then a Latin tutorship at Harvard in 1829. He is appointed College Professor of Greek in 1832 and in 1834 he succeeds Dr. Popkin as Eliot Professor of Greek. Henry finds in him a mirthful, loud-laughing, gentle-minded companion who has mastered the whole classical literature of Greece and whose nature is therefore curiously veined with bright streaks of the ancient pellucid pagan zest in living. Second to Felton and within a short time to be Henry's dearest friend is Charles Sumner, at this time a lecturer in the college law school. Henry, it will be remembered, first saw Sumner in Felton's quarters on his historic trip to Cambridge to settle the business of his professorship. Sumner is immersed in books, in the acquisition of culture, and that fierce eventful political career which is to carry him to the Senate and place him for all time among his country's statesmen is far in the future. His law partner is George Stillman Hillard and of course he is drawn into this small coterie, becoming the third member of the Five of Clubs. Then there is Henry R. Cleveland, formerly a comrade of Felton's in the school at Geneseo. Cleveland is of a sickly nature, highly susceptible to new impressions and easily moved to joy or sorrow. Already the seeds of the dread disease that is to destroy his lungs and carry him off, the first of the Five of Clubs to go, are implanted. This sensitive creature is the only one of the five who has seen Europe, excepting Henry, and this is a bond between them. They can expatiate on France and Italy to their hearts' content and Henry can describe that land of dreams, Spain, which he is never to see again.

These five men meet usually on Saturday afternoon, although they are constantly running across one another during the other days. Fond of good cheer and wine they are yet moderate in their habits and a simple, respectable Bohemianism ensues during which literature is discussed animatedly and a deal of kindly criticism of one another's ventures is passed about. Later, when they begin to extol one another's books in print, they are dubbed the "Mutual Admiration Society" and it is obvious that they are "set," so to speak, to puff each other. They are quick with excitement over new literary ventures. They are, so far as letters go, sentimental-minded. We must always remember this little inner group, for it is the background against which all of Henry's early gestures are to be made. It is a source of comfort and confidence for him. The four friends form a sort of Greek *choros* of praising disciples. Closely allied as they are, their plans, their most intimate betrayals, become mutual property. They dine together constantly. They hold what Henry is fond of referring to as a *gaudiolum* every few days. They run to each other with vast designs. They pat each other's backs and soothe each other's feelings.

This, then, is the inner ring. But besides these young men there are others, near and far acquaintances, with whom Henry continues or newly establishes those terms of intimacy which are to so bulwark him with an admiring audience as Time gathers speed and carries him along with it. There is Washington Allston, the painter, who comes from Cambridgeport to share the Johannisberger and roasted hare at Craigie House. There is the *bon vivant* and wit. Sam Ward, brother of that Julia who is to marry Dr. Howe, hurrying in from the brighter, more insouciant scene of New York and saluting Henry with a loud German kiss on each cheek and on the mouth. Sam is a relict of those sad Heidelberg days that follow so hard upon the death of Mary. He brings with him literary gossip of all sorts, jokes, criticism, and unofficially he serves as liaison officer, bearing back to

New York, to Halleck, to the *Knickerbocker* or the *Arcturus* or the *New World*, the precious manuscripts from Cambridge studies. And but a year or so after he has settled down to his professorial duties, there is the shy, reticent Hawthorne making his brief visits to Henry. Nathaniel Hawthorne has been living like a hermit in Salem for ten years or more, meditating, "feeling his way through the twilight of dreams," weaving those brief fancies that have appeared so sporadically in the periodicals of the day. It is in 1837 that he sends a copy of *Twice-Told Tales* to Henry with a quaintly courteous little note. And in response to Henry's cordial reply he writes: "Since we last met, which you remember was in Sawtelle's room, where you read a farewell poem to the relics of the class,—ever since that time I have secluded myself from society; and yet I never meant any such thing, nor dreamed what sort of life I was going to lead. I have made a captive of myself, and put me into a dungeon, and now I cannot find the key to let myself out; and, if the door were open, I should be almost afraid to come out." It is a somber man writing to a sunny man, a man who knows that trouble is the next best thing to enjoyment. Henry, with that instant response, is generous and shortly after this kindling of a vague sort of friendship—which, by the way, had never really existed at Bowdoin—he writes a review of *Twice-Told Tales* which appears in the *North American Review*. "To this little work we would say, 'Live ever, sweet, sweet book,'" he cries. The review touches Hawthorne and thereafter there are infrequent meetings between the two men, friendly notes interchanged, dinners and casual conversations. Henry, it is to be expected, never really understands the Salem wizard. He feels the strange-

ness of an unearthly nature in him, something quite
alien to his own sanguine outlook, and though regularly, as each new book by Henry appears, there is
the usual graceful tribute from Hawthorne, we can
not say that this acquaintanceship travels much beyond
the situation during college days, except in so far as
words are concerned. The spirits of the two men
are poles apart.

Still another acquaintance who never becomes part
of the intimate circle is Ralph Waldo Emerson, who,
according to Henry, "mistakes his power somewhat,
and, at times, speaks in oracles, darkly." Henry recognizes the brilliance of the man, but he is never to
become more than casually familiar with any of the
so-called Transcendental group. They belong to a
different sphere. Cambridge is neither Concord nor
Boston and though Henry may visit both places, particularly Boston, where so many of his evenings are
passed in pleasant homes, at concerts, or in the theater,
he remains steadfast Cambridge to the last. Dr.
Samuel Gridley Howe must not be forgotten either,
for he is to take the place left vacant by Henry Cleveland in the Five of Clubs when that young man succumbs to tuberculosis. Howe is one of the most fascinating figures in this scene, a man who has fought for
the Greeks and who directs with great genius the Perkins
Institution for the Blind. In 1843 he marries Julia
Ward, the blithe young woman who meets Henry in
1837 and describes him as "remarkably youthful in
his appearance. I remember well his clear, fresh complexion, and the bright chestnut of his hair." It is
among these varying degrees of friends that Henry
now passes his days, finding them a welcome release
from his onerous college duties, his lectures, the prose
articles he is writing for the *North American Review*,

and the poetry which begins to come back to him after
he has settled himself in Craigie House.

IV

With 1839 Henry reëmbarks, so to speak, on his
career as a writer, stimulated by his friends and freed
from the shifting kaleidoscope of European travels.
It has been four years since *Outre Mer* was issued
and that book, after all, was not creative in the true
sense of the word. It was descriptive, a volume of
stylized memoranda, a rag-bag wherein Henry might
thrust the experiences and joys and sadnesses of his
first momentous pilgrimage to Europe. But now a
differing aspect of his nature reasserts itself. The
young poet who seemed to languish and pass away so
long ago, whose demise was heralded in the woeful
paragraph to the dead Elizabeth, comes to life. From
1837 on, Henry's muse has been fluttering tentatively
and various "psalms" have resulted, "psalms" written
in the calm Cambridge twilights or the bright summer
mornings when the young Professor sits between the
two windows at the small table in the corner of his
chamber. This reawakening of the poet after so long
a somnolence requires some explanation. Why has
he been poetically silent for more than a decade? It
is extraordinary; for these years of silence are assuredly the most impressionable—and generally the
most productive—of the average poet's career. There
are various reasons. Part of this time has been passed
in Europe and the young man has been drinking down
copious draughts of the foreign scene and so impregnating himself with them instead of giving out anything. He has been filling himself much as a reservoir is filled. The desire for expression that is the

spiritual backbone of every writer has satisfied itself
in prose and translations. Then there are the busy
years at Brunswick where he has been almost wholly
concerned with the objectives of building up a curriculum in the wilderness and orientating himself to a
domestic existence. There has been his second trip to
Europe, the excitement of his appointment at Harvard, and the lamentable death of Mary. There has
been the first season of adjustment to the Cambridge
scene with its bewildering array of social functions,
new friends and the more arduous duties of directing
half-a-dozen instructors.

All of these things have contributed to his silence,
but if we look still farther there is possibly a psychic
reason to be discerned. Henry, it will be remembered,
emptied himself of the slight efforts of his youth in
a semi-illiterate environment so far as culture went.
Having done so there was no vast urge within him
to strike fire against his sensibilities and so flash into
being new ventures. He was hollow, hollow but receptive. Then came the discovery of Europe and all
that Europe stood for, ages of mellow culture, social
graces and the devastating "sense of the past." At
first it appalled the young man. Against that rich
world he observed the charlatanism of so many
writers, and because an old Puritan integrity permeated him through and through, he could not stoop
to the idle gestures of secondary creatures. Gradually, however, the subtle essences of that rich world
began to seep into his receptive nature. He comes
back to Cambridge brimmed with a thousand and one
juxtaposed impressions of England, France, Spain,
Germany, the Scandinavian countries, Italy, and it
becomes obvious that, given the comparative peace of
release from excitement, new vistas and sorrow, these

impressions will grate against one another, will mix, interflow and eventually rouse from its lethargy the poetic impulse of the young man, an impulse that needs no more than sentiment, didactic reasoning and the color of foreign atmospheres for its props. This is what happens after Henry settles in the Craigie House, selects his friends, adjusts himself to the college scene and otherwise bestows upon himself a long sedentary acceptance of life. The mingled impressions begin to clarify, a calmness of the spirit proves fallow soil for the little green shoots of didactic observation, and Henry's poetic urge rises deliberately to its feet.

It does not achieve rhythmical structure immediately but may be sensed in the curiously Germanicized romance, *Hyperion*, which appears in the summer of 1839. But it is completely visible in *Voices of the Night*, published in the autumn. In October, 1837, the first of these poems, *Flowers*, is written, and it is the linking poem with that boyhood work beyond which Henry has now traveled. At first the reborn poet writes sparingly, as though he were slowly adjusting himself to the creative urge which his pleasant surroundings in Cambridge are invigorating. Together with these casual poems goes the composition of *Hyperion*, a book wherein he inserts a hint of the new affection that has come into his life (Frances Appleton returns to Boston in 1837 almost simultaneously with Henry's rebirth as a creative writer, and this is significant), a number of odd literary comments, a wordy panegyric of Jean-Paul Richter, and a mass of badly digested travel notations, didactic commentaries and melancholy musings shot here and there with a poetic flash. It is a curious book and when it appears in 1839 it receives a mixed reception, part of its audience accepting it with some pleasure because of the love story implicit in it and its atmosphere of German life now presented to American readers with some clarity for the first time.   Henry, as usual, ignores the caviling and turns to the praise.   The young man still regards himself as a liberal, as not too "New England," for to his old friend, Greene, who is in Italy, he writes: "I have been rending asunder some of the Boston cobwebs of prejudice and narrow-minded criticism by publishing a strange kind of a book, which I have the audacity to call a *Romance*." Orestes A. Brownson's review in the *Boston Quarterly Review* for January, 1840, may be taken as an example of this "narrow-minded criticism," for there he wrote, "I do not like the book.   It is such a journal as a man who reads a great deal makes from the scraps in his table drawer.   Yet it has not the sincerity or quiet touches which give interest to the real journals of very common persons." Orestes has a keen eye but Henry dismisses this with, "I understand there is a spicy article against me in the *Boston Quarterly*.   In *Hyperion*, he claims, are his cherished thoughts of three years.   The attacks by the Boston papers please him, he avers, for they prove that the book is good, a curious reasoning that sounds most modern in its implications.   He desires Greene to get the book noticed in foreign journals, for Henry is only too aware how eagerly the American public accepts what has been roundly praised in Europe. Indeed, all his life he has an eye out for publicity. He likes it and there is no reason why he should not like it.

On December 10, 1839, Henry's first book of poems, *Voices of the Night*, appears and it immediately strikes the fancy of the public.   Within a few

weeks the edition is exhausted and a second one is on
the press. This book is fashioned from the various
poems he has written in the last two years, five early
pieces rescued from the maw of the past, and several
translations which had appeared in *Outre Mer* and
Hyperion. It is a small book but it is big in the
sense that it is the opening shot from a writer of verse
who is to dominate his era for forty years to come.
Among the poems in this book are several of the prime
favorites which are to hold their own for years, indeed
until excessive familiarity and repetition has rendered
them so trite as to obscure whatever values they may
have had in the beginning. There is, first of all, *A
Psalm of Life,* so Germanic in its origins, but yet
so new and vital to the Americans of 1840. Then
there are *Hymn to the Night, The Reaper and the
Flowers, Footsteps of Angels,* and *The Beleaguered
City.* One of these, the last, is to arouse the
jaundiced Poe to fury. It is impossible to level
any criticism at this work for it has passed beyond
criticism. One might as well criticize the shape of the
letter A. The fact that these poems are drenched in
German sentimentality, that they are mathematically
mechanical in technique, and that they are almost un-
believably ordinary in what they have to say, does not
dispose of them. Time alone can do that. They are
"Henry," first of all. These pieces are shafts of
light into his nature and his attitude toward life. But
Henry is not just Henry. He is something more than
that. He is important because he is the mirror of the
first urbane culture in the Republic, even though it
is a borrowed culture, and his career is a revelation
of the growth through which the country is passing.
Like a great child America is grasping at opportunities to imitate, to mimic, to respond artlessly to the

tunes played on European pipes. Henry is not ahead of his period. He travels with it. Hawthorne may be ahead and so may Emerson and Thoreau and Margaret Fuller. But Henry travels with the popular taste of his time. He is a great bourgeois and if he is more European than American in his outlook we must remember that the American outlook, so far as any refinement or culture goes, is more European than anything else.

Henry, therefore, puts out his Richter-like *Hyperion* and his Germanic *Voices of the Night* with a kindling sense of their sufficiency. Disturbed as he is at this time by troublous attacks of dyspepsia and an aggrieved warfare with the Harvard College authorities over a French instructor, he yet manages to inject some degree of virility into his advent upon the American scene as a purportedly mature writer. Of course he is not mature at all, but he has his zealous friends about him to assure him that he is and it is to be suspected that he receives the adulation of these friends a trifle too unctuously. "I have the approbation of those whose approbation I most desire; and, of course, do not much care how others abuse," he writes to his father about *Hyperion*. Now that this book is out (the publisher fails, by the way, and only half the edition is sold) and *Voices of the Night* is almost ready for the press various designs seethe in Henry's head. He will write a history of English poetry. He will do a series of studies in the manner of Claude Lorraine. He will write a novel called *Count Cagliostro*. He will write a long poem called *The Saga of Hakon Jarl*. He will write two more volumes of *Hyperion*. He will do a drama on Cotton Mather. It is with such superabundance of mental vitality that the publication of these two books animate him. None of these plans come to anything but they serve to show that Henry is again burning with that old creative urge which had died down years before. It is also evident that he is still equally divided in his mind between prose and verse. He does not know whether he is a poet, a prose writer, or both.

It must be remembered that this poetic energy runs abreast with a disaffection occasioned by his treatment at the college. He regards himself as overworked, and perhaps this sense of being crowded is somewhat aroused by a desire to have more time to labor at his poetic ventures. There is so much in his mind now. Having created so emphatic an impression on his immediate public he is kindled to further endeavors. "My work here grows quite intolerable," he has already written to his father, "and unless they make some change I will leave them—with or without anything to do. I will not consent to have my life crushed out of me so." On October 4th, 1839, he writes in his journal, "Poetic dreams shaded by French irregular verbs! I wish I were a free man!" and the entry for the next day is "Wrote a new Psalm of Life. It is *The Village Blacksmith*." That unrest that is to give sporadic vent to itself for the next fifteen years is already in evidence. Henry's inclinations are all rushing one way and the age-old struggle between the dream and the business is to be reënacted as it has been done in countless lives before and since. The idea that he might cut adrift, although vaguely formulated in words now and then, is never taken too seriously by Henry for he is possibly aware that his very being desires that certain modicum of comfort that a penniless life as a free lance writer will not give him. He is not ready to forsake all for the love of letters. His waistcoats and Johannisberger mean too much to him.

No sooner is *Voices of the Night* off the press and in the hands of the public and running through edition after edition—it reaches four in a single year—than Henry is formulating plans for new publications. He continues to write short poems between the busy scenes of college life and social intercourse. On December 17th, 1839, he is planning three ballads, *The Skeleton in Armour, The Wreck of the Hesperus,* and *Sir Humphrey Gilbert.* On the thirtieth he sits smoking by his fire and at midnight suddenly starts up and composes the entire *The Wreck of the Hesperus.* These lunges of action soon bring into being a body of work which shapes into another book of short pieces. A brief nationalistic urge accompanies these activities; early in 1840 he is writing "The national ballad is a virgin soil here in New England; and there are great materials." He is right, but he does not know how to go about it. A few weeks later he is diving into early Spanish drama, Lope de Vega, Cervantes and Calderon. He reads Lope de Vega's *El Major Alcalde el Rey* and *Moza de Cantaro.* The next day he is rushing through the *Comedia Aquilana* of Torres Naharro and that night he writes, "A good idea! Yes, I will write a comedy—*The Spanish Student!*" It is as easily as this that his nationalistic urges are dissipated by the bright charms in foreign books. He runs to and fro, figuratively speaking, having no basic design to his poetical activities. Spain cries to him louder than New England and he must needs forsake his own grim hills and wave-torn shores for the brighter sun of Andaluzia. After all, Spain is his land of dreams, his lost country of cloudy palaces. So back there he goes.

The first part of 1840 is full of Spain, many plays read, lectures before his classes and musings over *The Spanish Student*. Before the year is out the play is written and put aside until the poet's ardor cools and he may read it in a more critical frame of mind.

The year 1841 passes to furious labor and various surprises. Mrs. Craigie lays down her Voltaire, retires to her bed, and passes away grimly. She is stubborn to the last and refuses the aid of doctors or nurses. "My system is not adapted to medicine," she declares. And so she dies as she lived, in Henry's words, "pretty much in her own way, without regard to the opinions of others." After her death it is discovered that she suffered from a cancer in the breast. Poor, lonely, turbaned, grim relic of a dead and courtly world! Joseph Worcester, the lexicographer, takes over Craigie House for a year and Henry continues on, not much lonelier than he was before. He essays horseback riding and apparently likes it, which proves how far away he is from the timorous young man who used to spar at an effigy of himself drawn on the closet door. He corresponds with Poe. He observes a student rebellion at Harvard that lasts two days. He visits Nahant and converses with Sparks, Prescott, Bancroft, the Eliots and Lowells, and a dozen other bulwarks of New England. Of course, the Appletons are there, and somewhere in the background is Frances, the Mary Ashburton of *Hyperion*, now full apprized of Henry's passion for her and possibly weighing the virtues of the flamboyant young professor. "Cold roast Boston," is what Mr. Thomas G. Appleton (or is it G. W. Curtis?) calls Nahant. Henry begins to consider another book of poems. "The 'Skeleton,' with the few other pieces I have on hand, will, it is true, make but a meager volume. But what then? It is important to bring all my guns to bear now; and though they are small ones, the shots may take effect. Through the breach thus made, the 'Student' may enter the citadel in triumph." *Excelsior* is written and despatched to the jolly Sam Ward in New York. In November the idea comes to Henry to undertake a long and elaborate poem by "the holy name of Christ; the theme of which would be the various aspects of Christendom in the Apostolic, Middle and Modern Ages." It is to be ten years before the second part of this trilogy is completed and thirty years before the complete project is finished and offered as the crowning achievement of Henry's life. In December, *Ballads and Other Poems* is printed and Henry's second "shot" takes immediate effect.

Ballads and Other Poems, following *Voices of the Night,* after a decent interval of two seasons, serves to consolidate the position Henry had achieved with the first book. Here, for the first time between covers, he offers his public *The Skeleton in Armour, The Wreck of the Hesperus, Excelsior, The Village Blacksmith, Endymion, To the River Charles,* and *Maidenhood,* among others. It is a rich handful to the American public of 1841, and though there may be cavilers such as Edgar Poe and Margaret Fuller waiting just around the corner to pounce upon Henry's weaknesses, for the most part this book is devoured with gusto. Letters of praise are showered upon the young man. William Prescott, John Neal, Washington Allston, a host of kindly disposed intelligences, extend cordial felicitations. It becomes apparent now that a new planet has soared into the American skies. He is neither deep nor passionate but he is simple, orderly, didactic and rhythmical. He is sensitive to colors and melody, and he is never above the intelligence of the average high-school boy. Therefore he suits his public admirably. Bryant, at last, has an equal. These poems are to be printed and reprinted, to pass from hand to hand and mouth to mouth. They are to be translated into a dozen languages and so made familiar to Europe. The Europeanism which Henry has imbibed perco-lates back to Europe again, slightly colored by the American channel through which it passes, and the Old World accepts it as the achievement of a good lad who knows what models to follow. Henry's assiduous labors, his flittings about to Philadelphia, New York, Portland, Nahant, have wearied him, and his health is in a decline but he is happy for all that. Guarded so excellently and praised so wholeheartedly by his own little group, represented so ably in New York by Sam Ward and Nathaniel Willis, he has little to fear so far as his immediate career is concerned. He may suffer from dyspepsia but he hardly feels the old pangs of his own mental feebleness.

v

The genial, flowery, sentimental, vulgar, inspired Charles Dickens burst upon Boston and Cambridge like a comet, coming to view the barbaric Americans and make notes on their customs and deportment. Henry is enchanted with him. "He is a glorious fellow. . . . He is a gay, free-and-easy character. . . . He went with Sumner and me to hear Father Taylor preach. . . . We took him to Copp's Hill and to Bunker Hill. . . . The other evening he was at the theater; and was received with nine cheers, and forced to come forward in the box and make a bow." Henry is now part of the great American reception committee to famous foreign visitors. It is important to remember this, for Charles Dickens is but one of the first among an endless galaxy that will associate Henry with America and naturally turn their steps to the Craigie House, there to pay their respects to one who —as far as they are concerned—is representative of American letters. He pleases foreigners for he is content to receive and to follow. It is easy to understand the mutual attraction between Charles Dickens and Henry for both are sentimentalists of the most facile type, although Henry possesses none of the Englishman's enormous vitality and inspiration. "Have no home but mine," writes Dickens expansively before he leaves America with the material for those *American Notes* which are to arouse such a furore of indignation in certain patriotic quarters, "see nothing in town on your way towards Germany, and let me be your London host and cicerone." Henry, it will be deduced, is considering another European trip. This is so. Ailing in health and run down because of his vigorous activities in writing, teaching and social movements, he decides to take a cure in Germany, and during this spring of 1842 he obtains a six months' leave from his duties and goes abroad to take the "water-cure" at Marienberg. He sails from New York, sped on his way by a poem in the *Boston Advertiser* from the pen of George Hillard.

> Ye gales that breathe, ye founts that gush
> With renovating power,
> Upon that loved and laureled head
> Your gifts of healing shower!
> And jocund health, that loves to climb
> The breezy mountain side,
> Wake with thy touch to bounding life
> His pulse's languid tide!

After three weeks of gray Atlantic tides, Havre. Then, one of the unforgotten diligences to Paris. Again the winding roads, the French peasants, the little inns, the green foliage. It is a famous author who is venturing upon Europe now, one who goes back to old familiar scenes, scenes last tinged with the mists of sadness, enfeebled in health but more exhilarated in spirits and certainly with a prospective happiness, of which he must be aware, looming in the near future. Henry loiters in Paris several days seeking out old acquaintances and revisiting the scenes of past episodes in his life. There is the Countess de Sailly's hand to kiss and Rachel in Racine's *Mithridate* to thrill over. George Sumner, Charles' brother, is there, too, and there is much converse about the militant young statesman, converse that starts certain liberalistic tendencies moving in the back of Henry's mind. From Paris he goes to Brussels armed with one of his usual letters of introduction from George Ticknor, this time to Count Arrivabene who welcomes the author most cordially. He gives Henry a dinner "at which were present an Italian philosopher and a Belgian poet." Henry's linguistic training stands him in good stead here. From Brussels he takes "a run through Belgium." There is a day at Antwerp full of exciting thoughts, where Henry is touched to the soul by "the antique streets, the chiming bells." Cologne is the next stop and here he takes steamboat to Marienberg. On the boat is a lady with "four daughters, each with a little straw hat without any trimming whatever." And at Marienberg he settles down in a chamber overlooking the well, determined to regain his flagging strength.

His life here is quiet. At four o'clock in the morning he is awakened and wrapped in a wet sheet, then

in a blanket, then in a mass of bed quilts. For an hour
he lies there until he perspires freely. Then he is
wheeled in an armchair to the bathing room and
plunged into a large bath of running water. After
this thorough inundation he dresses, walks for an hour
in the garden and drinks four or five glasses of water
from the fountain. A breakfast of bread, butter and
milk, and occasionally strawberries, is followed by another walk. At eleven o'clock he stands under a spout
and receives a *douche*. Another walk. A *fliessendes
sitzbad*, or flowing bath. Walk. A frugal dinner
without wine. Then a choice of sitting, walking or
billiards until five o'clock. Another *sitzbad*. Another
walk. Supper, which is the same as breakfast. And at
ten o'clock, to bed. "You will think the treatment quite
barbarous," Henry writes to his father, "but it is not
half so much so as it seems. To me, indeed, it is extremely pleasant." Outside of reading, writing letters
(he composes but one poem, apparently, while he is
here) and billiards, there is little beyond the strenuous
water cure to occupy Henry's time. He reads huge
quantities of the younger German poets, possibly urged
thereto by his fortunate meeting with Ferdinand Freiligrath while on an excursion to St. Goar, an excursion,
incidentally, where he saw the first beautiful woman
he had ever seen in Germany. Then there are the
characters at Marienberg to amuse him, the old Dutch
Admiral who thunders along with a huge cane, the
pale young Jewess who is carried out in her chair every
morning to sit on the terrace, the gouty English
surgeon who rides into his bedroom on a donkey and
tumbles from that perplexed steed directly into bed,
the pretty girl who walks like Ellen Tree in the
Bandit's Bride, the prima donna of the Dusseldorf
theater whose tin dipper is gallantly filled by Henry

every morning, the Russian colonel who roars like a
maniac when the cold *douche* descends on him, the
music master who sings in bed, and (how the impressionable youth with his flute in his knapsack wandering along the Loire crops out here!) "thee, sweet
Jacobina, born on this river of romance, and now just
under the eaves of twenty, looking forth upon the
world, with thy tender eyes, dark hair, and green
album." It is to be wondered how many times Henry
writes his name in this "green album."

The friendship with Freiligrath must be emphasized, for although the two men are never to meet
again, they are to correspond frequently, translate each
other's work, and treasure the memory of each other.
Freiligrath at this time is one of the most promising
of the younger German poets. He is romantic in
appearance, with long black hair, a mustache and beard
all flowing into one another. The two men meet at
St. Goar and gabble away like schoolgirls, for Henry
is European in the warmth of his affections for chosen
friends, although he may be a trifle cool toward mere
acquaintances. Freiligrath translates *The Skeleton in
Armour* and *Excelsior*. He sends Henry papers and
letters. He extends himself in every way to render
Henry's tenure in Germany a pleasure.

Time flows along and Henry grows unpleasantly
aware that his leave of absence from Harvard is drawing to a close. He remembers Charles Dickens' warm
invitation and decides to go to England, although the
doctor at Marienberg urges him to stay and complete
the cure. But what are water cures compared to
Charles Dickens? So about the middle of September
Henry is off, armed with newly arrived letters of introduction from Charles Sumner to personages in
London. "You know I am to stay with Dickens while

in London," he writes proudly to his father, "and beside his own agreeable society I shall enjoy that of the most noted literary men of the day,—which will be a great gratification to me." Up the Rhine he goes and by the twenty-fourth of the month he is in Nuremberg, tracing Albrecht Durer and Hans Sachs. On the twenty-eighth Charles Dickens is writing to him: ". . . Your bed is waiting to be slept in; the door is gaping hospitably to receive you." Early in October Henry is installed in the bosom of the Dickens family, dividing his time between conversing with literary personages, reveling in the English atmosphere of the Dickens milieu and rushing about London purchasing new garments, boots, hose, trousers and coats, all of the latest fashion. For a fortnight he sits at the Dickens' table, listening to the chatter of the novelist, of George Cruikshank, of Maclise, of Macready. He breakfasts and dines with Samuel Rogers and at his table meets Thomas Campbell, the poet, and Moxon, the publisher. Campbell disappoints him; he finds him small and shrunken, nipped by frosty age and wearing a "foxy wig." Talfourd, Tennyson and Milnes are among those whom Henry desires to meet, but, alas, they are out of town. He must do without them. Behind all this urbane chatter and airy English persiflage moves a shadow that beckons to Henry's moralistic inclinations. In the back of his mind the positive arguments of Charles Sumner begin to shape themselves and the abolition movement from which he has kept himself detached, heretofore, fills his thoughts with as near a semblance of passion as his calm and somewhat lackadaisical temperament may command. He feels that he should do something. As he purchases his neatly cut trousers he thinks of the slaves in the fastnesses of the Great Dismal Swamp hiding from the baying bloodhounds. Between the fair pattern of his new waistcoat and himself creep dark faces and brown uplifted hands. For a brief moment Henry realizes that there are terrible things in life and that the Republic is tottering on the edge of an abyss. He bids a fond farewell to London, to the smoky streets, to the bubble of St. Paul's, and departs, pausing long enough at Bath to dine with the old ferocious critic, Walter Savage Landor. The next day he takes passage for his troubled native land on the *Great Western* from Bristol, and as the ship lurches into the maw of a blustering wind vext thoughts of Abolitionism and political turmoil boil and bubble in his usually serene mind. The ship groans in tempest and Henry is not out of his berth for more than twelve hours during the first dozen days of the trip. Stretched out in the forward part of the vessel he listens to the great waves breaking against the ribs of the ship and shouting with voices of thunder. During these stormy sleepless nights he meditates on Slavery, and each morning he sets down the fruits of his meditation with a pencil. He remembers Benjamin Lundy's *Genius of Universal Emancipation* in his father's house at Portland. He recalls planning a drama on Toussaint l'Overture while he was installed at Brunswick. Pacifically minded as he is he determines to follow Sumner, to come out openly as an Anti-Slavery man. The great waves bellow about the ship and there is a strained creaking of cordage. Perhaps he first conceives that simile of the Union as a "ship of state" on this turbulent voyage. Anyway, stretched out in his narrow berth and guided by the dim light from a solitary porthole he begins to write and by the time the *Great Western* eases into New York harbor—where the beloved Felton and the

equally beloved Sumner are waiting impatiently on
the pier—he has to his credit seven anti-slavery poems.
They lack the iron of great controversial poetry. There
is nothing in them calculated to rouse passion and
strike home a truth in such flaming wise as to stir
the multitude. But Henry's intentions are in the right
place and if his verses are rather insipid, or, as Margaret Fuller is to dub them, "the thinnest of all Mr.
Longfellow's thin books," that is because he is congenitally debarred from any strong attitude. There is
no ferociousness in his nature, none of the dynamic
thunder that is in the humorless Sumner, for example.
The verses are what they are, innocuously handled
and gentle little attempts to grapple poetically with a
problem that already calls for giants, for a mature
Sumner, a Garrison, a Lincoln. Still it is to Henry's
credit that he takes this stand, for the Cambridge of
1842 is not a den of heroic liberators as one might
think, but a rather timid-minded parish, if we except
certain personalities who are not Cambridge-like at
all in their evolution. He is no sooner back in Cambridge than he turns over these abolitionist poems to
his publisher, John Owen, and they are immediately
issued in a thirty-one page pamphlet. A mixed reception greets them. Sam Ward writes that he is
"fresh from among the negroes" and pities "the
masters more than the slaves." "When the Eastern
negrophilists are prepared to pay a tax, they will have
a right to dispose of the property of their Southern
brethren," he adds. Henry Ware, Jr., is enthusiastic
about the poems. Nathaniel Hawthorne, just married,
is gently surprised at this exhibition of life on Henry's
part. "You have never poetized a practical subject
heretofore," he remarks. Charles Dickens waits
anxiously for the promised pamphlet. Henry, how-

ever, is glad of his stand. And now that he is back
in Cambridge as Smith Professor it is natural to think
that he will consolidate this, for him, dynamic gesture
on a question that is being so violently agitated. Instead of this, he turns away from life again, uncon-
trollably drawn to those far-away, dim, romantic vistas
of the imagination. *The Spanish Student,* which he
had written some time before, must be made ready for
the press. And a great change in his mode of living
looms imminently before him.

"Of late my heart has quite turned my head out
of doors," he writes to a friend in May, 1843. The
romance which presumably began so long ago in Switzerland when the heartbroken young professor was
endeavoring to stifle his grief over Mary is about to
culminate. On July 13, 1843, Henry is married to
Frances Elizabeth Appleton, the Mary Ashburton of
Hyperion. This spring courtship is the postlude to
a declared passion of seven years before, and it is
the most natural thing for Henry, essentially domes-
tically inclined, to do. Whether it is wise for the
modicum of talent which he possesses is another
matter. Frances Appleton is a kindred type. She is
didactically minded, essentially "New England," and
sans reproche. If Henry had married some foreign
woman, some Jacobina with alien views on existence,
it might have shifted his talent somewhat and brought
out that vein of luxuriousness that evidences itself in
bright gloves and waistcoats and rare wines. But even
so it is difficult to argue that Henry would have shifted
very much from the gentle, moralistic creature that he
is. The New England impulse, the old impulse of
Portland, is too deeply implanted in his nature. It is
possible that he would have been intensely unhappy
with a more worldly-minded wife. Frances is, after

all, the proper, the eminently proper, choice for him
to make. Besides, she is well off and socially secure.
Henry is bulwarking himself with a vengeance, although it is his heart that indubitably leads him and
not his cleverness. He is not clever in that sense; he
is merely following the ingrained instincts of his
nature which calls him to a "good" type like Frances
Appleton.

After a fortnight's seclusion in the Craigie House
(which Nathan G. Appleton purchases and presents
to the newly married couple) Henry and his wife pay
a filial visit to Portland and another to Nahant. Then
there is a trip to the Berkshires to visit other Appleton
connections, and on their way they made a wide detour
to the Catskills, passing through the rolling valley
of the Connecticut. Charles Sumner, who has acted
as "best man," travels with them throughout a part
of the journey. At Springfield they visit the Arsenal
and the new Mrs. Longfellow exhibits her tempo in
likening the burnished stands of arms to organ-pipes
and suggesting a "peace poem" to Henry. As he is
already filled with Sumner's recent utterances on peace
the idea lures him and *The Arsenal at Springfield*
results. Henry's eyes are troubling him; he has strained
them by reading in the twilight and he is compelled
to put himself in the hands of an oculist. It is months
before the abused eyes resume their full labors. In
the meantime Frances acts as amanuensis and much of
Henry's correspondence at this time is put down by
his wife. This unfortunate eye trouble compels him
to forego a deal of his work, and it is partly because
of this that he calls upon Felton in the fall of this
year, to aid him in the preparation of a new undertaking, an anthology of *The Poets and Poetry of
Europe*, which has been proposed by Carey and Hart

of Philadelphia. It is to be a big book and in its hundreds of pages will give Henry a chance to revel in foreign lyricism to his heart's content. It is to be an important book, also, one that introduces to the American reader a host of alien names and measures and the lyrical urges of half-a-dozen European countries. Besides this venture Henry nibbles at the *Divine Comedy* of Dante and by November 24, 1843, he writes Freiligrath that he has translated sixteen cantoes.

Henry now is adjusted to that long domestic scene, not to be actually broken until the tragic catastrophe of 1861. Settled in the Craigie House he has his classes to attend, his arguments with the college faculty to pursue, his translations, his original poems, his lectures, his summer trip, his friends—always, of course, his precious Five of Clubs, and, to crown all, the happy duties of a father. On June 9, 1844, his first son, Charles Appleton, is born, and on November 23, 1845, a second son, "a little wandering musician, with a remarkable talent for imitating with his mouth the penny trumpet and the wooden dog," comes into the world and is christened Ernest Wadsworth. Time moves along, sunnily, urbanely, and the poet sits back in his charmed studio, glimpsing the River Charles, the salt marshes, and the Brighton hills from his window, and meditating on the good fortune that has befallen him. He would seem to be quite prepared now for a golden era, a period of unstemmed creation fertilized by the constant praise of his immediate associates, and in a sense, this is so. It is true that his labors at the college irk him a bit and the far-off vision of an existence devoted wholly to the creation of poetical fancies hovers before his sparkling blue eyes; but such momentary irritations and fair vistas do not impinge too drastically upon his nature as yet. He is too busy and facile to be dissatisfied. Attending to his voluminous correspondence, keeping his journal, putting together the work which is to form the prospective new volume of verse, *The Belfry of Bruges and Other Poems,* and considering plans for *The Poets and Poetry of Europe* and the de luxe illustrated edition of his collected poems which Carey and Hart are dangling before him—still another milestone on the way—Henry finds himself swimming boldly and easily down the stream. Time slips along and the year 1845 looms on the threshold and with it come warnings as well as prizes.

VI

A dark cloud no larger than a man's hand and in that hand a pen moves across those fair alien skies which shine so brightly above the New World. The Southerners, the New York group, the New England cliques, gesticulate blandly, echo one another, dip graceful hands into the rich cornucopia of Europe and draw forth what they please in spirit, essence and matter. A flock of miniature Mahomets turn to the Mountain and each one of them returns to the banks of the Potomac, the Hudson, the Charles, holding aloft a polished stone and offering it as the bread of life. Henry, well placed, happily married, astonishingly popular, stands benignantly at the head of these minor prophets. He is barricaded by mellifluous-tongued friends, "insured in the Mutual." But the dark cloud no larger than a man's hand and in that hand a pen moves steadily across the skies. Henry does not see it. He continues to exist, as he will exist all his life, in a Palace of Song builded of borrowed

bricks. "A national literature is the expression of
national character and thought," he enunciates, "and
as our character and modes of thought do not differ
essentially from those of England, our literature cannot. Vast forests, lakes, and prairies cannot make
great poets. They are but the scenery of the play, and
have much less to do with the poetic character than
has been imagined. Neither Mexico nor Switzerland
has produced any remarkable poet." It is as easily as
this that he pushes aside three thousand miles of
tangled wildernesses, mushroom cities, clashing communities, majestic river-reaches, vast lakes, and blood-
stained soil. The influence of environment on character is a mystery to the dapper gentleman seated in
his Cambridge study and surrounded by his calf-bound
tomes. "When I go out of the precincts of my study,
down the village street to the college," he writes (the
year is 1845), "how the scaffoldings about the Palace of
Song come rattling down." Henry is bounded by his
books and he cannot see beyond them. He does not
possess even the vigor of the Quaker, Whittier, who,
but a few months before, has urged him to run on the
Liberty Party ticket for Congress. "Partisan warfare
becomes too violent, too vindictive for my taste," he
responds. Suddenly the dark cloud no larger than a
man's hand and in that hand a pen resolves itself into
the nervous hand of Edgar Allan Poe.

Poe is the first great original writer in America. He
is original in that he demands a beginning that evolves
out of itself and not out of a predicated atmosphere.
But he is caught like a rat in a trap of the "colonial
expansion" theory of literature, and his weaknesses
reduce his strength so fatally that he cannot tear
clear of it. An abiding sense of his own grievances
arouses a personal jealousy. He carries his critical

theories, theories formulated upon Coleridgean logic, to a *reductio ad absurdum*. He loses his balance. But behind all his drastic errors of passion and pride and loneliness looms an essential *rightness* that is ominous in its implications to the teetering future of American letters. Henry, armored in the invincible faith of the justice of his position—a justice bolstered by the undeniable sweetness and integrity of his limited mind, is hardly disconcerted by this phenomenon who, after all, speaks with the rancorous voice of a jealous-minded New Yorker who is on the "outside." He can afford, so he imagines, to maintain a dignified silence while the mad dog rages, and there is no response from Craigie House to accusations from Poe which open 1845 so momentously for Henry. After all, he has certain settled convictions regarding Poe, for this is not the first time that a vindictive shot from the Southerner has whistled his way. Poe has reproached Henry for using so crudely in *Hyperion* material capable of being highly wrought by art. As early as 1840 Poe attacked Henry for plagiarism, basing his onslaught upon the similarities between Tennyson's *The Death of the Old Year* and the New Englander's *The Midnight Mass for the Dying Year*. In a review of *Ballads and Other Poems*, he stated that Henry's "conception of the *aims* of poetry *is all wrong*" for the reason that "didacticism is the prevalent *tone* of his song." And in 1841 Poe had written to Griswold pointing out what he considered a plagiarism of his *The Haunted Palace* in Henry's *The Beleagured City*. It is true that less than two months later Poe was writing Henry begging contributions to a magazine and ending his letter on this note: "In conclusion, I cannot refrain from availing myself of this, the only opportunity I may ever have, to assure the author of the *Hymn*

HENRY WADSWORTH LONGFELLOW, 1842
    From an old print

EDGAR ALLAN POE
(From one of the Pratt Daguerreotypes)

to the Night, of *The Beleagured City,* and of the
Skeleton in Armour, of the fervent admiration with
which his genius has inspired me; and yet I would
scarcely hazard a declaration whose import might be
so easily misconstrued, and which bears with it, at best,
more or less of *niaiserie,* were I not convinced that
Professor Longfellow, writing and thinking as he
does, will be at no loss to feel and to appreciate the
honest sincerity of what I say." Poe may have
been talking through his hat in this letter although
niaiserie may equally be a touch of sly genius. If
one chooses to credit Poe with slyness his remarks
may be read: "I like certain of your poems, which
is a foolish statement, but you, being a simple fellow, will credit me with sincerity." However, this
is possibly going too far, for Poe is on serious record
as placing Henry at the head of the American poets
of his long generation. This does not bespeak much
for Poe's idea of that generation.

In that curious correspondence with Lowell—curious because of the personalities of the two men—Poe,
in 1843, speaks of the inferior quality of Henry's
genius but goes on to say, "Mr. Longfellow . . . by
no means equals you in the true spirit . . ." which
seems to be a clear case of soft soap. The next year
Poe tells Lowell that Graham, of *Graham's Magazine,*
kept back his review of Henry's *The Spanish Student* for almost a year because of the proof in it of
palpably plagiarized passages from the Southerner's
Politian. Poe is now actively girding himself for
his open attacks on the New Englander and the book
which breaks the critic's back (to grow wildly figur-
ative) is *The Waif,* a collection of stray pieces edited
by Henry and published during the last days of 1844.
In concluding his review of this book in *The Evening*

Mirror, New York, for January 14, 1845, Poe writes: "We conclude our notes on *The Waif* with the observation that, although full of beauties, it is infected with a *moral taint*—or is this a mere freak of our own fancy? We shall be pleased if it be so; —but there *does* appear, in this little volume, a very careful avoidance of all American poets who may be supposed especially to interfere with the claims of Mr. Longfellow. These men Mr. Longfellow can continuously *imitate* (*is* that the word?) and yet never incidentally commend." The so-called "Longfellow War" is now on.

Henry sits silently in Cambridge although various of his friends bestir themselves in his defense. He can afford to sit silently, for already he is preparing his collected poems for the press, a publication which, before this crucial year of 1845 has run its course, is to arouse a new and unexpected attack from a different quarter. As for Poe, he has a full season before him. It is to be an *annus mirabilis* in a way; it is to be starred with the publication of *The Raven*, the appearance of his complete collected poems, and the publication of twelve of his tales in a single volume—a rather shabby volume, by the way. Indeed, it gives a poignant picture of the positions of the two antagonists to set this little volume of tales beside the illustrated edition of Henry's collected poems, issued by Carey and Hart of Philadelphia. Poe leaves the *Mirror* shortly after his opening fusillade at Henry and the columns of that periodical contain the protests of Henry's ever zealous friends, some editorial comment in reply—extenuating on Willis' part (the nobby Nat Willis who, not so many years before, was hobnobbing with the Duchess of St. Albans) and vindicatory on Poe's. Willis eventually withdraws from the discussion in a card in which he intimates his entire dissent from "all disparagement of Longfellow." Nathaniel, it is to be inferred, likes to play safe. Then the "Outis" letter appears, a long letter attacking Poe's attitude and valiantly defending Henry and those of his colleagues in *The Waif*, who have been accused of plagiarism. "Outis" is a mystery. He is certainly not Henry. It is fairly established that he is not one of Henry's friends. Perhaps "Outis" is Poe himself anxious to bring forth new arguments and answer certain rebuttals that have been floating about in the somewhat excited literary circles.

Anyway, Poe finds the letter an excellent punching-bag and begins his reiteration of the charges of plagiarism against Henry, James Aldrich, and one or two others, in *The Broadway Journal*, beginning them on March 1, 1845, and continuing them for five installments. It is futile to go into the particulars of these accusations, for they are concerned with details no longer of any importance. It is the spirit of the matter which reflects on Henry's life. Poe accuses him of lifting thoughts and paraphrasing lines from other writers and adduces himself, Tennyson, and the Scotch ballad, *The Good George Campbell*, as instances. This Scotch ballad which Henry had put forth as an original translation from the German is unfortunate, but there is no reason not to accept Henry's statement that he was unaware that it existed in English, that he thought it to be an original poem by the German singer, Wolf, and that he translated it from a collection of German poems, *Deutscher Sänger-Soal*, while he was passing up the Rhine. If anything it is a reflection on his loose scholarship and his inability to immediately perceive that *The Good George Campbell* was a translation from the Scots tongue. Neither do we need to take seriously Poe's personal grievance that Henry had plagiarized from *Politian* in *The Spanish Student* and from *The Haunted Palace* in *The Beleagured City*. There are superficial likenesses here to be sure, but that is all. The case of Tennyson is somewhat different although it is, perhaps, the spirit of the imitation and not the actual poems in themselves that matter. Indeed, as it has been inferred already, it is the spirit of the Poe attacks that matter and not the details. Poe indubitably lays his finger on a colossal crack in Henry's armor. Through this crack we see the man as he is. He is but the larger development of his younger self. He is the chameleon, coloring to his books if not so much to his surroundings. He represents to a huge degree the very things in American literary history which Poe hated, objectives which the Southerner made his particular points of attack, though more often than not he weakened his offensive gestures by insistence on too personal a note. Poe forgot that he was fighting for the non-existent quality of American letters and remembered only that he was fighting for himself. But in back of his most scurrilous and personal attacks walked certain doughty principles. He hated secondary genius in poetry. He despised sentimentality. He detested and, it may be, feared the monstrous log-rolling of the New England group. It must be remembered that Poe was not "insured in the Mutual." The didactic element in letters nauseated him. Henry represented to him all these things, and Henry was a bright and shining mark, a beloved of the gods who had his books elaborately presented, who had his zealous disciples ever ready to write about him, who received large prices for his poems, and who lived in comparative affluence. For the moment the New England poet could afford to sit back in a benignant silence and play the injured but forgiving man. Poe's race was nearly run. Within a few seasons the doleful Raven was to pass on his way, and Henry, remaining the uncrowned king, was to grow in seeming permanence while Griswold nosed at the wretched dead Poe's bones. Decades later Henry is to stroke back his flowing white hair, lift his blue eyes to the adoring young William Winter and gravely say, "My works seemed to give him much trouble, first and last; but Mr. Poe is dead and gone, and I am alive and still writing—and that is the end of the matter." It is not the end of the matter and it is to be hoped that Poe, the harassed, poverty-stricken, Time-smitten Titan so inconsistently mingled of the elements of strength and weakness, knows it now.

Following hard on the heels of the Poe attacks come other onslaughts, for Henry has now developed into a shining mark for aggrieved sharpshooters. In December of this year of wordy battles, 1845, William Gilmour Sims, the Southern novelist, lets loose what Henry terms "a very abusive article." "I consider this the most original and inventive of all his fictions," blandly notes the idol of Cambridge. Two days later he is scribbling in his journal, "Miss Fuller makes a furious onslaught on me in *The New York Tribune.* It is what might be called 'a bilious attack.'" "A bilious attack," indeed! It is compact with the soundest criticism that he is to receive during his lifetime but so strongly bucklered is he with friends and an innate self-approbation that Margaret Fuller has her "bilious attack" in vain. It does not divert Henry into any new channels of endeavor, indeed, why should it? He writes with that ever flowing facility which is unstemmable. He has his "poetic mornings" now

with a serene gusto. Margaret Fuller's trenchant comments fly off into space and Henry polishes up *To a
Child,* decides to write a poem for Fanny's birthday
and, instead, writes *To an Old Danish Song Book,* puts
on paper *The Bridge Over the Charles,* the *Occultation
of Orion, To the Driving Cloud, The Evening Star,*—
this, by the way, being Henry's only love poem—*Birds
of Passage,* and so forth and so on until the end of
1845. At the same time he is flirting with the idea of a
long poem in hexameters tentatively called *Gabrielle*
but which is soon to be offered the world as *Evangeline.*
He is also proof-reading *The Belfry of Bruges and
Other Poems.* To be succinct, he is an extraordinarily
busy poet entirely unselective but kept within bounds by
an ingrained taste and essential "safety" of expression
which is to raise his gentle ambling verses—so shot
through with that to-be-desired European culture—to
a degree of popularity entirely disturbing to the few
and scattered critical minds in America. Margaret
Fuller is one of these few intelligences. Her keen-
ness is unquestioned, although it is to be doubted that
Henry thinks her keen. She is merely "bilious." Besides that she is a Transcendentalist, and the Trans-
cendentalists do not think so much of Henry. It is
equally certain that he does not think so much of them.
After all, he has been in Germany, he has read German philosophy and he is not to be blamed if he refuses to accept at their face value certain notions put
forward by the Fuller faction as original when he
knows that they are not. It would be unwise to underestimate his intelligence here. He is not so simple as
he looks. Margaret Fuller's transcendentalism, however, does not invalidate the pith and point of her
criticism. Her ideas on American letters are sound,
to the point, and exceedingly acute for 1845. "It does

not follow," she writes, "because many books are written by persons born in America that there exists an American literature. Books which imitate or represent the thoughts and life of Europe do not constitute an American literature. Before such can exist, an original idea must animate this nation and fresh currents of life must call into life fresh thoughts along its shores." This is excellent generalizing and Henry, raising his eyes from *To an Old Danish Song Book,* might well have wriggled uneasily. There is not a wriggle out of him, however. "That day will not rise till the fusion of races among us is more complete," goes on the trenchant voice of Margaret Fuller, speaking like a Sibyl into space. "It will not rise till this nation shall attain sufficient moral and intellectual dignity to prize moral and intellectual, no less highly than political freedom, not till, the physical resources of the country being explored, all its regions studded with towns, broken by the plow, netted together by railways and telegraph lines, talent shall be left at leisure to turn its energies upon the higher department of men's existence." This is not a jaundiced woman speaking. There is no biliousness here. Neither is there any conscious dislike of Henry as a man in the direct remarks she has to make on his work. She strives to be impartial and she is impartial, much more impartial than Edgar Allan Poe had been during the opening months of this year. "Longfellow is artificial and imitative," she declares. "He borrows incessantly, and mixes what he borrows, so that it does not appear at the best advantage. He is very faulty in using broken or mixed metaphors. The ethical part of his writing has a hollow, second-hand sound. He has, however, elegance, a love of the beautiful, and a fancy for what is large and manly, if not a full

sympathy with it. His verse breathes at times much
sweetness; and, if not allowed to supersede what is
better, may promote a taste for good poetry. Though
imitative, he is not mechanical." She is striving des-
perately here to be impartial, even to the degree, it is
to be suspected, of affecting a sympathy which is hardly
existent within her keenly analytic mind. That little
word "supersede" is the key to the fervor of her feelings. It tells us much about her. It tells us that she
sees in Henry something ominous creeping upon
American letters and clogging the ways. "Never was
a time," she cries, "when satirists were more needed
to scourge from Parnassus the magpies who are devouring the food scattered there for singing birds."
And there we have it. Margaret Fuller perceives
what literature has suffered from since its genesis, the
clever magpies who catch the universal ear and drown
out those solitary lofty voices which speak most intensely to the mind. But there are magpies and magpies. There are the magpies who, of their own noisy
voraciousness, devour the food of the singing birds,
and there are the magpies who have this food thrust
upon them by the eager, obvious-minded well-wishers
and disciples who hear their repetitious notes and enthusiastically react to old ever-comprehended echoes.
Henry, perhaps, is in this second classification. He is
a magpie but an innocent one. The rich food is being
brought to him. Margaret Fuller is aware of this, as
indeed, she seems to be aware of everything, for she
writes: "Yet there is a middle class, composed of men
of little original poetic power, but of much poetic
taste and sensibility, whom we would not wish to have
silenced. They do no harm, but much good (if only
their minds are not confounded with those of a higher
class), by educating in others the faculties dominant

in themselves. In this class we place the writer at present before us. We must confess to a coolness to Mr. Longfellow, in consequence to the exaggerated praises that have been bestowed upon him. When we see a person of moderate powers receive honors which should be reserved for the highest, we feel somewhat like assailing him and taking from him the crown which should be reserved for grander brows. And yet this is, perhaps, ungenerous. It may be that the management of publishers, the hyperbole of paid or undiscerning reviewers, or some accidental cause which gives a temporary interest to productions beyond what they would permanently command, have raised such an one to a place as much above his wishes as his claims, and which he would rejoice, with honorable modesty, to vacate at the approach of one worthier. We the more readily believe this of Mr. Longfellow as one so sensible to the beauties of other writers and so largely indebted to them, *must* know his own comparative rank better than his readers have known it for him. . . ."

Henry, however, does not grasp the peculiar position in which he has been placed by time. There is no reason to believe that praise has unduly turned his head, though it is plain enough that he enjoys the felicitations of his friends. It is "smoothness" of life, the gentle turn, the warm comfortable aspect of existence which calls to him in a sweetly Germanic voice and he responds with as much ardor as he can muster up. In the back of his consciousness move the vague forms of great endeavors but he can never quite approximate them to himself. He knows that he burns for eminence, but it is no furious fire which consumes him. Three years before, while at Boppard on the Rhine, he had written:

Half of my life is gone, and I have let
   The years slip from me and have not fulfilled
   The aspiration of my youth, to build
Some tower of song with lofty parapet.
Not indolence, nor pleasure, nor the fret
   Of restless passions that would not be stilled,
   But sorrow, and a care that almost killed,
Kept me from what I may accomplish yet;

Though, half-way up the hill, I see the Past
   Lying beneath me with its sounds and sights,—
A city in the twilight dim and vast,
   With smoking roofs, soft bells, and gleaming lights,—
And hear above me on the Autumnal blast
   The cataract of Death far-thundering from the heights.

At that time he had behind him *Outre Mer*, *Hyperion*, *Voices of the Night*, *Ballads and Other Poems*, *The Spanish Student* and *Poems on Slavery*, a meager enough showing and yet one starred by his most popular brief pieces. A sense of his own shortcomings, we must believe, was with him through all these early years, and this sense was dulled only by the continual praises showered upon him at Cambridge. It is no fierce passion of regret speaking in the above-quoted sonnet but rather a pensive wistfulness, putting the blame on "sorrow and a care that almost killed." There is a sanguine note here also; he intimates that he "may accomplish yet" that lofty tower of song. He believes in himself, therefore. Behind his kindly and somewhat removed exterior is a confidence yet to be vindicated by achievement. And because of this confidence he can read Margaret Fuller's castigation with a degree of tolerance, dismiss it in a phrase, and march off light-heartedly to hear Mr. Emerson lecture on "Great Men." Margaret

Fuller, for her part, can dismiss Henry as airily. "And now farewell," she writes, "to the handsome book, with its Preciosos and Preciosas, its Vikings and knights and cavaliers, its flowers of all climes, and wild flowers of none. We have not wished to depreciate these writings below their current value more than truth absolutely demands. We have not forgotten that, if a man cannot himself sit at the feet of the muses, it is much if he prizes those who may; it makes him a teacher to the people. Neither have we forgotten that Mr. Longfellow has a genuine respect for his pen, never writes carelessly, nor when he does not wish to, nor for money alone. Nor are we intolerant to those who prize hothouse bouquets beyond all the free beauty of nature; that helps the gardener and has its uses. But still let us not forget—Excelsior!"

The embittered Poe is pleased with this onslaught even though he is no friend to Margaret Fuller. "In my opinion," he writes, "it is one of the very few reviews of Longfellow's poems ever published in America, of which the critics have not abundant reason to be ashamed. Mr. Longfellow is entitled to a certain and very distinguished rank among the poets of his country, but that country is disgraced by the evident toadyism which could award to his social position and influence, to his fine paper and large type, to his morocco binding and gilt edges, to his flattering portrait of himself, and to the illustrations of his poems by Huntingdon, that amount of indiscriminate approbation which neither could nor would have been given to the poems themselves." There is a little too much emphasis on the physical appearance of Henry's first collected edition here, for it predicates a personal rancor on the part of Poe, but there is an element of underlying truth in what the bitter critic has to say.

It is true that Henry is bulwarked by position, friends, morocco bindings, and all the elaborate appanages of kindly fortune. But he accepts these things tacitly. He is not aware of them as particular gifts, and indeed regards himself pretty much as a Byronic figure in his solitary moments, although that unceasing didactic impulse within him cautions him strenuously against too much bewailing at fortune. One must believe that behind the clouds the sun is shining.

So 1845 comes to its end, a year filled with ominous warning for Henry. He does not read any writing on the wall. There is none there for him to see. Margaret Fuller's warnings are "a bilious attack." Sims' castigation is an original and inventive "fiction." Poe's harsh criticism he never attributes to anything but "the irritation of a sensitive nature chafed by some indefinite sense of wrong." There is a flash of intuition in this dismissal of Poe, but only a flash. Henry does not see the man in large. He observes but the troubled outward vesture (undeniably there) which weakens Poe's attacks. Surrounded by his family and students in the pleasurable milieu of Cambridge he will go on as he has gone on heretofore. He will ignore attacks and welcome praise. Speaking of critical clippings some years later to William Winter, he declares, "I look at the first few lines and if I find that the article has been written in a kindly spirit, I read it through, but if I find that the intention is to wound, I drop the paper into my fire, and so dismiss it. In that way one escapes much annoyance." Already Henry is getting to be like Queen Victoria. His Balmoral is the Craigie House and he dips his hands in life as he pleases, pleasantly conscious that he need heed no warnings. At the conclusion of 1845 he writes: "Not many hopes deceived, not many illusions scattered, not many anticipations disappointed; but love fulfilled, the heart comforted, the soul enriched with affection." Other minds may be passionately concerned about American letters, but he has his log-fire, his books, Fanny to hang on his words and point out to him the moral implications of living, and himself. What does it mean to him that Margaret Fuller cries out, "The reason of his being over-rated here is because through his works breathes the air of other lands, with whose products the public at large is but little acquainted," when he himself has already said that "vast forests, lakes, and prairies cannot make great poets"? Can he read behind that sentence and realize that he is feeding a vast semi-literate, hungry audience choice foods from foreign platters newly cooked by himself? And can the bulk of that audience realize that these ingredients have been used before? Henry's position is safe as long as culture remains in Europe. He is, if the phrase may be used without offense, the missing link between barbaric America and literary Europe.

VII

By this time Henry has become a familiar figure but not the white-bearded patriarch who is to dominate the school books of the years to come. He is a well-built man of medium stature, with square shoulders and a jaunty walk. His bearing urges some college wit of the day into composing a doggerel which includes:

> With his hat on one whisker, and an air that
>   says, "Go it,"
> You have here the great American poet.

257

His face is clean-shaven except for the mutton-chop side whiskers which are already tinged with gray; that whiteness which is to come upon Henry starts early in his life. His hair is long, parted in the middle behind, and brought forward over the ears in the fashion of the period. His mouth is large and sensitive, his nose slightly aquiline, his forehead broad and intelligent, his eyes blue and sparkling. Carefully dressed always —for the dandy in him persists to the end—he emanates an aura of benignity, sweetness, self-aplomb, aristocracy. He is *l'homme a la mode,* the brightly furbished expression of a tradition and sufficiently endowed with personality to arouse respect and admiration amongst his numberless friends. Put him beside the out-at-elbows, dark, morose Poe and note the difference. The domesticity of the man is evident in his methodical nature. He has a place for everything. He folds up and puts away wrapping paper. He unties, never cuts, string and deposits it in a drawer from which it may be drawn forth when he sends one of his frequent books to a friend. He keeps huge quantities of cartridge paper, cut to an exact size, upon which he indites his poems in that surprisingly plain round handwriting which is so evenly spaced. He keeps a carriage and a pair of dapple-gray horses, and he becomes a spectacle of domestic nobility as he drives through Malden and Lynn on his way to his summer quarters in Nahant, his wife and his children beside him. Europe has not stemmed the old Puritan in him despite the many changes time has wrought, and Sunday is still a day of awful respectability in the Longfellow ménage. Special books are permitted for the occasion and uncomfortable Sunday clothes adorn the children who must refrain from frolicking on this day of days.

Tranquillity marks his life now. It is true that the distress of onerous college duties puts him out of sorts at moments, but on the whole he is of too sanguine a temperament to protest fiercely against his lot. He makes the best of things. The anti-slavery papers attack him for omitting his *Poems on Slavery* from the Carey and Hart collected edition but within a few months a cheaper collected edition is issued by Harper's and there the seven disputed poems may be found. Henry is not fearful of consequences. He is merely "easy." These poems on slavery may be regarded as the initial evidence of a new strain in Henry's work, a strain that attempts to express an Americanism lying somewhere beneath the European surface of his nature. This Americanism is thin and theoretical, in a sense, but it befools the public at large, who cannot as yet recognize autochthonous impulses when they see them. Perhaps the attacks of Margaret Fuller and Edgar Allan Poe stimulate Henry to a more emphatic exhibition of what he regards as his Americanism.

The idea—not a new one, by any means—of expressing various facets of the American scene creeps into his mind but for some reason (and this must be because of the essentially romantic tinge to his thought) he turns to the historical or legendary. The years that now follow, up to his resignation from Harvard, are filled with the enterprise of two major works, *Evangeline* and *The Golden Legend*. Threading the interrupted activity with them are such byproducts as *Kavanagh*, a curious and forgotten tale of New England life, and *The Seaside and the Fireside*, a book of short pieces including *The Building of the Ship*.

Hawthorne gives Henry the idea for *Evangeline*. In his notebook for October 24, 1839, he has entered: "H. L. C—— heard from a French Canadian a story of a young couple in Acadia. On their marriage day all the men of the province were summoned to assemble in the church to hear a proclamation. When assembled, they were all seized and shipped off to be distributed through New England, among them the new bridegroom. His bride set off in search of him; wandered about New England all her lifetime; and at last, when she was old, she found her bridegroom on his deathbed. The shock was so great that it killed her likewise." Hawthorne, dining at Craigie House and having with him H. L. Connolly—the H. L. C—— of this notation—gives the theme freely to Henry when the poet, touched by the sentimental features of the story, asks for it. With intuitive wisdom Henry recognizes that here is a plot fitted exactly to his talents, an opportunity for the development of those pathetic strains and gentle descriptions wherein his kindly muse is most efficacious. By November, 1845, he sets about the poem in earnest and labors upon it intermittently for more than a year. The first draft is finished on February 27, 1847, and the poem is published in October of the same year. From the first, and against the advice of several friends, he determines to employ the difficult hexameter, a verse measure that is not adapted to the English language and which at this time is pretty much of an innovation. It would be a dull matter to enter into a thorough critical survey of *Evangeline*, to expatiate on the fact that Henry never saw Acadia and that he gathered his atmosphere from such sources as Haliburton's history of the dispersal of the Acadians, Fremont's *Expedition to the Rocky Mountains*, Sealsfield's *Life in the New World*, Darley's *Geographical Description of Louisiana*, and a dozen other sources including a diorama of the Mississippi River (was it Banvard's?) which was exhibited in Boston. The careful reader, too, will notice an echo of Scandinavian landscapes and country life creeping into the poem at times. Henry, therefore, borrows his plot, "lifts" his color from books and otherwise shows his dependability upon library sources for an idyl which is somehow successful in spite of this habit of leaning and the extraordinary employment of hexameters. It is, at least, an American theme treated with some degree of extension, a theme that uses Acadia, Louisiana, Philadelphia and the barbaric West. Its success is immediate and during Henry's lifetime it continues to hold its own as the most popular product of his popular pen.

The personal picture of Henry throughout this period is the usual one. His eyes are dim from the old ailment and Time passes too swiftly for him. He goes to the opera in Boston often, attends lectures by Emerson, Whipple, Sumner and other oratorical lights, reads the novels of Dickens as they come out, returns again and again to his dear Richter, welcomes the young James Russell Lowell into the charmed circle, witnesses the passing of Josiah Quincy and the installation of Everett as President of Harvard, goes to Papanti's Assembly without his wife and finds that "the lights seemed dimmer, the music sadder, the flowers fewer, and the women less fair," reads the lectures of Fichte and exclaims: "And this is a German philosopher! Why, there is more of the soul of Christianity in these lectures than in the sermons of all the rebel crew of narrow-minded, dyspeptic, so-called *orthodox* preachers who rail against German philosophy, should they preach from one end of the year to the other!" He decides that his most interesting books are the histories of individuals and individual minds, "all autobiographies and the like." The War with Mexico comes along and he views it from a distance with disdain. "So little interest is felt here in this shabby and to us disgraceful war with Mexico," he notes, "that the New Orleans paper in our reading room has not been cut open for the last two weeks." The laborious trial of his professorship impinges more and more drastically upon his mind. "I am in despair at the swift flight of time, and the utter impossibility I feel to lay hold upon anything permanent. All my hours and days go to perishable things. College takes half the time; and other people, with their interminable letters and poems and requests and demands, take the rest. I have hardly a moment to think of my own writings, and am cheated of some of life's fairest hours. This is the extreme of folly; and if I knew a man, far off in some foreign land, doing as I do here, I should say he was mad." He still possesses his friends, his climbing fame, his wife and children and home, his quiet summers in Portland, Pittsfield and Nahant, but the weight of life is upon him now and it is bowing him down. And then death comes, not as a solitary and exceptional visitor but in a series of sporadic forays on the sheltered life of this poet. On April 7, 1847, Frances had given birth to a little daughter and the next year the baby dies. Henry is benumbed for a time and the blow seems to paralyze his love for his other children. On August 3, 1849, his father dies and there are long sad days in Portland previous to this. Henry wanders about Portland noting the loveliness of his native town. After the funeral he visits the dusty deserted law office and runs over page after page of unpaid charges, the record of Stephen Longfellow's generosity. On March 12, 1851, as he is departing for his college duties a boy runs up to him bringing a telegraphic

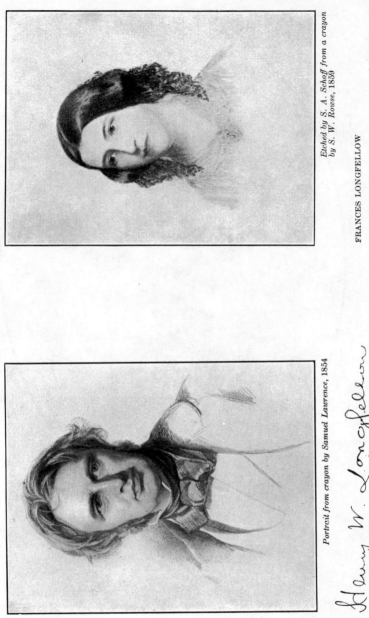

Portrait from crayon by Samuel Lawrence, 1854

Henry W. Longfellow

*Etched by S. A. Schoff from a crayon
by S. W. Rowse, 1859*

FRANCES LONGFELLOW

LONGFELLOW'S DAUGHTERS

despatch. It reads, "Your mother died to-day suddenly." He goes to Portland, sits all night by the body, attends the funeral and comes back to Cambridge in a dazed dream. These griefs deepen the mournful strain already implicit in his nature. But if there is death there is life as well. For during these active years which intervene between the Poe attack and Henry's resignation from Harvard more children come to lighten a home peculiarly adapted to children. They are girls, first Alice, then Edith and eventually Anne Allegra. It is in this way that Life plays its continual see-saw with Henry, taking away, then giving with unstinted generosity. In the broader, more flamboyant sense of the word, these years are eventless. There are no visits to Europe, no sudden and astounding decisions. Perhaps the high peak is the complete success of *Evangeline* and its unusual acceptance in Europe, for this poem serves as the culminating gesture that quite definitely places Henry in the fore-rank (and a bit ahead) of his coevals. Sam Ward may gag a bit at the measure and mumble something to the effect that he prefers plain verse, but Felton is right at hand to strengthen Henry in his attitude, and there is also Holmes, the blithe bright little Holmes.

Indeed, the Cambridge circle is completed. There are no new faces to be introduced, unless it be young Mr. William Dean Howells from Ohio or the hulking figure of Bayard Taylor. These men are but minors, however, so far as the group goes. What we might denominate as the great New England group is marshaled, matured and accepted. There is Henry, Mr. Emerson, Mr. Hawthorne, Mr. Thoreau, Mr. Felton, Mr. Sumner, Mr. Howe, Mr. Ticknor, Mr. Fields, Mr. Holmes, Mr. Lowell, Mr. Norton, Mr. Prescott—one pauses out of breath. They are all there, however, gracious, idealistic, old-fashioned in courtesy and essentially cultured, visiting from home to home and study to study, criticizing one another's work, listening to one another's lectures, reading one another's books, writing dissertations on one another's personalities and literary achievements. This particular milieu must be understood if Henry is to be made plain. One must see Cambridge—of course, not all of the galaxy of names adduced belong to Cambridge—in the pleasant sunlight of 1850, for instance, stretching out small and village-like, crowned by trees and splashed with greenery. There is a meditative somnolence impregnating the air, a scholarly atmosphere. The carriages rattle along the roads behind glossy horses. The placid houses stand back from the streets. The river glistens and sparkles. Across the salt marshes the blithe wind blows through the bright air. There is a miraculous mingling of the new and the old here, a joining together of phantom hands stretching from cultured Europe and the stillness of the woods. A sense of the intellect is formulating itself here. It is true that this intellectual gesture is influenced by European urges, but this may well be understood in a community based on English traditions more emphatically than any other section of the Republic. These men are the descendants of Puritans and the old blood still lingers in their veins.

A new and perplexing passion is slowly seeping into this community. The vexatious question of slavery is agitating certain minds and prophets are uttering disturbing warnings regarding the future of the Republic if the state of affairs in the South be permitted to continue. Sumner, like a new John the Baptist, is crying out in this pleasant wilderness. Since he has been made a member of the Whig State Committee in 1845

he has been much in the public eye, for he is an orator
of the old-fashioned type, flowery and fierce in his
denunciations.   In 1846 he had loudly advocated with-
drawal of the U. S. troops from Mexico and by the
opening of the fifth decade of the nineteenth century
he has been running for the Senate; at first unsuccess-
fully, but by 1851 he is installed in that august body
at Washington and fighting with all the oratorical fervor at his command for the equality which he regards
as necessary for the preservation of the Union.   Henry
is the thin and pleasant echo of Sumner.   He sees in
the statesman a bright and anointed crusader, and he
is wholly devoted to him, accepting implicitly the
judgments of the slightly younger man.   Cambridge,
however, does not view Sumner in so sanguine a light.
A greater part of the community adjudges him a fire-
brand, a radical, a man who is stirring up a hornets'
nest of trouble, and Cambridge does not like trouble.
It is possible, therefore, that Henry's close friendship
with Sumner causes the more sedate authorities at
Harvard to view him with a slightly suspicious eye.
Henry must sense this, just as he senses that he is being overworked, that his poetical activities are being
cramped because of a plethora of pedagogical duties
which might just as well be in the hands of a younger
and, for the time being at least, less ambitious man.
The last four years Henry passes as Smith Professor
are disturbing years because of this dissatisfaction and
the feeling that time is rushing along at too furious a
pace.   He thinks more and more about resignation and
especially is this train of thought strengthened by the
indubitable success of *Evangeline*.   He discusses with
his friends and his wife the possibilities of retiring,
but for some time he hangs on, either because of the

innate deliberateness of his nature or because of a fear of too drastic a gesture.

In the meantime three books come rapidly from his pen. There is *Kavanagh, The Seaside and the Fireside,* and *The Golden Legend. Kavanagh* appears in 1849, two seasons after the publication of *Evangeline.* It is a slight tale with a thin atmosphere and so mild a flavor that there is small need to resuscitate it. It is written in Melville House, Pittsfield, Mass., and it aims to be a revelation of New England life and customs. The absence of plot and the procrastination of the hero militate against its success and its readers are few. Indeed, Henry's prose seems to be dwindling away. He does not understand the true function of fictional narrative and wisely enough he makes *Kavanagh* his last excursion in prose. If he loses ground, however, with this vacuous little novel he gains new territory with *The Seaside and the Fireside,* which appears the next year, in 1850. There is to be yet a decade of troubled peace before the Republic is ripped apart by mounting passions but Henry, because of his close intimacy with Sumner, is already viewing the future with a startled eye. The outstanding poem in this new volume, therefore, is one concerned with the Republic. It would be sheer effrontery not to admit that *The Building of the Ship* is a dramatic and finely conceived work. There is a grave warning implicit in it. To understand this the poem must be set against the time. The Free-Soil party had just been formed and Massachusetts is in a turmoil of political excitement, conventions, speeches and the like. The Whigs, having lost their vital rallying principle, dwindle to a mere faction. Fillmore, the president, however, is a Whig and little suspecting what passions he is to turn loose, he signs the Fugitive Slave Bill. This Bill is like a red rag before the already snorting Bull of the North. On Oct. 3rd, 1850, Sumner lifts his voice in Faneuil Hall, Boston, against this iniquity. Henry is caught up in all this swirl of excitement. It is true that he is still a Whig, but Sumner's influence with him is a mighty one and though he may vote the Whig ticket on State matters he is willing to go beyond it when Palfrey runs for Representative to Washington. But by this time *The Building of the Ship* has been written and published. It is the sort of poem which shows Henry at his best, simple and direct and rising to an extraordinary climax that loses nothing but rather gains by the didactic implications. It may be oratory, but it is better oratory than Sumner's or the lost Webster's. Having risen to this burst of feeling over contemporary matters—and it may be pointed out that this is the only dynamic poem in a book containing *The Secret of the Sea, The Fire of Driftwood* and the ever popular *Resignation*—Henry abruptly turns his back on contemporary life and ducks back into the middle ages. This is exactly what he did after *Poems on Slavery* was published, concerning himself then with the already written *Spanish Student* and plunging into *The Poets and Poetry of Europe*. This time he turns back to that dream of a great work which has occupied his mind for some years. Having corrected the final proofs of *The Seaside and the Fireside* he notes in his journal: "And now I long to try a loftier strain, the sublimer Song whose broken melodies have for so many years breathed through my soul in the better hours of life, and which I trust and believe will ere long unite themselves into a symphony not all unworthy the sublime theme, but furnishing 'some equivalent expression for the trouble and wrath of life, for its sorrow and its mystery.'" In this

solemn notation Henry is referring to the plan to write
a grand symphonic poem to be called *Christus*. It is
to be in three parts and it is the second part upon
which he immediately starts to work. *The Golden
Legend* moves swiftly. By September 8, 1850, it
is "nearly finished" but on March 28, 1851, he is
rewriting it and "putting the blank verse into rhyme."
By October it "creeps slowly through the press" and
in November it is issued. It goes well, the first edition
of thirty-five hundred copies selling within a month.
This poem is based on *Der Arme Heinrich* of the
minnesinger, Hartmann von der Aue, and it tells a
typical medieval tale of a sick Prince, aided by Lucifer
and then saved by a pure maiden. Being part of a
larger pattern any specific comment on it may be saved
until Henry has completed his vast structure and offered it as his "monument of song" to his huge international audience.

This is the last book to come from him until he has
severed his connections with Harvard. Four years of
silence now ensue. He is to embark upon another
long poem just before he is free, but in the meantime
the political unrest of the time and his college duties
combine with a growing household to fill his hours.
He sighs frequently and fondly for time to himself
but it is always done gently. He views the turmoil of
public life with some perturbation. "I am glad I am
not a politician," he notes, "nor filled with the rancor
that politics engenders. The Whigs are beaten—
horse, foot, and dragoons. This is owing to their
dereliction from their avowed principles of freedom.
I think Daniel Webster has broken up the Whig party
in Massachusetts; and those who have been so active
in upholding his 'Fugitive Slave Bill' speech, and trying to ride over every one who differs from them,

must thank him and themselves for this signal defeat." He may be glad that he is not a politician but there is frequent evidence that he discusses the perplexing situation with Sumner, advises him as best he may, and takes, on the whole, a more vigorous and feverish interest in the state of affairs than might be thought. The Republic rushes along recklessly and small men talk loudly on every corner. The quiet of Cambridge is disturbed and the placid trees wave above a muttering atmosphere. Henry's boys begin to grow up and one of them, Charles, betrays an adventurous frame of mind. The poet begins to lay his plans for retirement.

The seasons pass and Cambridge (at least in Henry's eyes) sprouts from a village into a city. New faces are to be seen on the streets and some of the old ones, among them Andrews Norton's, pass away forever. Some of these new faces prove pleasing to Henry and chief among them is Louis Agassiz who joins the faculty of Harvard in 1847, and is soon a familiar visitor to Craigie House. Agassiz is a pleasant, voluble French-Swiss, a distinguished naturalist and an amusing companion. He is a cosmopolitan and this fact in itself is enough to warrant Henry's interest. Agassiz drifts more and more intimately into the Longfellow circle as the years roll along and soon he, too, has his summer home at Nahant, that sacred Nahant where the Chosen gather to idle away the hot months. This addition of Agassiz to the Harvard Faculty speaks much for the college; indeed, the college is beginning to spread its wings a little. The secularization of the institution is under way and liberalizing influences are at work—one among them being Henry's own activities—to broaden the Unitarian atmosphere. Even though Harvard is growing and gradually turning in the right direction it does not solve Henry's problem of proper adjustment to a poetical career. There is only one way to solve that problem and early in 1854 he takes it. "How barren of all poetic production, and even prose production, this last year has been!" he notes at the end of his journal for 1853. "For 1853 I have absolutely nothing to show. Really, there has been nothing but the college work. The family absorbs half the time; and letters and visits take out a huge cantle." Of course, this state of affairs cannot continue. Henry is in a blind alley. He has reached an impass. It is no longer appealing to him to vindicate his poetical existence through brief lyrics flung off at odd hours. He has tasted the joys of long productions, of *Evangeline*, of *The Golden Legend*, and he desires the time to bury himself anew in vast designs. He begins his negotiations with the faculty, therefore, and at a time when Sumner, now a Senator in Washington, is holding forth fierily on the Nebraska Bill which would open all the United States territories to slaveholders and so invalidate the shaky Missouri Compromise of 1820. The faculty are undoubtedly cognizant of Henry's close comradeship with Sumner and it is possible that this has something to do with the ease with which they permit Henry to depart from those halls where he has been a shining light for eighteen years. Anyway, at the Commencement of 1854 he finishes his long task and walks from Harvard Square freed of the laborious routine that has cramped his creative endeavors. On April 19, he notes: "At eleven o'clock in No. 6 University Hall, I delivered my last lecture—the last I shall deliver here or anywhere." A tremendous feeling of freedom settled down on him and together with it went a vague excitement, the prospect of long years of exciting intellectual occupation ahead. He is now forty-seven years old, no longer the "Flashing Sickle" of 1836—the twenty-nine-year-old professor bowed down by the sorrow of Mary's death. He is an experienced man now, a settled husband and a father, a personage in the country and known in foreign lands as well. About him gathers the inner circle of friends and beyond them is that huge outer ring of well-wishers who see in him the apex of American letters.

CHAPTER SIX
Darkness and Apotheosis

HENRY is free. He is free of the troublous duties of an uncongenial professorship, uncongenial only in that he imagines it diverts him from those great creative enterprises which swim somewhere in the back of his brain. He is also free of formidable antagonistic criticism, for Poe lies forgotten in the graveyard at Baltimore and Margaret Fuller's bones crumble beneath the ocean waves. It is true that detractors still spring up in all quarters, men and women who lose no opportunity to assail Henry's poetical shortcomings, but he is so superbly fenced from them now that their onslaughts can make but small difference to his serene progress. He is no longer the esquire in the antechamber of art. He is the knight now, a "very parfit gentil knight," who has broken lances with his peers, whose *Evangeline* has appeared in the same year with Tennyson's *The Princess,* whose books sell in such quantities that he is assured a fair-sized yearly income, who is, perhaps, the handsomest, wealthiest, kindliest, best-mannered author in the Republic. His health has improved and he has the pleasure of observing half-a-dozen personal friends clamoring for the professorship he has left vacant, a post speedily occupied by the younger, more sophisticated James Russell Lowell. He has nothing to do now but write poetry and enjoy himself. At least, that is the way the fair vista appears for a time. It is true that the clouds above the Republic are somewhat stormy, that Sumner is fulminating furiously against the injustice of slavery, that escaped blacks from the south are upsetting the equanimity of Boston, and that the bewailed apostasy of Daniel Webster has deeply

272

wounded and estranged the closest of friends, but all
these things are on the outside, so to speak. They are
not a part of the inner life of Henry. He can follow
Sumner in rising to a patriotic passion, but he needs
to be led, and his scholarly instincts always partially
divert him from the more vital scenes of contemporary action.

Even before he has cut the final threads of red
tape binding him to Harvard he has plunged back into
that bookish life which so engrosses him. He happens upon the Finnish epic, the *Kalevala,* and sweeps
through it with gusto, relishing the unrhymed tro-
chaic diameter with its echoing parallelisms. An old
idea begins to ferment in his brain and the various
tag ends of thoughts gather about it. He will write
a long poem which shall be a coördination of the Indian myths and he will do it in the tripping, tinkling
measure of the *Kalevala.* This shall be the great work
which will mark his complete emancipation from college duties. Henry immediately looks about him for
material. The idea has been latent in his mind for
decades although not in the definite form which now
outlines itself before him. One must go back to his
college days to note the inception of his interest in the
American Indian, an interest which betrayed itself in
that forgotten dialogue wherein he took the part of
an Indian defending his right to the rolling miles of
the American wilderness. Then there was his plan to
write the tales of the Quoddy Indians. There were
the attempts to explain the aborigine to his Scandinavian friends during his second trip to Europe.
There is his interest in an Ojibway chief, Kah-ge-ga-
gah-bowh (somewhat of a poseur, it is to be suspected),
who calls upon him from time to time in Cambridge.
He has also read a number of books concerning the

273

Indian and his customs, but from first to last Henry approaches him romantically. The poet is as thin-blooded so far as reality is concerned as James Fenimore Cooper. At the same time he is more of a scholar than that older novelist and he makes it his business to find chapter and verse for his projected epic.

No sooner, therefore, has he hit upon his subject than he writes to Sumner in Washington for Schoolcraft's work on the Indians. However, he must have found a copy in the Harvard Library, for the next day he puts himself on record as looking over the three huge quartos, ill digested and without any index. This work, *Algic Researches*, and another, *History of the Indian Tribes of the United States*, both by Henry Rowe Schoolcraft, form the mine from which Henry dredges his preliminary information and situations. There he finds the various culture myths which will constitute the backbones of his poem. He turns to other writers on the Indian, Tanner and Heckelder among others, and finds various hints, words, customs and color for the long poem upon which he promptly begins work, a poem which he first calls *Manabozho*, but which he later and definitely entitles, *Hiawatha*. The work progresses slowly through 1854, for Henry determines this time to create a water-tight poem, so far as scholarship is concerned. By February, 1855, the first draft is completed and during April and May he rewrites it for the press. Early in June he receives proof-sheets and on November 10 the first edition of 5,000 copies is published by Ticknor and Fields. *Hiawatha* creates an immediate furore and by December 11 the poem is in its eleventh thousand.

Although Henry has taken great pains to be faithful to his subject in this arrangement of Indian myths he

is guilty of serious errors. Perhaps the greatest of
these is his failure to be faithful to the Indian spirit.
He selects his material and unifies it in a way which
the originals do not warrant. Still he *uses* the real
Indian legends. There are two types of errors which
may be noted briefly, factual and errors of spirit. The
most glaring of the former is his identification of
Manabozho, demigod of the Ojibways and their Al-
gonquin kinsmen, with Hiawatha, an Iroquois historical personage, a chieftain and statesman who existed
about the year 570. This error is not really Henry's,
for he finds the confusion of characters in Schoolcraft's
material. He continues it, however, and as a result of
thus following Schoolcraft's misapprehension *The
Song of Hiawatha* is not concerned with Hiawatha at
all but with the tangled Ojibway myths of Manabozho. Now Manabozho was not the pure-minded
person Hiawatha was. He was a trickster and dupe
as well as a culture hero, and whenever Henry finds
any situation which does not seem quite noble enough
for his hero he transfers it to Pau-Pau-kee-Wis, the
boaster of *Hiawatha*. He calmly omits all the elements that make his Indian hero a malicious trickster
as well as a hero, a didactic move the Indians would
not understand at all, and the result is a white-washed
hero. To sum up, he humanizes the demigod to a
great extent, takes the name of his Ojibway hero from
Iroquois annals, fashions his poem on the form of the
Kalevala and even receives certain suggestions for
some of the situations from the Finnish epic. The
animal attributes of Manabozho—or Hiawatha, as
Henry calls him—are dropped and an element of
romance, absolutely alien to the Indian mind, is in-
fused into the poem. The love affair between Hiawatha and Minnehaha, for example, is entirely

Henry's invention, and it is introduced because the poet insists on sentiments that find no place in Indian psychology. This poem is an excellent revelation of Henry, both as poet and as scholar. It shows that limpid fertility which never seems to desert him, although as he progresses through life it grows thinner and thinner. It reveals the indubitable command of color and a rather obvious musical quality that cause his best work to slip so easily into the mind. It manifests the power which his congenital sentimentalism—undoubtedly a growth from his equally congenital didacticism—has upon his scholarship, a power which draws him to view life, its phenomena, its physical and spiritual emanations through curious mental spectacles which somehow avoid the darker realities. And yet it is not quite right to affirm that Henry avoids the darker realities. Rather does he translate them into something which they are not. Just as Hiawatha, the pure Indian, is not Manabozho, who is a trickster as well as a hero, so is Henry's revelation of life not life as it really is or as it should be seen through the eyes of a great poet who may entertain all its vast and perplexing conflicts and clashes, but as a gentle spirit would like to imagine it. It is true that *Hiawatha* as a conceived work is a decided notch higher than anything he has done before. Hawthorne, writing from England to Ticknor, is quite correct when he remarks, ". . . it puts my estimate of his originality a peg higher; and I love to see him still on the ascent." It is this question of originality that is Henry's *bête noire,* for all through the closing years of his life he is to meet criticism anent it, accusations that he is lacking in originality, and for the most part these criticisms are justified. Just as he relied on Connolly's outline and a dozen books for *Evangeline,* so does he rely on

Schoolcraft for *Hiawatha* and so will he rely on Puritan annals for the New England tragedies and the romance lore of a dozen lands for the *Tales of a Wayside Inn*. He is an expert embroiderer and arranger, a builder with bricks that are not his own, but his solitary personal gifts are those implicit in his general nature, sweetness, limpidity, a moral suasion and a certain innate good taste.

Hiawatha scores a tremendous success. It is praised and damned right and left. Its novel form lends it easily to parody and it is not long before the comedians of letters put forth ridiculous travesties on it. But all this is excellent publicity. It serves to spread the poem far and wide. Curiously enough, there is another parallel here between Tennyson, the demigod of Victorian England, and Henry, the demigod of Victorian America. Just as the Time-Spirit thrust *Evangeline* before Henry while Tennyson was creating *The Princess,* so does *Hiawatha,* an epic based on the only autochthonous American myths, come at a time when Tennyson is busy with the *Idylls of the King,* a series of poems which may be said to have their basis in a portion of the autochthonous mythic substance of England. It may be noted here that there is a mutual regard between these two poets who represent such similar trends on both sides of the Atlantic, although it is to be suspected that Henry's ardor for Tennyson is far more than that of the somewhat dour Englishman for the American poet. Tennyson considers *Hiawatha* Henry's most original poem, and Henry himself thinks highly of the *Idylls of the King.* "Rich tapestries," he writes James T. Fields, "wrought as only Tennyson could have done them, and worthy to hang by the *Faërie Queene.*" Henry is never to be as great

a poet as Tennyson, but on his lower American plane,
a plane that cannot avoid indebtedness to foreign
sources, he represents pretty much the same thing that
Tennyson does in England. He stands at the fore-
front of the American singers now, having to his credit
two major works, a portion of another one, *The Golden
Legend,* and an inclination to turn to the Puritan annals of old New England as a source for future work.

Surely, it will be put forth, Henry is now orientated
to his America. Has he not written *Evangeline,* an
American poem? And *Hiawatha,* an American epic?
And is he not turning to annals which will produce
The New England Tragedies and *The Courtship of
Miles Standish* and *The Ride of Paul Revere,* besides one or two shorter pieces? True, he is striving with all good will and the power of scholarship to reveal an America, but his America is a ghost
that walks through the dusty pages of books. It is
not the New England which even at this moment is
rising unsteadily to giant feet and preparing to halt
the slave progress in the Southern States. That is not
the America adumbrated in Henry's poems, although
he is most intimately acquainted with it, particularly
through his friendship with Charles Sumner, who, after
all, is the oratorical mouthpiece of that New England.
Instead of this we find an Acadie which never existed,
an idyllic Indian life that could never be, and a senti-
mentalized Puritan atmosphere which, in spite of its
sentimentalization, comes closer to being American
than any of the other efforts. No, Henry is still—as
he is to be all his life—dominated by a romantic impulse that is less American than European. He may
not be un-Americanized (that, perhaps, is too strong
a word for it), but he is certainly Europeanized. Just
as Scandinavian impulses and colorings peep through

Evangeline so does the Finnish *Kalevala* peep through the monotonous length of *Hiawatha*. Something is accomplished in spite of this dependency, however. Henry is possibly responsible for a smoothing of rough corners, a lifting from the crudities of a life less than fifty years from pioneer existence, an introduction of the limpidities of European culture, a revelation of the graces inherent in the study and of the felicities of a scholarship that may not be deep but which still is potent with a mellow surface charm. And he has his huge public to follow him and to feed from his graceful board. By 1857 his sales in America alone result, in round figures, as follows: *Outre Mer,* 7,500 copies; *Hyperion,* 14,550; *Voices of the Night,* 43,550; *Ballads and Other Poems,* 40,470; *The Spanish Student,* 38,400; *The Belfry of Bruges and Other Poems,* 38,300; *The Golden Legend,* 17,188; *Kavanagh,* 10,500; and *Hiawatha,* 50,000. It is an imposing array of figures, totaling 316,308 books. His English editions which sell widely are not taken into consideration at all. Surely but few poets in the world could stand at the peak of fifty years and look back on so generous an acceptance by the public. Henry, therefore, must not be belittled. His period wants him and it takes to him with avidity. And it takes to him because he gives it what it desires, because he has opened an hundred and one doors for it, doors through which that public may view the great sparkling world of culture. But the Time-Spirit, observing Henry on this peak, is disturbed. It reaches down a finger and muddies the pool of life and the dark ripples break up the luster. It is nearly time for destruction to run amok and create havoc in this western world, which is striving so zealously toward all that is implied by the word culture.

II

There is a brief breathing space before this happens, however, and Henry profits by it to add to his felicitous gestures as the great American poet. E. V. Scherb, the German poet from Basle who is now living in Cambridge and, if not a friend, at least an intimate acquaintance of Henry's, suggests to the poet that he write a poem on the Puritans and Quakers. The idea sounds good to Henry but it appeals to him more as a possible tragedy than a narrative poem.

Within a few days he is looking up source material, plodding through Besse's *Sufferings of the Quakers* and investigating dusty tomes on Puritan life in the college library. By April 2, 1856, he is composing a scene in a drama tentatively called *The Old Colony*. He does not get very far with this—a few notes and speeches, perhaps—when an unexpected disaster overtakes his friend, Sumner, and so upsets Henry for any considerable concentration for some time. On the twenty-third of May as Henry is walking in his garden John Owen, his friend and publisher, rushes in and in a voice broken by sobs, informs him that Sumner has been assaulted and brutally beaten in the Senate-Chamber. For an instant the placid garden swims in a haze of blood before Henry's eyes. He hurries indoors distraught and the next day finds him in Boston mingling in the feverish excitement aroused by the assault. Through various channels the story comes with all its vindictive sidelights and all its ominous prophecy of the future.

There is the picture of the leonine-headed Sumner, his flowing locks fallen over his collar, sitting at his desk in the Senate-Chamber, resting from his unremitting attacks on Douglas and on Butler of South

HISTORIC CRAIGIE HOUSE AT CAMBRIDGE, MASS., FORMERLY
WASHINGTON'S HEADQUARTERS, AND LONGFELLOW'S HOME

LONGFELLOW'S SEASHORE RESIDENCE AT NAHANT—FROM A
PHOTOGRAPH BY SILSBEE, CASE & CO.

BOSTON STREET SHOWMEN AND MUSICIANS.

"Our artist has here sketched expressly for the *Pictorial*, one of those scenes that have become characteristic of the street life of modern Boston, which is fast becoming cosmopolitan in its spirit. We have here an itinerant showman and musician, with a wonderful performing monkey whose dexterity always attracts crowds whenever the "enterprising proprietor" sets up his table and exhibits the animal's proficiency in the programme which has been taught him."

From *Ballou's Pictorial*, September 19, 1857.

Carolina, both of them champions of the slave states. There is the slighter form of Preston S. Brooks, a representative from South Carolina and nephew of Butler, standing behind him and clutching the heavy-headed cane with which he is to protect the honor of the South. The cane rises and falls with horrid force and Sumner, blood streaming down his neck, starts upward in anguish, tearing his clamped desk from the floor. He falls prostrate and Brooks rushes from the chamber toward the eager felicitations of Southern sympathizers who see in him a new Brutus. There is more in this attack than a foul assault upon an individual. Cornewall Lewis, in England, hearing of it, declares: "That outrage is no proof of brutal manners or low morality in America; it is the first blow in a Civil War." Brooks, after two mock trials, goes free except for a slight fine and resigning his seat returns to South Carolina, a hero, a translated being, a Roman champion. Sumner for months lies at the point of death and, to the end of his life, carries the results of this onslaught. Henry, hurrying through the afore-time quiet streets of Cambridge and Boston, hears rumors of war and cries for revenge. The subterranean lavas are mounting toward the crater and it will not be long before they burst forth. For his own part Henry is now wide awake to the dangers of the time. He sees the writing on the wall. Reading Sumner's fierce speeches again he writes to him: "You have torn the mask off the face of traitors; and at last the spirit of the North is aroused."

It is during this momentous summer that Henry nearly goes to Europe for the fourth time, perhaps to escape the new chaos that has befallen his native country. Europe is ready for him. Has not Lowell written, "Over here it is more of a reputation to *know*

Longfellow than to have written various immortal works." Alas, Henry does not go. His staterooms are engaged and his tour planned, but he smashes his knee and the surgeon gravely advises him against any trip. So all preparations are canceled and Henry returns to his beloved Nahant. It is here that he rests, works aimlessly at his New England tragedy and reads Cooper. He sits on his piazza in the morning and watches the barks beating up the harbor, and his mind goes back to his first sea voyage so many years ago, thirty of them in all, when he sailed for France filled with youth and hope and enthusiasm. There are few connecting links left of that old time. Greene, of course, is an ever-present reminder, but Greene has been away for long periods, and it is not until now when both men have aged that the ancient comradeship is frequently renewed by pleasurable meetings. Little things fill his days during this brief interim. Two of his children have their little sailboat smashed in a squall. A sunset delights him. A few friends gather on the piazza and talk of the times. He returns to Cambridge, welcomes back Sumner from his sick bed, and takes part in the statesman's triumphal entry into Boston. The orator is a national hero now. He stands for a furiously thrusting urge and though he must soon leave America on a weary pilgrimage in search of health his name and the memory of the attack upon him serve as oriflammes for the militant-minded Northerners.

Four years of comparative quiet now envelop Henry's days. Men come and go and the face of Time changes imperceptibly. The winter snow piles about Craigie House and Henry senses a curious shifting of elements in the air. Christmas is not the same.

He is clever enough to discern that New England is in a transition state. "The old Puritan feeling prevents it from being a cheerful, hearty holiday," he notes, "though every year makes it more so." And, again, he is to note: "After all, holidays are hard things to manage in New England. People cry for more of them, but when they get them, they don't know what to do with them. It is not in their hearts to be merry." He sees the old granite wall of Puritanism, therefore, and comprehends what difficulties attend its breaching. At the same time he notes the ingress of a new liberalism. This newborn liberalism is true of the Sabbath in a lesser degree. Life is broadening in certain ways but in others it is as narrow as ever. The old era sits about Papanti's and watches the young ones dance to livelier measures. Ever so far away, is that Portland of 1813 with its guns booming, its drums playing, and the small boy climbing Munjoy's Hill beside the sturdy old General of Revolutionary fame. The General too is as far away, as far away as 1829 when he folded his hands, his labors done, and passed away just as the young Henry entered upon his first professional duties at Bowdoin. All of that time has gone. It is done with. It lies in the grave with the General and George Pierce and Stephen and Zilpah and Mary. It was a world more spare in material comforts perhaps than this nascent era of the Craigie House and dappled grays and universally renowned books and ample leisure, but it was a good world, simple, frugal, and always pious. Henry must think of those past times more than once as he swims deliberately down the broadening stream of his days. The comparison is too vast and pleasing not to be noticed.

Few highlights spot these four years that intervene

before the Republic answers boldly the challenge implicit in Preston Brooks' brandished cane. There is the slow completion of *The New England Tragedy*, written in prose and first called *The Old Colony*, and then *Wenlock Christison*, but this can hardly be called a highlight for the play is never really published. A few copies are printed and the effort is flung aside, there to lie forgotten for nearly eight years, until Henry again takes it up and entirely rewrites it in blank verse when it is sent out to the world under the altered and better known title of *John Endicott*. Perhaps the chief highlight so far as poetical composition goes is *The Courtship of Miles Standish*. Henry first conceives this as a play, starting it in 1856. For a year he keeps it by him and then starts anew, beginning a poem which he calls *Priscilla*. The theme grips him and he finishes the script in four months. On October 16, 1858, the book is published in a first edition of 10,000 copies. In one week 25,000 copies have been sent forth and Henry has another extraordinary success to his credit. There is the usual laudation from friends and disciples and the usual few dissenting voices. Lowell, writing to Miss Norton, declares: "I like *Miles Standish* better than you do. I think it in some respects the best long poem L. has written. It is so simple and picturesque, and the story is not encumbered with unavailing description, which is a fault in *Evangeline*." It is unnecessary to pay more than brief attention to *The Courtship of Miles Standish*. The poem suffers from Henry's failure to achieve a plane of passion commensurate with the theme, and the love of Priscilla and John Alden becomes no more than a sort of treacly affair without the dignity that might have saved it. Henry is incapable of expressing strong emotions and the better portions of this poem, notably

Standish's expedition to the Indian camp, are those descriptive passages wherein the poet may amble on about nature in his questionable hexameters. There is a certain grace and prettiness implicit in the poem, but this very prettiness invalidates it as a picture of a dramatic climax of Pilgrim days. The Pilgrims were not pretty. Here again is the weakness of Henry exposed in the most obvious manner. The innate felicitousness of the poet cannot make up for the failure to grasp high emotions. He insists on smoothing out, on romanticizing, on deliberately eschewing the flaming heart of his inspiration. It is an agreeable surface—at least for the mentality of his particular time—that he polishes, but that is all.

Another high light of these quiet years is a launching of *The Atlantic Monthly*. There had been nothing like it in American letters and it served immediately as a rallying point for the New England group. It is on April 28, 1857, that Lowell calls upon Henry to interest him in a new magazine, to be started in Boston by Phillips and Sampson. "I told him I would write for it if I wrote for any magazine," notes the poet in a half-hearted manner. On the fifth of May he attends a dinner at Parker's in Boston, with Emerson, Lowell, Motley, Holmes, Cabot, Underwood, and the publisher, Phillips, to discuss the magazine. Henry is still half-hearted about it. "I am not so eager about it as the rest," he remarks. However, he is generally present at the dinners which take place once a month and he is generous in the number of poems which he turns over to the magazine after it is started. Among these efforts are *Santa Filomena*, which appears in the first issue, *Sandalphon*, *The Golden Milestone*, *Catawba Wine*, *The Birds of Killingworth*, *The Children's Hour*, *Paul Revere's Ride* and *The Bells of Lynn*. The literary history of New England, the New England of the middle period, is implicit in the names of the men (contributors, of course) who attend *The Atlantic Monthly* dinners. Lowell is editor of the new sheet and among the varying attendance of the first two years are Agassiz (for whose fiftieth birthday Henry writes one of his most successful short pieces), J. Eliot Cabot, John S. Dwight, Emerson, Felton, Holmes, Judge E. R. Hoar, Dr. Estes Howe, Charles E. Norton and Edmund Quincy. Motley goes abroad shortly after the first dinner but he never fails to manifest his interest. Whittier comes at rare intervals, although his delicate health, capricious appetite and dislike of the tobacco smoke that succeeds the dinner disturb him so much that he rather fails to enjoy himself. Whipple and Trowbridge show up occasionally and now and then there is a foreign guest. Only once are the women contributors invited. Henry, as always in gatherings, listens rather than talks. It is Agassiz, full of vibrant cosmopolitan bonhomie, and Lowell and Holmes, witty and brilliant, who carry on the burden of the conversations about the table. These dinners usually take place at Parker's in a large front room, but the scene is changed occasionally. Once the contributors meet at Fontarive's and sit down to a dinner that becomes historical as a feast of Lucullus. Another time they go to Porter's in Cambridge and partake of flip and canvas-back ducks and the mongrel goose. Here, as the flip starts its warming work, the hilarity becomes general. Holmes tosses compliments about with the greatest abandon and Henry being the recipient of a large share of them and remembering Holmes's statement that authors were like cats, sure to purr when stroked the right way, interrupts with

"I purr! I purr!" They are all purring by the time
the party breaks up and streams out to a road a foot
deep with new fallen snow. Back to Old Cambridge
they tramp, the younger men chanting Dr. Palmer's
"Puttyrum" as an accompaniment. Henry does not
approve of all of these dinners, for after one of them
he notes: "Felt vexed at seeing plover on the table at
this season, and proclaimed aloud my disgust at seeing
the game-laws thus violated. If anybody wants to
break a law, let him break the Fugitive Slave Law.
That is all it is fit for."

Time passes in such ways for Henry. There are
letters to answer and callers to receive. He goes to
the opera and to musical soirées. He plays with his
little girls and achieves comradeship with his sons. He
is liberal with autographs and chary of emphatic advice. He goes to Nahant in the summer and he makes
infrequent trips to Portland. His throne is his chair
in the study and the white sheets of cartridge paper
spread before him compose the heaven to which he
constantly flies from a world of all-too-mundane affairs. The books pile up about him, books from the
four quarters of the civilized world and in all tongues,
and he reads them through. Although the muttering echoes in the streets outside the quiet Craigie House
must filter through the waving curtains he strives to
keep as apart from them as he can. His action is in
words and not in gestures. It is in the printed page.
It is in this way that he passes through the brief interim between two storm-clouds, between the assault
on Sumner and the assault on Sumter. He is the representative of a scholarly urbanity that is, perhaps,
misplaced in the America of the late fifties where a
more dynamic type is needed.

III

It is not without foreknowledge that the Republic pitches over that ominous precipice of political agitation into fratricidal warfare early in the momentous year of 1861. Prophets have been crying at the street corners and the enflamed Time spirit has hovered above those meeting-places where more than two or three men have gathered together. Henry has heard these voices. He has listened to Charles Sumner. He remembers the foul attack in the Senate Chamber. "It is now too late to put the fire out," he exclaims on the twenty-eighth of January after hearing that six Southern states, led by South Carolina, have seceded from the Union. "We must let it *burn* out." The days pass slowly. The South continues arrogant. The North is like a giant weak in the knees. As the dissolution goes on Henry hears the indistinct murmuring of negro slaves like a Greek *choros*. They are crying, "Woe! Woe!" Abraham Lincoln is inaugurated and the antagonistic factions draw apart sullenly. The volcano is quivering now with the fierce lavas of uncontrolled passions. Fort Sumter is attacked and suddenly ferocious armies spring up like dragon's teeth. Henry walks about a crumbling world with a sinking heart. He sees regiments of boys mustering on Boston Common. The faces in the streets are stern and serious. Drums sound in the by-ways and horsemen gallop across the cobbles. Before the Capitol two red-cheeked lads bowed beneath their muskets stand gravely on guard. There is a flaunting of flags, a rumble of many footsteps, a muttering of interminable voices. Henry strives in vain to secrete himself from all this terror. He walks before breakfast to hear the birds sing. In the tranquil moonlight he tramps out to Cambridge from Boston with Lowell. He turns from the strident newspapers to Calderon and discovers in the Spanish dramatist "a far-off, dreamy sound, like the ringing of church bells in a little Spanish village." The contrast is too much and his May is bleak and cheerless. The flower-decked children seem to him like little victims.

What has become of his world, his simple Paradise of books and poems and friends and family and European dreams and sleepy Cambridge in the quiet New England sun? It is passing in the whirlwind and vanishing in the storm. An unrest seizes him. He cannot work. He walks about with the solemn-faced Sumner, who, after all, is one of the foremost players in this tragedy of nations. He goes to Papanti's ball for children and can think of nothing but the slim youths on guard at arsenals and forts. He watches the Harvard students drill and even reviews them with Felton. He discusses the tone of England and her newspapers and tries to read Maurice de Guerin. Unseen by him a dark shape draws near; it is time for Henry's calm world to crash into pieces as well as the greater world of the Republic. And suddenly, like a fierce and cruel bolt of lightning, the Craigie House is smitten with an unforeseen horror.

It is the ninth of July and the day is Tuesday. The late afternoon sun plucks at the windows of Craigie House. Fanny sits by the library table sealing up some small packages of her children's curls. Her light summer dress flutters faintly as she moves, leaning forward and backward, smiling to herself. It is peaceful here even though the streets outside are raucous with warlike preparations. Fanny strikes a match and heats the bar of wax and the match falls unnoted from her hand. It lands on the floor near her, its tiny flame lifting by the edge of her frail dress. The small flare reaches toward the gossamer garment, attaches itself to it, and suddenly bursts upward. In an instant Fanny is enveloped in fire and she rises, screaming, from her chair. Henry, at work in his study, hears her cry and rushes to the library. He flings a rug about her to smother the merciless flames, burning himself badly in a last endeavor to save her. But it is too late and though doctors are hastily sent for, Doctors Wyman and Johnson of Cambridge and Doctor Henry J. Bigelow of Boston, and everything that surgical skill may devise is done, the dark shadow has its way. That night Fanny and Henry lie under the influence of ether and toward eleven o'clock the next day Fanny dies. The news is broken to Henry as he lies bandaged in his bed. Three days later, on the anniversary of her wedding day, Fanny is carried to Mount Auburn for her last rest. Henry, confined to his chamber by his burns, hears the body borne from Craigie House.

It is impossible to estimate the damage done to Henry by this tragedy. For a time it seems to have wrecked his life entirely and all through the years that are to follow the shadow of a great sadness is never very far from his gentle mind. The buoyancy that once invested his character so charmingly has gone and though he never obtrudes his sorrow on others few friends can gaze upon his patriarchal face without understanding that he has passed through the deepest valleys of torment. Between his liberation from Harvard and this dark moment he had vindicated himself, at least in his own eyes and certainly in the eyes of his coevals, with *Hiawatha* and *The Courtship of Miles Standish*, works larger in import than anything he had done previously, except possibly

Evangeline. He had gone on to those vaster projects that had been his ambition. Even the dislocated
aspect of the Republic had not diverted him from his
ambitious scheme of letters. But now his world is
smashed to pieces. As soon as he is able to get about
again he walks through the anxious circle of his friends
in silence. He has nothing to say to them, nothing to
put into rhyme and so ease the dull pain that gnaws
at him in the haunted rooms of Craigie House. One
day after Fanny's funeral, July 14, Nathan G. Appleton, her father, dies as the result of a long illness.
So the blows fall not singly but rapidly, one after the
other. Henry's outbreaks are few. To one friend
who mutters some hope that he might be enabled to
"bear his cross" with patience, he replies, "*Bear* the
cross, yes; but what if one is stretched upon it!" This
is not so much bitterness at the fierce shafts of fortune
as an intense inward agony. He goes to Nahant to
rest and in September returns to the desolate Craigie
House. "How can I live any longer!" he notes in
his journal, after he has walked through the rooms
which Fanny has dominated for eighteen years. These
rooms are filled with too many phantoms. His friends
flock about him. Sumner comes and Dana and Fields
and Dr. Holmes, himself frantic about the fate of his
son who is on the Potomac with the Massachusetts
Twentieth. Visitors continue to flock to his door,
Bakunin, the Russian, and Anthony Trollope and
J. S. C. Abbott among others. But though he is
charming with them, generous in hospitality, and apparently glad to see them, a famine of the heart consumes him. He must do something to remove his
mind from the obsession that sits behind it in a veil
of fire and tortures him throughout the day and night.
It is then that he bethinks himself of the translation

of Dante which he had projected long ago and he takes up the *Divina Commedia* again, striving to lose himself in the splendor of the Tuscan's vision. It had been in 1843 that he had begun his translation of Dante, the year of his marriage, but he had laid it aside when his new happiness came to him. Again in 1853, ten years later, he had returned to it, being weary of trying to write any creative verse while the arduous labors at Harvard ate up his days so mercilessly. But freedom from Harvard had come and he had laid it aside again. This time he takes it up quite determinedly, disregarding the earlier attempts apparently and applying himself to it as zealously as he may for two years, years interrupted by bloodshed and the chaos of civil war.

The dark years still loom before him. His personal life is to run parallel with the travail of the nation. On February 27, 1862—his fifty-fifth birthday— word comes to him that his old friend Cornelius Felton has died in Chester, Pennsylvania. Felton, the oldest of them all, the Cornelius who lived and laughed beneath him in the old house on Kirkland Street when Henry first settled in Cambridge, fresh from the sorrow of his first wife's death in Europe! He stays indoors translating and the snowdrifts about Craigie House and the windy trumpets sound over the chimney-tops. The war snatches up his son Charles and a fresh care is laid upon the already overburdened spirit of the man. The daily papers filled with their martial headlines assault his eyes and he strives in vain to flee from them to the seclusion of his study. Letters from friends, from strangers, from America and Europe pour in, requests for information, for aid, for autographs, and the lonely man, gracious to the last, attempts to attend to everything. To one commiserating friend he writes, "I can hardly tell you how changed Cambridge has become to me. Felton, too, is gone; one of my oldest and dearest friends. It seems indeed as if the world were reeling and sinking beneath my feet." To Freiligraph he writes that he has no definite plans for the future but that he drifts along from day to day through the bitter waters, that it is difficult to build up again a life as shattered as his has been, but that he is patient and that his children comfort him. It is true that his world is reeling and sinking. The old New England is foundering in these stormy waters. The Republic is reeling and though it will not sink it will come out of its fiery bath another thing altogether. All the old ease and leisure are to vanish. What is the old New England is to shift, slowly at first, but furiously as it gathers pace, into a commercial commonwealth that includes but the faint echoes of the ancient Puritanism. There are a score of years yet before Henry and perhaps he misses the real tragedy of New England, a tragedy at least to him and men like him, but the prime reason for this astigmatism is the completely set character of his mind. He grows no more after the Civil War. His greatest exertions antedate it and nothing to come can possibly heighten the fame which he enjoys.

In June of this year, 1862, he takes a trip to Niagara Falls with a party of friends and his sons. The trip seems to profit him and he recovers a faint measure of his light-heartedness. Returning from the roaring Falls in whose sound he has slept and whose thunder unnerves him and gives him a vague sense of terror and unrest, he travels by way of Toronto and Kingston and so down the St. Lawrence and to Montreal. By the sixteenth of June he is home and preparing for the summer at Nahant. The summer colony, his precious "cold roast Boston," is solitary and deserted this year and the echo of war fills the cloudless days. In the fall he hits upon the idea for a connected series of tales in verse which is to turn into *Tales of a Wayside Inn*. He applies himself to this simultaneously with the Dante which is now going along at a fair pace.

Both the Dante translation and the *Tales of a Wayside Inn* prove to be fit occupations for a scholar set down in the midst of chaos. In each case the writer is not wholly relying on himself but on a frame-work of extant material. Putting the *Divine Comedy* into English is a difficult task, but it is not so difficult as attempting to create poetry. And although several of the tales in the Wayside Inn series appear to be entirely original, by far the greater number of them are dredged from those rich mines of literature that line the walls of the Craigie House study. The expedient of fitting the stories into so charming a mosaic is a happy one but it is not original with Henry. There are suggestions of Boccaccio and Chaucer here. Henry takes for his scene the old Howe Tavern in Sudbury, Massachusetts, a hostelry that has been in existence for more than a century. Out to it goes Henry together with Fields and in a lovely valley he finds the rambling, tumble-down building which had once served as a house of call for all travelers from Boston westward. The ancient aspects of the place please him and he has but to create the characters who will sit in imagination around the huge fireplace and narrate the various tales which are to form his book. Naturally he turns to his friends. The Musician,

> Fair-haired, blue-eyed, his aspect blithe,
> His figure tall and straight and lithe,

> And every feature of his face
> Revealing his Norwegian race,

is Ole Bull. Bull is to marry a Miss Thorp whose brother marries one of Henry's daughters and in this way the two families are drawn together. Professor Luigi Monti serves for the Sicilian,

> In sight of Etna born and bred,

and the Youth,

> Of quiet ways,
> A student of old books and days,

is Dr. Henry W. Wales, a liberal friend of Harvard College. The Poet, whose verse "was tender, musical, and terse" is Thomas William Parsons and the Sicilian Jew is Israel Edrehi of Boston. There is some doubt about the Theologian who may be Samuel Longfellow, Henry's ministerial brother, or Prof. Trowbridge or Prof. Daniel Treadwell, but the Landlord is certainly Lyman Howe of Sudbury. Having found his place and his characters Henry has but to put the appropriate tales into their mouths and his scheme is complete. He works swiftly on the book and it is to be suspected that this immersion in his project is intensified for three reasons: a desire to shut himself off from the terrific chaos of the times about him, an instinctive urge to forget the recent tragedy of Craigie House, and a reborn delight in these old romantic legends drawn from the generous sources of half-a-dozen different literatures. Several of the tales included had been previously published and Henry has but to fit them into his scaffolding. Among these pieces, evidently written with no idea of making them blocks in a larger structure, are *The Saga of King Olaf, Paul Revere's Ride* and *The Legend of Rabbi Ben Levi.* The book moves at a rapid pace and by April 16, 1863, it is in press under the title of *The Sudbury Tales.* Sumner cries out against this title, and in August it is changed to *Tales of a Wayside Inn.* The book appears in November in an edition of 15,000 copies. There is nothing more interesting than this wide sale of Henry's books during a time when most people would seem to be too excited by contemporary events to do much reading. Perhaps they find in the pleasant romanticism and bookish turn of Henry's work a relief and an escape from the devouring problems which are leaping about them like gaunt half-starved dogs. Anyway, the book is successful. No sooner has Henry done with it, however, than he finds himself again engulfed by the turmoil and anguish of the time. If he has sought an escape it has proven to be but a temporary refuge, for he calculates without the ardor of his oldest son, Charles, who has run away and joined the army. There is this to worry about and there is also the fact that he finishes the translation of Dante and so deprives himself of that cool retreat from a vexed world. It is true that there are many notes to formulate, many corrections to make and a deal of discussion to take place before the work appears—it is held off until 1865, that year being the six-hundredth anniversary of the birth of Dante—but the complete absorption has gone. There are a few major and minor happenings to please him, the emancipation of the slaves has gone into effect, he has thrilled at the sight of a regiment of blacks marching through Beacon Street, George W. Curtis writes a laudatory article about him in *The Atlantic Monthly,* Lowell and Norton take over the

Henry W. Longfellow

editorship of *The North American Review*, Gettysburg is fought and Lincoln's speech seems to him "admirable," a rather curious way of estimating one of the greatest speeches ever made. The shadow of death continues to hover over Cambridge, for early in October of this year George Sumner dies. Then on December 1 Henry receives a telegram from Washington bluntly notifying him that his son, Charles, has been severely wounded. The distracted poet, together with his youngest son, Ernest, immediately departs for the South.

There is an intensely dramatic aspect to this spectacle of the New England poet, the leisurely scholar, the sedate man of fifty-six years, setting forth on a pilgrimage to a son who has been shot down in action and whose condition is a matter of grave doubt. He goes to Washington on the Fall River boat and as there are no staterooms or berths he is compelled to sit up all night in the saloon. At Washington, weary as he is from his sleepless night, he hurries about striving to obtain information. A supercilious clerk at the War Office insists that there has been no battle and that only a little more than a thousand men have been killed and wounded in the advance. A Doctor Knapp of the Sanitary Commission aids Henry as much as he can and eventually he discovers that a train of wounded soldiers is expected at Alexandria the next day. Down to Alexandria the poet goes, passing through the Russian fleet on the way. Charles is not there. Disappointed and fearful he returns to Washington. For two days he waits, fuming with impatience and feverish surmises, and then he is told that a train is expected at the station on the Washington side of the Long Bridge. There he goes and finds a tumble-down telegraph station. After a two hours' wait a train consisting of a baggage car draws in slowly. In it are sixteen wounded men lying or sitting on the straw-covered floor. Charles is among them, his wounds undressed for three days and in anguish from the bumping car. He has been shot through both shoulders, an Enfield ball entering under the left shoulder blade and passing directly through the back, taking off one of the spinal processes and passing out under the right shoulder blade. For three days Henry stays in Washington while the surgeons inspect and dress Charles' wounds. There is little that Henry can do. He talks to the doctors, goes with Sumner to the Senate and witnesses the opening of Congress and visits a few friends. By the ninth of December he reaches Craigie House with his wounded son, Dr. Wyman is called, quiet days of invalidism follow and the year 1863 draws to a sad close.

Naturally there is no thought of poetry throughout this feverish period. Henry, generally so fenced from the barbarities of life, is wholly at the mercy of this bloody and fluctuating phantasmagoria of days. He is caught up through his own flesh and blood, as in 1856 he had been caught up by the assault on Sumner and compelled to stare Life straight in the face. That he does it with some measure of self-command is a direct testimonial to the inward strength that carries him through. His sensitivity reacts violently to anguish, but the inborn faculty of absorbing grief in such a way that it does not destroy him is manifest to the last. The Henry who stood beside Mary's bedside in Rotterdam and the Henry who recovered from his grief in Heidelberg are inextricably intertwined. Though his life be smashed to pieces for the moment as it undoubtedly was when Fanny died he possesses a curious interior strength that lifts him above the eventual sloughs of despond. It is, perhaps, not so much that he does not feel grief deeply—for he indubitably does—but that he is balanced by a sweet sanguinity, a didactic serenity that must make the best of things as they are. His mind may be autumn-hued now, but there is a mellowness in it that removes it from the darker and starker aspects. Life for him continues to be a matter of vast surfaces rather than unfathomable depths.

IV

Early in 1864 Hawthorne, who has been living in Concord since his return from the Liverpool consulship three years before, writes a letter to Henry that ends with an ominous paragraph. "I have been much out of sorts of late," he states, "and do not well know what is the matter with me; but am inclined to draw the conclusion that I shall have little more to do with pen and ink. One more book I should like well enough to write, and have indeed, begun it, but with no assurance of ever bringing it to an end. As is always the case, I have a notion that the last book would be my last, and full of wisdom about matters of life and death,— and yet it will be no deadly disappointment if I am compelled to drop it. You can tell, far better than I, whether there is anything worth having in literary reputation; and whether the best achievements seem to have any substance after they grow cold." Henry does not know it but Hawthorne, his classmate at Bowdoin and the one man who stands in New England fiction where, for the moment, Henry stands in poetry, is dying. On the nineteenth of May, Henry, returning to Craigie House with Greene, finds a note apprizing him of the death of Hawthorne. Another name has vanished from the shining circle that makes up this New England. It is impossible to estimate the depth of the intimacy that existed between Henry and Hawthorne but it is to be suspected that it was, for the most part, always a trifle formal. They possessed an honest admiration for one another, although at times Henry seems to have been somewhat impatient with the underlying note of sadness implicit in Hawthorne's work; but they never met upon those terms which existed between Henry and Felton and which exists to the end between Henry and his aging friend, Greene. Hawthorne was a mystery. He walked in an impalpable mist of shadows and Henry could see him but indistinctly through them. Yet the poet, inspired for the moment, creates one of his loveliest elegiac lyrics for his dead friend.

If the flowering May of New England is thus shadowed by Hawthorne's passing, it is also lightened by favorable news from the embattled South. Grant is driving Lee before him in Virginia and a corner of History seems about to be turned. Henry, therefore, may suspect the vindication of Sumner's career with some degree of justice. In November Lincoln is reëlected and the poet breathes freely. "The country will be saved," he declares. In the meantime he busies himself with his Dante translation, pruning, revising and making notes. Besides this major labor he writes a few short poems, poems that will take their places in those series of *Birds of Passage* that are added to his later volumes of short verse. These poems which appear in five flights have already made two appearances in *The Courtship of Miles Standish* and *Tales of a Wayside Inn*. Three are to follow in *Aftermath* (1873), *The Masque of Pandora and Other Poems* (1875), and *Keramos and Other Poems* (1878). In them Henry expends his remaining lyrical pence. They are to his later years what the short pieces of *Voices*

of the Night and *Ballads and Other Poems* were
to his younger period. The note of freshness is lacking in this later work; Henry has shot his bolt as a
lyrical writer. He is a trifle jaded now and the sparkle
is forced. The technical workmanship evinced in the
Birds of Passage poems is higher than that in those
earlier strains but this excellency is not sufficient to
carry the poems to the common reader with the old
appeal. Henry, it is to be feared, is on the verge of
outliving himself, but only on the verge as yet. He
still has seventeen years before him and during this
period his apotheosis is to take place.

His life is sedate enough now except for the unrest
of the war which shakes Cambridge even as it shakes
all parts of the country. Sumner is with him part of
the time. Greene comes up from Rhode Island and
they converse together about that Italian past which
is now so far away. Greene is growing old rapidly.
The time comes when he is stricken by paralysis and
must be led about the house by his old friend. A
young man named William Dean Howells, formerly
a consul at Venice, comes to Boston and eventually
moves into a cottage at Cambridge that is covered with
vines and mortgages. He is immediately taken into
the charmed circle. Henry strikes a new height of
poetry with several sonnets inspired by his Dante
translation. The children grow and flower with health.
The *Divina Commedia* begins to go through the
press, book by book; and Henry establishes the Dante
Club which meets on Wednesday nights at Craigie
House and goes carefully through the translation, suggesting emendations and notes. After the discussion
there is a late supper at which cold turkey or a platter
of quails or a haunch of venison or braces of grouse
form the *pièce de résistance*, bulwarked by a huge bowl

of salad. The most regular members of this club are Norton and Lowell, Norton himself being at work on his English prose version of the *Vita Nuova*, but others are present as well, including the young Howells, now an assistant editor of *The Atlantic Monthly*, who sits modestly at the feet of his elders and offers an infrequent suggestion now and then. Occasionally the meetings are diverted by a descent to Henry's wine-cellar where row upon row of cobwebbed bottles line the shelves. Tokay is Henry's favorite wine, incidentally. Letters continue to pour in, from Emerson, from the aged Bryant, from a hundred and one lesser lights. There are books to read and there are a few plays and concerts to attend. Grant corners Lee, Richmond falls to great rejoicing and pealing of bells in Boston, and the war ends. A week later Lincoln is assassinated. But these tragedies do not seem to affect Henry so deeply now. He has retreated again to his quiet library. Of course he is immersed in his Dante translation at this time, his letters and journals being full of it. But one would expect a fiercer glow, a wilder reaction to these epochal episodes of history. Instead he burrows into his Dante material and arranges his poems for a household edition. *Flower-de-Luce*, a small volume of lyrics containing but thirteen pieces, is also in hand. It appears in 1866, the same year that *The Complete Works of Henry Wadsworth Longfellow* in seven volumes comes from the press of Ticknor and Fields. *Flower-de-Luce* is Henry's farewell to his youthful lyric strain. Though other volumes of short poems may come from his pen—and six do, including the posthumous *In the Harbor*—he is never again to strike the note of freshness or quite recall the urbane

ripple that made *Voices of the Night* and *Ballads and
Other Poems* so pleasurable to innumerable readers.

It is in 1867 that the three volumes of the complete
translation of *The Divine Comedy of Dante Ali-
ghieri* are issued. Some of the most tragic years of
Henry's life are interwoven with this huge endeavor
and yet the calm, uninspired though scholarly rendering suggests nothing so much as the labors, painstaking and overly pedantic, of a placid professor shielded
by library walls. In the first place Henry's temperament is not the temperament for a translation of Dante
any more than Cary's had been. This is evidenced in
every book of the *Divina Commedia* translation but
particularly in the rendering of the Inferno. The
flash, the divine meeting of creator and of translator,
is missing. It is the scholar, a limpid scholar it is
true, who is omnipresent. The passion of Dante is
lost in philological peccadilloes. A second reason for
the comparative failure of this undertaking is, perhaps,
the means employed by Henry to achieve a faithful
version. The idea of forming the Dante Club, of
having its members suggest emendations, of making the
translation a party affair instead of the gesture of a
single individuality is not wise. It may seem to be a
laudable method of reaching accuracy but it is also
a sure way of debilitating whatever spontaneity may
be implicit in the rendering. It is easy to picture the
Dante Club at work. Henry announces that it is time
for school to begin and the members, primarily Norton
and Lowell, with the bland little echo of Howells behind them, gather for the discussion. Henry produces
his proofs and reads slowly while the listeners follow
his version from Tuscan originals which they hold
before them. A word, a phrase, or a line jars upon one

of them. Lowell interrupts with his idea of the rendering. Norton follows suit. There is a brief argument. Henry either notes the emendation on his proof or he insists upon his reasons for letting it stand as it is. In this way Dante's divine work is pursued to the very end. Now as the *Divina Commedia* is the work of a single man, so should the translation be the sole labor of a solitary individual if a unity of mood is to be the objective. It should express, even with all its flaws and personal quirks, the result of a single man's rendering of Dante. Only in this way may it carry through without revealing an altogether ominous deliberation in the translation. Henry's version, therefore, with its emendations by other minds, its multitude of notes, its chastened formulation and its somewhat pedantic air, is pretty much of a failure. His temperament is an equally strong factor in the non-success of this poem as a revelation of Dante. Yet the very faithfulness of the poem so far as mere words go give it a certain value. Scholars hail it with admiration. It appears in the same year with Norton's *Vita Nuova* and Parson's translation of the *Inferno* and as the mode in scholarly circles at the moment is Dante, it receives more attention than it deserves.

Having put Dante behind him Henry is for the moment at a loss as to what he might do next. Vague thoughts of a European trip nip at his mind and the desire to revisit those scenes of his youth is intensified by the arrival of Charles Dickens late in 1867 for a series of readings. It has been twenty-five years since he last saw Dickens and astonished that great Englishman by his hurried descents on various London haberdashers. Dickens does not see the same man whom he entertained so many years before. He sees now a patriarchal personage, bearded and more subdued in raiment. He sees a Homer without the strength of Homer, a handsome face with no iron in it. Yet the old Henry is there to please him, to laugh at his jokes, to set before him the cobwebbed bottles of rare wine and delight him with various New England delicacies. Henry on his part probably sees his youth in the aspect of this Dickens who also has grown older but who yet represents that murky London wherein Mary was so happy. "I am seriously meditating a flight to Europe in the spring or early summer," he writes to Sumner. He takes up his New England tragedy again and remodels it in verse. During this month of February, 1868, he finishes *John Endicott* and a new tragedy which he calls *Giles Corey of the Salem Farms*. These done he puts them aside and returns to the idea of his European trip. On March 9, 1868, he writes to Sumner, "The European expedition is taking shape. We are going at the end of May—probably in the *Russia* on the 27th. I do not like the breaking up of home and drifting about the Old World; but I suppose it is for the best. I hope to come back better in body and mind. I need a good shaking up, and expect to get it." He sends the New England tragedies to the printer, although at first he had meditated putting them away for future consideration, and early in April they are set up. Only a few copies are printed, enough for Henry to take to Europe and to give to his nearest friends. Neither one of these plays are important for Henry lacks the dramatic instinct, a fact that was obvious as far back as *The Spanish Student*. Dickens gives his last lecture and departs. Henry battles with influenza for a week. May comes with its flowers and sunshine and Fields gives a parting dinner for the white-haired poet, a dinner at which Greene, Holmes, Agassiz, Dana, Lowell, Norton and Whipple

gather about the ample board. Holmes reads a farewell poem. It begins:

> Our Poet, who has taught the Western breeze
> To waft his songs before him o'er the seas,
> Will find them wheresoe'er his wanderings reach,
> Borne on the spreading tide of English speech,
> Twin with the rhythmic waves that kiss the farthest beach.

v

The steamer *Russia* pulls out of New York Harbor for Liverpool on the twenty-seventh of May.
Henry stands on the deck surrounded by his family.
There is his son, Ernest, and that youth's young wife
(the marriage had taken place early in this month of
May), his three daughters, his two sisters, a brother, and
the breezy Thomas G. Appleton. Henry is like an old
monarch. How different all this is from that day
forty-two years before when Henry, a rather startled
and uncertain youth, sailed for the first time from a
barbaric native land to the vari-colored European
scene. Everything was before him then, including
mystery. But now it is an old tale. He is no longer
the young pilgrim in search of romance to whom all
things are new and wonderful. He is a man, sixty-one
years old, whose name and face are familiar throughout Europe. He is also a man who has passed through
a decade of tragedy and death and there is nothing
much that can startle or unnerve him now. Neither
fame nor dispraise can shake him much. He has known
the inexpressible delight of a secure domestic life and
he has been a victim of circumstances that demolished
that life in a flash. He is bucklered with a myriad of
friends. He is "the man" in Cambridge much as
Goethe was "the man" in Weimar. Strangers make

pilgrimages to him, and, in himself, he stands for the Cambridge spirit. He is the emblem of Victorian America, kindly, benign, urbane, moral, and safe. Seldom has it been the portion of any individual with so limited a creative faculty to be so adulated and yet it is possible to assert that Henry deserves all this. He has represented his era and represented it nobly. He has stretched out his hands to the east, across the rolling wastes of the Atlantic, and taken up the culture of Europe and brought it back and translated it into the language of his own people. He has been a transcontinental bridge across which the thousand and one nuances of foreign lands have come. He is the great fireside romantic who is cosmopolitan in his appetite. But being so much he cannot be more and so he writes in a thin ink which Time will fade. He inscribes for his day and his people and not for posterity. He is not an American in the sense that Walt Whitman (already a creature of scandal because of his "Leaves of Grass") is an American, brutally delivering himself of a chaotic utterance that is impregnated with the fecund soil and the sweating millions who travel across that soil. He is the library American, the sheltered enthusiast of a culture that is not congenitally American for the simple reason that there is no culture in America. Henry does not start at beginnings. He starts from a polished library table. All this work behind him is less the work of life than it is the work of books and because this is so it lacks that final vitality that might cause it to stand unquestionably upon its own feet. As the times and manners change the greater portion of this work will be dated. It will grow old-fashioned and dull and treacly and namby-pamby for the reason that the spiritual urge which it represented will cease to function as a vital quality in man except in rare instances of stemmed growth. A few things, mainly because of a graceful albeit thin sincerity, will last, some early lyrics that will continue to delight children, the Dante sonnets, perhaps some odd bits of *Hiawatha*. Memory will create emotional associations about some of these lyrics and the adult man will find them impressed upon his brain. The lost voices of childhood, thin as the trembling sounds from some old spinet, will call from behind these simple stanzas and the mature mind will hearken and turn back for a little. But for the most part this work will vanish as the old Cambridge—now that the war-years are over and a commercial ardor is settling on New England —will vanish. It will go with the calm old trees and the village atmosphere and Washington Allston's paintings and the horse-cars and crinolines and the cellar of wine and oratory as an art in itself and stocks and melodeons and beaver hats and the fireplace as a necessity and relics of the War of 1812 and Dioramas and all the vanished voices of the Grisis and Marios that once thrilled Boston.

But it is not to go quite yet for the age shifts slowly and if there are voices crying out against Henry and the blessed old world for which he stands they are few and indistinct at this point of time. The vitality of the urbane Puritanism of New England may have abated its vigor somewhat but only in degree. Life is more liberal, perhaps, but the ancient fetishes still maintain their ascendancy on the high altars of New England. Henry, therefore, surrounded by his family, stands on the deck of the *Russia* and gazes toward Europe as an old monarch might gaze toward a land which he is to revisit. He is not proud in the vulgar sense of the word but he is self-contained. He is no longer uncertain of himself. He goes to his apotheosis with the dignity of one king going to another, although in this case it is an uncrowned king going (unknown to himself, perhaps) to a crowned queen. The waves roll about the *Russia*. The days pass. The sun shines. Time observes this triumphant tour with a gentle humor.

Landing at Liverpool Henry and his entourage go immediately to the English Lakes, for he is fully aware of the green charm of Windermere in June. The large party finds some brief difficulty in securing quarters and at the Peacock Inn at Rowsley they fill the small hostelry to overflowing, much to the disgust of certain natives who regard the advent of the Americans as an imposition. Bowness and Furness Abbey are among the places visited and then Henry goes with his daughters to visit his friend, Robert Ferguson, at Morton near Carlisle. A public address of welcome greets him here and he responds briefly. "Being more accustomed to speak with the pen than with the tongue," he replies modestly, "it is somewhat difficult for me to find appropriate words now to thank you for the honor you have done me, and the very kind expressions you have used. Coming here as a stranger, this welcome makes me feel that I am not a stranger; for how can a man be a stranger in a country where he finds all doors and all hearts open to him? Besides, I myself am a Cumberland man—I was born in the County of Cumberland, in the State of Maine, three thousand miles from here—and you all know that the familiar name of a town or country has a home-like sound to our ears. . . . You can think then how very grateful it is to me—how very pleasant—to find my name has a place in your memories and your affections. For this kindness I most heartily thank you, and I reciprocate all the good wishes which you have expressed for perpetual peace and amity between our two nations." It is not a very brilliant speech but Henry has never been a speech-maker. Indeed, he has dodged public speaking rather warily, knowing full well that he is not an orator. Still, the address is pleasing enough to the good folk of Carlisle. From Carlisle he goes to Corby Castle and Eden Hall and Lowood on Windermere and then sets out for Cambridge, having been apprized of the honor to be done him there.

Here, on June 16th, "amid a score or so of Heads of Houses and other Academic dignitaries conspicuous by their scarlet robes," he is admitted to the honorary degree of Doctor of Laws. Victorian England is taking her own to her ample bosom. Loud cheers greet the appearance of the American poet in his long red robes, and a witness of the ceremony in noting the honored guest's appearance states: "Long, white, silken hair and a beard of patriarchal whiteness enclosed a fresh-colored countenance, with fine-cut features and deep-sunken eyes, overshadowed by massive eyebrows." Henry has achieved that appearance that is to be immortalized in endless steel-engravings. The Cambridge undergraduates are loud in their adulation of this favored visitor and Henry departs from the ceremony with cries of "Three cheers for the red man of the West!" ringing in his ears.

The series of triumphs has now definitely started. Long before this the social circles of London have been agitated about Henry's visit. In 1867 Abraham Hayward had written to Lady Emily Peel, "If Longfellow is in England, he has kept himself very close, for none of the literary men seem to have heard of him. I have asked Kinglake, Froude, Merivale, and others." But now that Henry actually is in England the public press takes immediate note of it. He is heralded by articles, encomiums, and—in the case of the conservative *Spectator*—a few satiric pin-pricks. It is to loud trumpet-peals, therefore, that Henry and his multitudinous family descend on London on June 26th and put up at the Langham Hotel. He is immediately besieged with a flood of hospitality, calls, cards, invitations, letters of welcome. He breakfasts with Gladstone, with Sir Henry Holland, with the Duke of Argyll. He lunches with Lord John Russell and receives midnight calls from Bulwer-Lytton and Aubrey De Vere. The indefatigable Abraham Hayward, presuming on old acquaintance, angles to get him for Lady Emily Peel and writes to her on the first of July, "With all my exertions I could not come to a clear understanding with Longfellow till this afternoon at Holland House. He leaves England on the 10th and has literally no meal free besides luncheon on Thursday, the 8th, and for that I engaged him for you. Why did you not come to Holland House? It was very amusing, and it fell to my lot to introduce Longfellow to both the Prince of Wales and the Comte de Paris. The Prince of Wales talked a good deal with him, which was right as regards America." Through this busy rush of days a few incidents stand out. Henry and his daughters spend a Sunday at Gadshill with Charles Dickens. By invitation of Dean Stanley he attends evening service at Westminster Abbey (where sixteen years later his bust is to be placed) and listens to a sermon by the famous Dr. Jowett. Afterwards he takes tea at the Deanery. He visits the Archbishop of Canterbury at Lambeth Palace. The American painter, Bierstadt, gives a great dinner for him at the Langham Hotel and hundreds of celebrities in literature and art, science and politics, come to meet him. Gladstone makes a speech and Henry makes one of his infrequent replies.

All this whirl and excitement take place in a few days and they are but the lesser notes in a complete British acceptance which reaches its apogee in the galleries of Windsor Castle. Lady Augusta Stanley comes to Henry with the tidings that the Queen would be sorry to have him pass through England without her meeting him. Therefore, on a fine day, Henry, accompanied by Lady Stanley, repairs to Windsor and after a brief wait in the hall a door opens and the short, stout Victoria, by the Grace of God, Queen of England and Empress of India, appears before him. Henry shakes hands with her and, in the words of his son Ernest, "they had a pleasant chat." It is a brief meeting but it is a symbolic one. Though Henry may have little to say about this meeting it comes to him like an accolade. His hand touching the hand of Victoria unites for an instant two great kindred urges flowering simultaneously on both sides of the Atlantic Ocean.

The Golden Years

66IT is in its international aspect that we rejoice at the
public honor done to Mr. Longfellow," remarked
the London *Daily News* after Henry received his honorary degree from the University of Cambridge.
"Familiar as his name is in the mouths of the people,
among us he represents his country. Such men come
among us on unofficial embassies of peace and friendship and good will. Their visits multiply the ties which,
as kindred peoples, bind us together. Our tendency is
more and more to cultivate our relationship to the
progressive and expanding West. Our language, our
literature, and our race have a great future here and a
great future there. Mr. Longfellow represents the
profound unity of sympathy, of home feeling, and of
moral aspiration which there is between us. That we
can each be represented by the same poet, and feel that
the same lyrics express our feelings and move our
hearts, is a strong tie of intellectual sympathy." Henry,
therefore, is recognized as an ambassador. He is the
representative of the New World in so far as that terrain is a shadow of the Old World and a definite
development of kindred ties. One wonders what
Henry thinks of it all, for during the Civil War he had
risen to heights of indignation, for him, at the unreasonable attitude of England toward the Northern States.
Even the Queen is made to see that Henry is not an
ordinary mortal, that he is, in fact, a crowned figure in
his own right, for to Theodore Martin she remarks,
"I wished for you this morning, for you would have
seen something that would have delighted you as a man
of letters. The American poet Longfellow has been
here. I noticed an unusual interest among the attend-

ants and servants. I could scarcely credit that they so generally understood who he was. When he took leave, they concealed themselves in places from which they could get a good look at him as he passed. I have since inquired among them, and am surprised and pleased to find that many of his poems are familiar to them. No other distinguished person has come here that has excited so peculiar an interest. Such poets wear a crown that is imperishable." Delightful Victoria! How sad it is that poor dear Albert could not have received this benign and bearded representative of the New World, that New World that had not been so popular a few years previously. Even the London *Times* joins in the pæan of welcome, expressing its friendliness in a poem by Mr. Charles Kent which opens:

> Welcome to England, thou whose strains prolong
> The glorious bead-roll of our Saxon song.

Henry is now on the high crest of the wave. He has attained his apotheosis. He has been taken to the bosom, figuratively, of course, of the Queen, and the entire Kingdom, so far as it is at all conscious of Henry, stands with open arms and a bright smile of welcome. It is true that a terrible young man named Swinburne is not to be found in the throng of hospitable intellectuals, but one could hardly expect to find him there. Algernon prefers Whitman to Henry, and Henry we may be sure finds nothing in the first *Poems and Ballads*. Indeed, did he not gag a bit at the unpleasantness of Mr. Thackeray's *Vanity Fair*, saying that it was a clever, cutting, amusing, disagreeable book that showed too much of the coarse lining of London life? Realism of any sort is not Henry's forte. He prefers his dear Jean-Paul.

He has one more visit to make, however, before he
can safely assure himself that he has been accepted by
England in toto. Though he has pressed the royal
hand of Victoria and the political hand of Gladstone,
there yet remains the poetical hand of Tennyson, for
he has adored "Saint Alfred" for a long time and, indeed, had sent him an Indian calumet as a token of
homage a year or so before this tour. So to Freshwater
he goes, to Farringford, with all his entourage, and
bursts upon the dour English laureate. Tennyson is in
an amicable mood. "Very English he is," he notes, regarding Henry approvingly. The Americans stay for
two days, though not at Farringford, and Tennyson
shows but little of that gruffness which so marks his
later years. He *does* catch one of Henry's daughters
turning over the leaves of a book of her father's poems,
prominently displayed upon the Tennysonian table with
more than usual tact, and growls, "Don't you have
enough of that at home?" much to the dismay of the
American girl. And he also grumbles roughly at his
boys during lunch for some fancied grievance, but the
bearishness is for the most part absent. Indeed, he
rather puts himself out for his American friends. He
takes them to the roof of the house to view the scenery
and hastily drags them down again when he sees a
woman and child hurrying across a distant field; swearing, as he does so, that the couple are running to get a
glimpse of him. He reads *Maud* in his peculiar
nasal sing-song voice. He discusses spiritualism with
Henry, a subject in which he is vastly interested at this
time. He even invites forty or fifty neighbors to tea
to meet the Longfellows, and Henry, observing Mrs.
Fraser Tytler's charming daughters, remarks, "It was
worth while coming to England to see such young
ladies." Henry even in his old age never loses his

315

delight in a pretty face. It is all quite charming and
Henry departs with the feeling that he has now seen
everybody worth seeing. He has been killed with
kindness as it were, and now he desires to revive on
the continent, among the unforgotten scenes of his
youth, during those brave days when he was twenty-one.

From the Isle of Wight and its Tennysonian atmosphere, therefore, the American party departs for Dover,
crosses the choppy Channel, and proceeds up the Rhine
to Switzerland, where the summer is passed with the
single interruption of a trip over the St. Gothard pass
to Lugano and Cadenabbia on the lake of Como. Old
ghosts pursue Henry but his gentle nature meets them
with that degree of benign valiancy that is so peculiar
a virtue of his nature. "The old familiar places sad-
dened me," he remarks simply in a letter to Fields, a
letter incidentally in which he directs the publisher to
go ahead and issue the *New England Tragedies*. It
is possible that wandering through Interlaken and walking in the ancient ways he met a rather Byronic albeit
fresh-cheeked young man recovering from the sorrow
of his wife's death in Holland. There is so much behind him now, so many hills climbed, so many views
forsaken, so many voices mute. The summer days
dream away in a pleasant heat and by autumn Henry
ventures into Paris, but the Paris of the Second Empire
is not particularly pleasing to him. There is nothing in
the contemporary literature to attract him. Hugo, for
example, is too extravagant and violent. He visits
Sainte-Beuve and finds the French critic so fat that he
can scarcely move. They talk of Chateaubriand and
Lamartine. "Take them for all in all, which do
you prefer?" inquires Henry. Saint-Beuve replies:
"Charlatan pour charlatan, je crois que je préfére
Monsieur de Lamartine." He dines with John Ruskin

at Meurice's and Ruskin finds him "a quiet simple
gentleman, neither specially frank nor reserved, somewhat grave, very pleasant, not amusing, strangely innocent and calm, caring little for things out of his own
serene sphere." Henry, on his part, is struck by the
quiet way in which the Englishman gives vent to his
extreme opinions. Of *course* Henry is strangely innocent. He cares nothing for things out of his own
serene sphere. Henry, after all, has ceased to grow.
He has nothing left now but the past upon which to
feed, and though that past is rich in foreign colors and
crowded with many faces it is still the past. The vitality has left it. He is an old man and he looks upon
the multi-hued, barbarously-shifting world as would
an old man, not comprehending and not caring for the
drastic twists of Time. What does it matter to him
now that new conceptions of art trouble the unresting
world of the mind? He, at least, settled the problem
long ago for himself. He goes to hear Molière's plays
at the Théâtre Française, explores some of the old lo-
calities of literary history, and pokes about among the
ancient books in the stalls on the quais, his white beard
drooping over the worn calf bindings as he chatters
excellent French with the peddlers. The autumn wind
blows along the Seine and there is a warning nip in it.
The mists above Notre Dame seem cold and forbidding.
This is enough for Henry and before winter sets in he
flees before it, setting off southward, still with his
family entourage, through Arles where the birds chirp
from the eaves of the ancient houses and along the
Cornihe into Italy. Ah! la bella Italia! Next to Spain
it is the land of his youthful dreams. Was it not here
that he dreamed with Greene of the mighty future that
stood pulsating just beyond his boyish orbit? Did they
not sit on the roof-top and gravely prophesy vast

317

achievements to one another? He pauses for a few weeks in Florence and then proceeds to Rome. There is a brief visit to Genoa but he does not stop at the old hotel where he once lived. He stops "at a newer and better one, close by." "I often took my girls to walk on the sea-wall," he writes Greene, "and pointed out to them our old terrace with its flower-pots and statues; though I confess that it had grown smaller and somewhat shorn of its former splendors." Perhaps the long perspective of Time has shrunk the ancient terrace. There is an autumn flavor over all his gestures now. The past is diminishing into a quiet picture drained of all fevers, and his activities are becoming simplified and less strenuous. In Rome, where he stops at the Hotel Costanzi above the Piazza Barberini, he does not go about so much. He is impatient of lingering in picture galleries, churches and ruins. It is true that he becomes a center of interest to the American tourists who crowd about him and vie with one another in adulation, and he also makes various acquaintances among the Italians, the Duke of Sermoneta, for example, and Monsignore Nardi, of the papal court. But he does not see the Pope and he does not seek too strenuously for the scenes of his youth. He is getting tired. Vague thoughts of the comfortable study in Craigie House come to him. Perhaps the high point of his pleasurable meetings here is his brief acquaintance with the Abbé Liszt. Healy, the artist, takes Henry to see the old composer, who is living in a convent at the side of the Forum, and in the twilight the door opens and Liszt stands at the head of the stairs, holding a lighted candle above his head, the tiny flame dancing over his black soutane. At a later meeting Liszt plays for them, his long fingers moving swiftly along the keys and his iron-gray hair brushed

back on his great head. Henry leans back and listens
as many voices thread the music.

Spring comes and travel is renewed, the party striking
southward to Naples. There is a night with the Bene-
dictines at Monte Casino and a trip to Amalfi. They
go to Pæstum and they pause at Sorrento. Perhaps in
the sun-shot silence Henry hears the far-away voices
of the sirens singing but the music is sad now and faint,
filled with the minor notes reminiscent of days and
times and faces that come no more. He turns his face
on it all for the last time, and the party strikes northward to Venice, and over the Brenner to Innsbruck,
Munich, Nuremberg and Dresden. Across Switzerland
they go to Paris, and thence to London and to Oxford
where he is given the degree of D.C.L. There is a
short tour through Devonshire and then to Edinburgh,
the Scotch Lakes and the Burns country. It is all over
now. Whether or not Henry suspects that this is the
last time he shall see his beloved Europe, his land of
romance upon which he has fed all his life, and which
has provided him with the particular sustenance which
his nature requires, it is patent that he has experienced
a dim feeling of restlessness and hurry. He has looked
for the past eagerly throughout this triumphal journey
and it is curious to note how little he is affected by the
present. New movements in letters, in art, in life, do
not attract him. These things belong to another world,
a world that is not the terrain wherein Henry walks so
leisurely. He has ceased to be excited by the Time-
Spirit except in so far as that inexplicable dæmon
affects his familiars, Sumner for example, or poor
Greene. So he arranges for his precious purchases of
wines and books and turns his face westward. By the
first of September, 1869, he is back in Craigie House,

setting about paying his taxes, thankful that he has returned his flock safely to the fold, and vaguely ruminating further poetic excursions from the vantage-point of his study chair.

II

The decade turns to the music of Tennyson's *The Holy Grail* and Lowell's *Cathedral,* and it is the sunny seventies. The Reconstruction period of the Republic is in full swing and indeed already far advanced, and commercial prosperity is mounting rapidly. The era of brownstone fronts, many equipages, and millionaires is at the door of Time, and Henry, settled back comfortably in the Craigie House, has before him slightly more than a decade of pleasant adulation. His New England is now perceptibly quickened by a curious commercial urge that has heretofore been lying semi-dormant in the minds of a canny folk who make it a point to seize opportunity by the forelock. In Washington Congress concerns itself with financial matters, with maritime interests, with the troublous question of extending the franchise to former slaves. Old wounds are healing and the readmission of Southern States to the Union is accomplished to a deal of palaver. President Grant issues a proclamation officially ratifying the Fifteenth Amendment and the conquered South mumbles and mutters and casts about for sly means of circumventing the suffrage of these millions of black men who once were slaves. In Cuba there is a violent insurrection against Spanish rule. Most of these affairs do not touch Henry, who passes a rather dull winter at home after the flare and color of his European tour. The dullness, however, is a sedative to his jaded nerves. He scribbles away at more tales for a new series of the

Wayside Inn, and, at the same time, finds himself conjecturing whether he will write any more, a rather fruitless conjecture for he commands an unstemmed facility that neither age nor lack of inspiration may impede. As long as there are books to be read there will be subject-matter for poems. Life grows quiet. Agassiz is disabled and cannot receive visitors, read or write. Palfrey is away. Lowell is busy. Sumner is in Washington delivering speeches on the refunding and consolidation of the national debt. Greene makes his occasional appearances from Rhode Island but these are, on the whole, dormant days. The snow falls and the icicles tinkle in the gutters. Nothing dynamic will disturb Henry now. There will be no more far travels and fierce crises of the soul, no more perplexing uncertainties. This quietude is, in a way, for the best. Though Felton, of the loud cheery laugh, and Hawthorne, dark and silent in his corner, are gone forever and though other friends become more and more immersed in their own affairs, Henry has his growing daughters about him and there are plenty of new friends, who, though they may never take the place of the old, serve to lighten his days and render this twilight end of Time a charming and urbane period. He sits at the study window and watches the light flare and die above this Cambridge that is not quite the old Cambridge but which is still compact with the intimate revelations and memories of long years.

There is something particularly graceful in this spectacle of Henry, returning from the flowery triumphs of Europe, and sinking so thankfully into the placid domesticity of his home. It is the quintessence of naturalism. If he possesses an undue pride in himself (and it is to be doubted) it is surcharged with an ease and assurance and an innate placidity that is

astonishing. He accepts his wreathe of laurels un-
ostentatiously and brings it home and hangs it up in the
study of Craigie House with all the other tokens of the
good will of a world that finds in him a peculiarly
appropriate subject for praise. After all, it is possible
that the great world sees in him a personification of
those gentle virtues of living that are so agreeable to
contemplate and so dull to put into practice. And yet
Henry, for instance, could be so much duller! He
might be a Total Abstainer. He might be an anti-
tobacco proselytizer. He might abjure bright waistcoats as the temptation of the devil. But he does none
of these things. Delightful streaks of liberalism
brighten the pale hue of his goodness. He sparkles
(faintly, to be sure) in a New England that grows its
yearly crop of fanatics. This is because he is aware of
more than his New England. And, being aware of
more than it, he is all the better equipped to enjoy its
finest flowerings.

Charles Dickens dies suddenly and Henry strolls
about Cambridge thinking of nothing but the figure of
the novelist lying lifeless at Gad's Hill. It has been
so short a time before that both men had been sitting
together and discoursing animatedly on life and letters.
Almost immediately, therefore, the Europe that Henry
knows so well begins to change. No sooner has he
sunk back into the quiet haven of Cambridge than the
faces begin to vanish and the old urges to diminish and
dissipate before new and monstrous phenomena. Disconcerting rumors of continental affairs reach Henry's
ears and he begins to speculate on the ways in which
the Time-Spirit is traveling. Bismarck's doctored telegram is published and infuriated mobs surge through
the streets of Paris shouting, "À Berlin! À Berlin!"
On the nineteenth of July Louis-Napoleon's govern-

ment declares war and great armies race, both from east
and west, toward the frontiers. Henry walks slowly
along the shore at Nahant and listens to the booming
of the waters while Weissenberg, Worth, and Spicheren
are fought. Maréchal MacMahon exerts himself to
the utmost for *la patrie* and the stout Bazaine remains
stationary, like a toy soldier, surrounded by his brightly-
uniformed regiments. Glistening helmets crowned
with horse-hair sway down the Champs Élysees.
Henry follows all this from a distance but calmly.
After all, the France of the Second Empire had not
thrilled him much. He winces at the idea of war and
calls it terrible (memories of his son, Charles, in the
freight-car outside Washington coming back to him),
but he hardly perceives that a new order is struggling
to militant freedom through these battles, that the fall
of the French Ministry and the slighting of Napoleon
"the Little" mean a new dominance of power in Europe
and the death of the ancient romanticism upon which
he has fed for so many decades. Indeed, he looks forward to the prospect of a French Republic. And
what does he think of his Germany, his Germany of
Jean-Paul and Freiligrath and Heidelberg students, as
he sees it transformed into a monster bristling with
steel? Is it possible for him to miss so palpable a
spectacle of the destruction of the springs at which he
drank as a youth?

The Germans overrun Lorraine and Moltke's strategy forces the Gallic armies apart. Colombey-Nouilly
and Vionville are fought. The Uhlans make their
charge at Mars-la-Tour. Gravelotte is contested.
Henry continues to dream placidly over *Wilhelm
Meister* (of all books!) and Dino Campagni's *Cronica
di Firenze*. It is the world of his imagination that
is being so desolated but he does not appear to

comprehend it. All those ancient desirable things which evolved him are being shattered to bits. The German armies close in around Metz and Beaumont is fought. The ghost of an Emperor goes to his doom with waxed mustaches and rouged cheeks. And then there is Sedan and *la débâcle,* the fleeing French legions, the riderless horses, the overturned wagons and guns, the débris of a smashed Empire. What does Henry think of all this ? Is he not sad at the thought of the deserted book-stalls beneath the plane trees along the Seine and the shouting mobs surging beneath the chestnut trees of the boulevards? What does he think of the mobbing of the Assembly, the flight of Eugénie from the Tuileries to England, and the proclamation of the Republic by a gathering of lawyers, demagogues, and journalists? Well, in his simple way he approves of it. "The Republic proclaimed in France!" he notes in his journal with the proper exclamation mark after the sentence. Although aristocratic in his personal predilections he approves and thrills to the huge phenomena of democracy. The lessons of Sumner have been well inculcated.

Leon Gambetta escapes from encircled Paris in a balloon and engineers his forlorn attempt to stem the tide of defeat with hastily formed troops at Orleans. It is futile, of course, a mere continuance of slaughter. There is mob-rule in Paris as the last desperate battles are fought, Beaune-la-Rolande and Champigny. Alexandre Dumas, perhaps dimly conscious that the romantic era has passed, dies and the German Empire is proclaimed. In the meantime, Mrs. Hamilton reads from her new novel, *Woven of Many Threads,* to the attentive Henry. The Commune overruns the boulevards along the Seine and MacMahon's troopers cut down the pétroleuses on the barricades. It is the beginning of the end. The greater part of the Tuileries, the library of the Louvre, and a portion of the Palais Royal have been destroyed. The Column of Vendôme is upset. In the streets of the city lie unburied corpses and the black ruins of fire-gutted houses yawn on all sides. Henry, lingering through the autumn at Nahant, thinks not so much of this lost city of his youth, in whose streets he once met Lafayette, as he does of those warmer southern climes. C. E. Norton is in Italy and to him he confesses that he is satisfied that he made a great mistake in not staying longer in Europe. "I am still hungry for more," he admits, but it is of Italy that he speaks and not of war-ravaged France. Even this Italy is changing, however, for Cadorna enters Rome with his soldiers and Victor Emmanuel delivers his ultimatum to the Vatican. And in Spain, that lost land of dreams which Henry never seems to dare consider revisiting, Amadeus mounts the throne for his exceedingly brief reign. The face of Europe is shaken and changed as it was shaken and changed when Henry was a small boy of eight, and all this has taken place within but a few months since Henry's last triumphal tour. The New Era is at hand, although Henry, perhaps, does not suspect it. And even as Europe is changing so is America, although in less drastic fashion, to be sure.

The sunny seventies in America open to this European uproar and that relatively long period of quiet insular growth has its inception, a period wherein villages shift imperceptibly into towns and towns climb to the proud estate of cities. Commerce quickens in cities where there are no tall buildings to hide the sun, where trees still grow in the streets, where communication is by post and not so generally by telephone or telegraph, although both exist, where no whirring automobiles clog the thoroughfares and where local travel is confined to carriages and horse-cars. To be precise, it is a world wherein men may still walk slowly. Behind all this looms the foggy shape of a restless giant, a giant about to crash through the happy insularity with fierce urges, a myriad of inventions to accelerate living, and a new materialistic thirst for the gold of the world. In the terrain of literature there is a brief breathing space between two modes. There is a dividing line here. Before the seventies poetry was the paramount division of American letters, although a race of novelists, Irving, Cooper, Hawthorne, had existed and partially colored the time to their personalities. It had been the era of Bryant, Whittier, Poe, Emerson, Longfellow, of a galaxy of singers. Now there is a pause while Mark Twain and Bret Harte begin their labors and Howells and James and a dozen younger men fumble toward a prose expression. Up to this time the American public, fed upon English fiction, has hardly missed an autochthonous fictional representation. But now an era of analysis and self-examination, crude and fragmentary enough at first, dawns and the gentle old epoch of semi-didactic poetry dwindles into a period of tentative prose ventures. The strength goes out of the poetry, except in so far as Walt Whitman stands as a dynamic protest against self-hypocrisy. There is, therefore, an almost imperceptible revolution in America.

Phenomena fleck the seventies. There is the great fire in Chicago and the "Boss" Tweed scandal in New York. Stanley, with the money of James Gordon Bennett, pierces darkest Africa and finds Dr. Livingstone. Gomez conducts his fierce insurrection against Spanish tyranny in Cuba. Henry follows these things with some interest but for the most part he continues to lead his quiet life, applying himself to his books, no less than six of which appear during this decade. Be-

tween 1870 and 1876 the greater part of this original
work appears. Cut from the same cloth, there is little
that can be said about them. The old felicities, smooth-
nesses, lyrical qualities, pleasantnesses are implicit in
them, always excepting that early freshness which first
established Henry as an American singer. There is no
growth here. *The Divine Tragedy* appears in 1871,
and it is followed by *Three Books of Song* (1872),
which contains the Second Day of *Tales of a Wayside
Inn* and the tragedy *Judas Maccabeus; Christus:
A Mystery* (1872), which is an arrangement of *The
Divine Tragedy, The Golden Legend* and *The New
England Tragedies* in a trilogy connected by inter-
ludes and prologues; *Aftermath* (1873), which contains the Third Day of *Tales of a Wayside Inn;*
and *The Masque of Pandora and Other Poems*
(1875), which includes *Morituri Salutamus.* It is
well to note the dates of these books for, with the exception of one of them, they may all be considered together. No new facets are evidenced. The life in them
is thin and though there may be odd lyrics of a pleasant
appeal the work as a whole is just what would be expected, the ambling product of a sheltered scholar. It
will not do to call it disappointing, for Henry has never
given any hopes of a higher perfection, an intenser
passion, or an increasing vitality. The time-honored,
unmistakable attributes are here, the delight and facility
in telling a story, the gentle lyrical running on, the un-
successful attempts at drama, and the pleasant though
for the most part theoretic joy in nature. The didactic
impulse is as strong as ever and it eats out the heart
of the matter as disastrously as it did thirty years back.

One book among these many books may be singled
out; on it Henry bases his highest poetical hopes. It is
Christus: A Mystery, and it is, possibly, the least suc-

327

cessful of all his works, the one towering monument of dullness. The dream of this book has been with Henry for decades but at the last moment he seems willing enough to put up with a hasty approximation of his theme. It has been his original intention to represent Christianity in three forms of development, its origin, its medieval power and its modern manifestation, but *Christus* does not do this. The first part, *The Divine Tragedy*, which is the last written, is no more than an uninspired retelling of the Gospels in blank verse in loose dramatic form. The second part, *The Golden Legend*, written first of all, is rather better, although even here there is none of the pleasing quality that may be found in Henry's slighter lyrics. For his third and concluding section *The New England Tragedies*, are made to serve, and it is difficult not to reach the conclusion that this hasty settlement is an afterthought, that when he made these two gloomy, dull plays from Puritan chronicles he had no idea of forcing them into the scheme of *Christus: A Mystery*. Indeed, he seems aware of the anticlimax of his work for he meditates still a third play, the scene to be laid among the Moravians of Bethlehem, Pennsylvania, to harmonize the theme. This is never written. It is unnecessary to point out that the origin of Christianity is much more poetically rendered in the Bible than in *The Divine Tragedy*, that *The Golden Legend* with its faintly charming medieval narrative of Prince Henry is hardly a fair aspect of Christianity in the Middle Ages, and that *The New England Tragedies* are representative of a phenomenon, a peculiarly localized attitude toward Christ. After all, these matters are not important when we think of Henry as a poet. We do not turn to *Christus: A Mystery* when we read Henry any more than we turn to *Judas Maccabeus*

or *Michael Angelo*. Instead of this, we look for the
shorter pieces of *Voices of the Night* and *Ballads and
Other Poems* and, perhaps, portions of *Hiawatha* and
Evangeline. It is not in monumental efforts that
Henry is himself. His thin lyrical faculty cannot cope with such high undertakings. But the mere
fact that he does strive to achieve such lofty conceptions
is revelatory of his own lack of self-adjustment toward
his medium. He outreaches his grasp time and again,
and his successes are to be found in those lesser moments
when he plucks some brief and fragrant flower of
fancy springing from his doorstep or from the calf-
bound tomes upon his library table. It is humble
enough but it serves.

Henry does not appear to be aware of his own limitations and, indeed, there is no reason why he should,
safeguarded as he is and coddled by loving friends who
pen ecstatic notes on every book that is conceived in
Craigie House. After all, he has ceased to be a figure
who may be impartially criticized. He is a monument
now and the sunny seventies form his calm afternoon of
living. The postman deposits his pile of letters at the
door each morning and Henry learns how well regarded
he is throughout the world. He turns from his mail
and passes the time in his pleasant study, writing slowly,
turning the pages of rare books, bowing his white head
over the much-loved type. Fields comes to see him and
they discuss new books. Toujours les livres! He
smokes his cigar and his blue eyes twinkle at the
thought of further efforts. Visitors come from all
parts of the earth. One notes with amazement the host
that turns in at the gate of Craigie House during this
golden decade, among them, to note the more famous,
Thomas Hughes, J. A. Froude, Anthony Trollope,
Wilkie Collins, William Black, Charles Kingsley, Pro-

fessor Bonamy Price, Dr. Plumptre, Dean Stanley, Athanase Coquerel, Lord Houghton, Lord and Lady Dufferin, the Duke of Argyll, Salvini, Christine Nilsson, Admiral Coffin, Lord Ronald Gower, Charles Fechter, Auguste Bartholdi, Carl Schurz, Martin Tupper, Sir Joseph Hooker, Mme. Modjeska, and even an Emperor, Dom Pedro of Brazil. They all come to pay their respects and Henry meets them with that unfailing courtesy, standing erect in his frock coat and dispensing his Tokay with an easy generosity. He is the uncrowned king of the Republic in a certain sense, although by this time the Republic is moving sluggishly forward toward other manners and leaving Henry and his Cambridge somewhat behind. Still he knows nothing of this. He cannot realize that there are huge tracts where his name does not mean so much as it did a few years ago. Around him, in his immediate vicinity, the incense is still burned and the delectable odors rise to the blue skies above him.

Samuel F. B. Morse dies and Grant defeats Greeley for the Presidency. Greeley passes away soon after. Henry hears that there is a tremendous fire raging in Boston and the next day he discovers that eighty acres have been burned and that $70,000,000 has been lost. Juarez dies in Mexico and Théophile Gautier dies in France. The rumble of change now sounds close to the doors of Craigie House. The world is shifting after all. In 1873 Agassiz dies and Henry is disconsolate for a while. Louis-Napoleon dies. Bulwer-Lytton dies. John Stuart Mill dies. Bells seem to be tolling this year and Henry, if he chooses to listen, may hear far-off measured footfalls as the bearers carry an era to its tomb. He begins to be haunted by dreams. He dreams of meeting Tennyson at a hotel in an Italian town. Tennyson is elegantly dressed and possesses the

easy manners of a man of the world.   Henry dreams
again that he is at a dinner party and that to reach the
dining room he must pass through a carpenter's shop,
climb out of a window and go over a roof.   There is a
clergyman there dressed as a woman in white.   He
dreams, too, of talking to the Emperor Napoleon who
asks him if he remembers the portrait which the Princess Charlotte, cousin to Bonaparte, drew of him in her
album at Florence in 1828.   These dreams show that
his mind is restless and laboring while his body sleeps.
It is grasping at curious phantasies, mingling forgotten
impulses with inexplicable impressions.

Early in 1874 Charles Sumner slips away from a
fierce and restless career and Henry, though he has expected the tragedy for some time, is intensely shocked
by it.   It is days before he recovers from this blow at
his immediate milieu.   Sumner has been an inextricable
part of his life and though as always he strives to rise
above his grief, he can never shake away the loneliness.
Lowell goes away and the Craigie House grows more
silent.   It is true that Norton and Emerson and Holmes
are still at hand, but Emerson, too, is aging and the
conversations are apt to be more regardful of the past
than of the future.   Emerson, moreover, is never a very
close friend.   Greene, the faithful Greene, comes frequently from his Rhode Island wind-mill, but Greene,
also, is old and feeble.   It has become a world of old
men so far as Henry is concerned, old men walking
slowly beneath the elms and feeling the caresses of the
sun with a vague disturbed pleasure.

Guizot and Michelet and Fortuny die.   These
bright-eyed brilliant boys who stood at the door of life
in 1807 have reached the end of their cycle and they are
passing, one by one, out of the world that is alien to
them.   Henry, in his late sixties, must realize that he

331

has achieved that lamentable point of time when his contemporaries will steadily drop from view, when they will vanish silently into history. And of course, the face of the era will change, although his own conception of that era, so fortified by the years, will remain the same. It is a serious matter when any writer who has been great among his own people continues to live beyond the age of sixty. Modes shift cruelly and Time alters accordingly. Henry is outliving his era now, for the young country in which he was once so admirable a prophet of foreign urges may now see for itself what Europe has to offer. It will take several decades adjusting itself to this new perspective but at the same time it will not want to be "told" things in the old primer way. As the country advances toward culture Henry's offering becomes more and more simple, therefore, and eventually is no more than pabulum for primary school boys.

The fiftieth anniversary of his class at Bowdoin comes around and he composes a poem for it. *Morituri Salutamus* he calls it, "we who are about to die salute you." He reads from the pulpit of the old church in Brunswick. It ends on a fine note of encouragement for these old classmates who sit beneath him, so many of them crowned with white hair, so many of them thinking as he does.

> What then? Shall we sit idly down and say
> The night hath come; it is no longer day?
> The night hath not yet come; we are not quite
> Cut off from labor by the failing light;
> Something remains for us to do or dare;
> Even the oldest tree some fruit may bear;
> Not Œdipus Coloneus, or Greek Ode,
> Or tales of pilgrims that one morning rode

Out of the gateway of the Tabard Inn,
But other something, would we but begin;
For age is opportunity no less
Than youth itself, though in another dress,
And as the evening twilight fades away
The sky is filled with stars, invisible by day.

And on this vigorous note Henry returns to Cambridge.

There are more than 50,000 people in Cambridge now and the aspect of the city has changed materially from what it was when Henry first came as a budding young professor. The tide of immigration, induced by low transportation rates, is in full flood and foreign quarters are building up. They rise like camps about the old New England strongholds and it will not be long now before those strongholds are in a state of spiritual siege. Most lamentable of all, the spirit of the city is changing. As Henry rides up to Craigie House he may sense this, but it is impossible for him to know that the day will come when the City Fathers of Cambridge will boast not that their community is the home of grave scholars, of Quincys and Everetts and Feltons, but that it is the headquarters of Kennedy's crackers, of the best soap, of Blake and Knowles Steam Pump Works and the Reversible Collar Company, of Mason and Hamlin organs and pianos and salted peanuts and the American Rubber Company and the Hews Pottery Company. The same condition, to a greater degree, maintains in Boston where the march of trade is under way, and though Anna Ticknor may strive to keep back the new raucous civilization with her Society for the Encouragement of Study at Home the erstwhile Athens of America will go on as the Time-Spirit directs it. It will evolve into a metropolis for the freaks of culture and the political ingenuities of hard-headed Irish politicians.

333

Henry steps briefly into the midst of this new world when the Philadelphia Centennial Exposition opens in 1876, recovering from his attacks of neuralgia sufficiently to leave the safe harborage of Craigie House for a week in the Quaker City. He considers it a charming vacation and he expresses his wonder at the sights, for he is placable to progress, not quite understanding that it is undermining his leisurely milieu. He stands before the Main Building—it is 1880 feet long—and gasps at its bulk. He walks for hours among the exhibits of mining and metallurgy, manufactures, education and science. Flags wave above him, blue for buildings erected by the Centennial Committee, red for United States and States buildings, white for foreign concessions, yellow for restaurants and places of entertainment, and green for miscellaneous edifices, whatever they may be. Not since the Vienna Exhibition of 1873 has such a momentous undertaking been successfully achieved by a country and never before in the Republic. It is the great gesture of the country, the notification to all the world that the United States is a grown-up country with vast manufactures and not so vast, perhaps, arts. And speaking of art, there is the Arts Building with its endless displays of paintings by such giants of the brush as G. H. Story, G. P. A. Healy, John La Farge, J. F. Cropsey and Eastman Johnson, its sculptures, its architectural designs, its loan collections of foreign paintings where the gaping visitor may study Cabanel and Courbet, and its applied arts such as miles of chromo-lithography and cameos and medallions and enamels and enamel paintings and wallpaper designs and inlaid book-cases and crochet and embroidery patterns and paintings on glass and silhouettes and bouquets drawn on silk and stained glass. Henry views it all and strolls about the Exhibition

grounds, admiring Bartholdi's fountain and the Catholic Total Abstinence Fountain, upon which a stone Moses smites water from a rock, and the Dead Lioness and the colossal statue of the American soldier which is twenty-one feet high and the monument to Bishop Richard Allen, who, it may be explained, is the founder and first bishop of the African Methodist Episcopal Church. Then there are the restaurants, the Great American, the Trois Frères Provençaux, the German establishment, Gaff, Fleischmann and Company's Vienna Bakery and Coffee House where the virtues of yeast are pressed on a reluctant public, and the New England Farmer's home of 100 Years Ago and Modern Kitchen, conducted by Miss Emma Southwick of Boston. There is Colonel Lienard's Georama to see, where the cities of Paris and Jerusalem are modeled in gypsum, and on George's Hill the West Point cadets, three hundred of them, are encamped with their band. The popcorn vendors shout and the hordes of people push to and fro, the women slanting their parasols against the sun and the men trickling into the beer gardens as often as possible. The nasal twang of the New Englander mingles with the lazy drawl of the Southerner. Henry's interest must flag as he is pushed about. He cannot find much to thrill him in the Shoe and Leather Building and neither can the monstrous array of triphammers, silk and cotton machines, boilers and gas generating apparatus, and hydraulic and pneumatic inventions appeal to him violently. Yet the new America is here, vulgar, shoving, loud-voiced, smart, essentially democratic, and it is difficult to understand how Henry does not sense it to some degree as he takes in the wonders of the Exhibition.

III

The few years that remain before the decade draws to a close are taken up with the compilation of the thirty-one volumes of *Poems of Places,* a huge garnering of short pieces descriptive of different lands and cities. It is the sort of work that would please an old man, and though Henry tires of it at times it serves to occupy a mind that now finds life not too rich in stimulating foods. He can browse through dozens of books, can make new translations, can arrange excerpts from his own works, and at the same time can relish the joy, a vicarious one, perhaps, of remembering those enchanted spots in Europe where he once passed young and full of the zest of the unknown. His sedate life fits in admirably with this long task, for there is little else that he can do. The thirty-one small volumes of *Poems of Places* stretch out over four years and they form a thread, as it were, to his mind during this time. It is peculiarly fitting that this thread should suggest the whole world and all its countries and cities and legendary places for it seems to emphasize the innate cosmopolitanism of Henry's mind so far as literature is concerned. In spirit he has wandered all about the globe and now in the twilight of life he traverses again the most outlandish terrains as well as the ancient cities of that Europe that transformed itself so madly immediately after his last journey across the Atlantic ocean. Occasionally his mind is diverted into some creative moment and a poem results, enough of them at last, indeed, to make possible in 1878 *Kéramos and Other Poems.* The title-piece is one of his more fortunate efforts from a financial point of view for *Harper's Magazine* pays him no less than $1,000 for it, the same price, by the way, which it paid for *Morituri*

Salutamus. This is not the highest price which Henry has received for a single poem for *The Hanging of the Crane* brought him $3,000 from the generous Bonner of the New York *Ledger,* an almost unheard-of honorarium for a solitary poem, no matter its length. Henry may now observe with some complacency the rise in his fortunes from those early days in 1825 when he was glad to receive one or two dollars for a poem although he really has no need of money now, a kindly destiny having thrust in his way one wife after another with more than the usual share of this world's goods. Still, it is pleasant to look back and note how like an arc his fortunes rise. The rainbow that rose in Bowdoin reaches its end in the Craigie House. In 1840 he was receiving fifteen dollars for *The Village Blacksmith.* In 1844 *The Arsenal* brought him fifty dollars. In 1850 he was getting one hundred to one hundred and fifty dollars for a single poem. Yes, Time changes. The value of genius mounts with the years. He looks upon *Kéramos and Other Poems,* therefore, with a kindly eye and continues to apply himself to the apparently unending *Poems of Places.*

His health begins to suffer now and it is impressed upon him that he cannot be quite so active as he has been heretofore. It is time for him to draw in sail a bit, and this is easy enough to do; the leisurely tradition enfolds him tightly and it merely means that he must not accept so many invitations, must not go to clubs, must not entertain his friends so often. True enough strangers both famed and obscure invade his privacy with either a relentless curiosity or a well-meant determination to express their admiration, and good-naturedly he permits himself to be put upon and receives them. He is incapable of saying "no," and congenitally debarred from such drastic returns to overtures as would injure feelings. The same is true of his correspondence. He plows through reams of silly and uninteresting letters and nearly achieves writer's cramp from his generous answer to the unending appeals for autographs. Remembrances of the past continue to greet him, a dramatization of Hawthorne's *The Scarlet Letter,* for example, or Pierce's *Life of Sumner,* and he walks slowly arm in arm now with the rich memory of things that were. He dreams that Emerson stands with his hands uplifted, saying, "The Spring will come again; but shall we see it, or only the eternal spring up there?" He takes part in the editing of Charles Sumner's collected works, and his mind wanders back to other springs when the flowers seemed to glow more freshly. The spring may come again, indeed, but not the spring of his youth and not the spring of literature in New England. He goes to the theater, to plays and operas, with a fair frequency, although once, at the *Vicar of Wakefield,* he catches cold from the ladies' fans behind him. It is as easily as this now that his weakened system reacts. He begins to meditate more and more about the past, and in 1879 he is amazed to discover how great a part the number eighteen has played in his life. He was eighteen when he received his college degree. Eighteen years later he was married for the second time. This happy marriage lasted for eighteen years. And now it is eighteen years since his wife died. For eighteen years he was a professor at Harvard. He has eighteen separate volumes of poems to his credit. It is during this period that he writes that affecting sonnet, *The Cross of Snow,* one of his few intensely personal utterances and a poem that stands among those highest in inspiration that he is to do.

In the long, sleepless watches of the night,
  A gentle face—the face of one long dead—
  Looks at me from the wall, where round its head
The lamplight casts a halo of pale light.
Here in this room she died; and soul more white
  Never through martyrdom of fire was led
  To its repose; nor can in books be read
The legend of a life more benedight.
There is a mountain in the distant West
  That, sun-defying, in its deep ravines
  Displays a cross of snow upon its side.
Such is the cross I wear upon my breast
  These eighteen years, through all the changing scenes
  And seasons, changeless since the day she died.

So he exists, sipping the past leisurely as he would sip the wine of Cyprus in his cellar. His first grandchild is born in the southwest chamber of the Craigie House, and the baby must be to him an epitome of that New World upon whose portal he stands but from which he is barred entrance. What times and manners will this child see, this child who will just be of age when the new century dawns? Henry puts his hand on the sleeping baby's face and he is a link between the American Revolution and the flashing twentieth century that is to be. There is a sudden shaft of memory, the memory of a small boy running beside a general up Munjoy's Hill to look for puffs of smoke from a British frigate. Time moves so wonderfully, after all.

His seventy-second birthday dawns and with it comes a gracious surprise, the presentation of an armchair made from the wood of the village blacksmith's chestnut tree. It is brought to him by the children of Cambridge and set down before him, and he welcomes it with one of his last gracious poems. And so the decade dwindles to a charming finale for him, although for

339

the world at large it has been a period of tremendous gestations and transformations. It would probably be too much to assert that the old order in New England passes with the passing of the seventies, but it is certainly well on its way by this time. For some reason the younger men are not of the same caliber as the older figures. There may be a Howells or an Aldrich or, to grow slightly facetious, a Higginson, but there will be no more Hawthornes, no more Emersons, no more Thoreaus. The soil that developed them has been over-tilled and though younger and spryer figures may spring up in their shadow these youths will be no more than shadows themselves. The pulse of New England (like the pulse of the rest of the Republic) beats too swiftly for contemplation. The fine old tradition will stagger on for a decade or two or three before it collapses, but already it is not quite the same thing that it was. Henry is both a part of the tradition and, curiously enough, a part of another,—namely, the Victorian. To be precise, both of them are wedded in him. At rock-bottom he is American enough but all his polished surfaces reflect a Europe that, for its own part, is also shifting into new ways. The old New Englanders, therefore, linger on in the world of their memories while the communities about them adjust themselves to mills and factories and manufacturing establishments. Shoes succeed sonnets and lathes displace lyrics. An unceasing growth of population raises urban centers and the life of the soil is shoved back into a secondary place. It is time to run now and no longer to stroll along at a leisurely pace beneath tall trees in an Endymion waistcoat and with a mind filled to overflowing with bright dreams of Europe. And in the few shelters protected from this increasing materialistic urge, this itch for swiftness of acquisition, and this

mania for a political equality and an economic inequal-
ity, silence falls. The old houses stand back from the
echoing pavements, having surrendered their vitality
for all time, and their draped curtains conceal an unperturbed and vanishing gentility. It is, after all, time for
the soundless footfalls of many ghosts.

CHAPTER EIGHT
Ultima Thule

THE shadow of Time droops above the Craigie House. The yellow dwelling is settling back again into that quiet haven of completed things wherein it existed before the young man in the Endymion waistcoat walked up the front path and lifted the heavy knocker. The ghosts that fled on that far-away day draw near now and seek their old accustomed haunts, for this house belongs no longer to the living. It has accepted a new tradition and must exist in the calm shadow of it for the rest of its days on earth. It is true that many footsteps sound on the piazza, that pilgrims from the four corners of the earth travel long distances—no longer by coach but by steam—to mount these steps, that children bearing flowers turn in at the quaint gate and ripple the air with their young laughter, but for all of that, for all of the sound and movement, the Craigie House has ceased to be a vital and vibrant hive from which emerges life. Life may come to it now. It will not give out life any more. The formidable ghost of Mrs. Craigie is to be succeeded by a kindlier if simpler ghost. The ghost of an amiable Victorian American is to haunt the chambers where once George Washington, the father of his country, planned to drub the English.

Henry observes the advent of 1880 calmly and begins the year with a folk-song. The next day he receives six Pennsylvanians and a Bostonian who call in a body. These people coming in arrays are an old story now and seven is not an unusual number at all. He has grown to expect them and they give him a certain pleasure; he sees in them a feeling for literature. It is also true that he is flattered, but he has been flat-

tered so often and so much, has gone through life so
decorated, as it were, with the warm ardors of many
friends and well-wishers that his pleasant portion in
the sunset of living is rather something to be expected,
something that has grown into his days. The fact that
fellow-passengers rise to their feet and doff their hats
when he steps from the horse-car, therefore, is a tribute
both to the abiding majesty of literature in itself and
to the fact that he has kept the faith, followed the light
as he has seen it gleaming before him through the
murky American skies. He has captured a secret that
is difficult to solve. He has, in spite of outrageous
circumstances, attuned himself to his era, wedded his
European culture to his indigenous mental efflorescences
and established a curious compatibility, and so orientated
himself in a milieu somewhat of his own concoction.
It is a state of mind not easy to present. The young
Henry James is puzzled by it and observes what appears to him to be a piece of the Old World fitted
smoothly into the new, and upon reconsideration, a
tight pattern that might be reversed and so be a piece
of the new fitted into the old. James was to inquire
later: "Did he owe the large, pleasant, easy, solution
at which he had arrived . . . to his having worked
up his American consciousness to that mystic point . . .
at which it could feel nothing but continuity and congru-
ity with his European?" It is a problem that must
have enticed, perplexed and semi-irritated the author
of *The American,* but it is also one which he could
not answer. The young James, after all, is so curiously constituted as hardly to recognize Henry for
what he is in himself. Indeed, it is to be doubted that
Henry himself can answer this question of his adjustment. He merely lives now and does not trouble his
mind too much about adjustments, which are not so im-

343

portant an intellectual topic in these pleasant 1880's, except for the disconcerting young James. The lyrics gush forth, not quite so fresh, not so memorable, not quite so many, and the aging poet welcomes them as of old with an urbane pleasure. He bethinks himself about another book and the ghosts of the Craigie House stir noiselessly about the still-lighted rooms as he seeks for a title and a motto. He finds the motto in Horace.

> "precor, integrâ
> Cum mente, nec turpem senectam
> Degere, nec citherâ carentum.

"My prayer is, that with mind unshattered I may pass an old age neither unworthy nor without song." He must find a title as well.

He sits like Priam at his desk in the pleasant study with the hundred and one knick-knacks about him reminding him of a hundred and one bygone things. His white beard falls like a cascade on his breast and his gentle blue eyes stare out of the window at the brown Cambridge fields. He muses, dreaming of a title for this new child of his, this book of verse from the heart and brain of a man who has passed seventy-three years. And the shadows pass. A multitude of unforgotten faces look down upon him. George Pierce, who died in the dawn of his early manhood. Mary, who passed away amid the alien scenes of Holland. The dark-eyed wizard, Hawthorne, freed forever from Custom Houses and consulates. Felton, his boisterous laughter stilled. Sumner, the leonine, the dogged warrior, safe from the assaulting canes of life. Fanny, beyond the reach of the cruel flames. Stephen and Zilpah, returned to their pioneer fathers. Agassiz, hidden in that earth that so perplexed his scientific curiosity. All these shadows pass, laughing, sighing, stretching out hands through the quietness of the study. They move against the dim vistas of an old world that has somehow ceased to be. Henry watches them go and above their mysterious laughter and sighs loom the towers of foreign cities, London, Rome, Paris, Berlin, Seville. He has been rich in friends, rich in his knowledge of many lands. He has reached his Ultima Thule, his land of endings where there is to be no beginnings. Slowly he draws the white cartridge paper to him and sets down the title of the last book he is to write. It shall be *Ultima Thule*. It shall contain but eighteen poems, a meager volume, but enough to carry cloth covers.

There is nothing left but the ground-swirl of autumn leaves and a new and barbarous generation springing up like armored warriors from the dragon's teeth sown by the Jason of the years, the Time-Spirit. Their impatient feet beat on the sounding walks somewhere outside the orbit of Craigie House but Henry is not unduly disturbed by them. He does not hear their uncouth ballads or wise jokes. If they are but gently radical, after all, he does not know it. The plush era in American civilization (natural successor to the pine-knot era) is stuffy but it possesses varying notions from Henry's. It is rather brisk and up and coming in a way, decidedly tinged with commercialism, and Henry, if he is aware, blandly ignores these revelations of a lessening spirit. He is still the possessor of the leisurely tradition. He is concerned with his own wistfulnesses now, twilight moods that fall at the end of day and which are as vague as the thin skeins of rain that fall upon his dwelling. As he broods upon this title, this *Ultima Thule* that stares up at him in quaint round handwriting, he is snatched up by memories and he visualizes himself sitting again on the house-top in Naples with Capri in a golden mist before him and Greene by his side and all his dreams sparkling in the bright Italian air. Yes, Greene is left, an old man creeping about his wind-mill in East Greenwich. And to this old man Henry sends a message, a hint of affection that shall introduce this last book, placing the letters slowly and carefully upon the pages.

> With favoring winds, o'er sunlit seas,
> We sailed for the Hesperides,
> The land where golden apples grow;
> But that, ah! that was long ago.
>
> How far since then the ocean streams
> Have swept us from the land of dreams,
> That land of fiction and of truth,
> The lost Atlantis of our youth!
>
> Whither, ah, whither? Are not these
> The tempest-haunted Orcades,
> Where sea-gulls scream, and breakers roar,
> And wreck and sea-weed line the shore?
>
> Ultima Thule! Utmost Isle!
> Here in thy harbors for a while
> We lower our sails; a while we rest
> From the unending, endless quest.

Ultima Thule is a small book and the poetry in it is of a meager quality but it is marked by that pleasant facility that seems never to desert Henry. He is echoing himself, repeating an old formula that is really a part of himself, for Henry in a certain sense is a formula. He is a placid and industrious repeater. He discovers the recipe for his lyrics as far back as *Voices of the Night* and the atmosphere which impregnated them is to be found in its sunset spell in these latest poems that drip so carefully from the ever-functioning pen. Though he may speak wistfully of an "unending, endless quest" in the nostalgic lines to Greene we may be sure that the quest he has in mind is for no tempestuous isles. It is for an imaginary sun-lit land of everlasting golden apples and it is possible that he would not demur too much if a golden text were inscribed upon each apple. That imaginary land is formed from idealized conceptions of England and Italy and Spain and Germany fused into a whole that is dominated by a gentle Puritanism. It is peopled with gentlemanly Indians and wistful Acadian maidens and young Germanic heroes who mount steadily toward the summits of life, and on each summit stands a personified ideal of Christianity, preferably the Unitarian brand. The turbid rush of life is unheard in Henry's imaginary land although exalted reflections of it loom from time to time through the pristine air. Henry knows that he is living, but like all great Victorians he permits no more than a certain few facets of his days to reflect themselves in his work. Literature for him, more often than not, is a series of remembrances of things past. It is nearly always the garment of an implied message. The rain falls and it becomes not a beautiful thing in itself, a sliding veil of pearl-gray magic, but a reminder that into each life some rain may fall. His public must be hungry for this didactic approach to living, for his popularity is unquestionable. He is the acknowledged ambassador of goodness and though strange voices are being lifted in this world he is still a potent influence. It is true that he is not accepted as unanimously as he had been twenty years before, but ensconced in Craigie House he can hardly be aware of any diminution of his fortunes. He despatches *Ultima Thule* into the world with the sanguinity of one approved and vindicated.

Curious honors devolve upon him from time to time. It is the era of a reawakened interest in pottery, for example, and extraordinary specimens are produced and dispersed among a huge public which is fumbling toward an art expression. The plates, jugs, bowls and statuary so conceived are often wonderful and fearful to behold, but they serve to placate an instinct that is still crude in its demands. Richard Briggs, a Boston dealer in pottery, is smitten with *Kéramos*, Henry's symbolic poem about a potter and his spinning wheel, and a brilliant idea—one is forced to believe that a measure of financial astuteness enters into it—dawns upon him. He makes a trip to England, to the world-famous works of Josiah Wedgwood and Sons, Staffordshire, and commissions them to make a "Longfellow Jug" in Wedgwood ware. The finished piece of pottery is about seven inches high, broad and capacious, holding five pints. There are two panels on the jug, one of them being a portrait of Henry and the other a quotation from *Kéramos*.

> Turn, turn, my wheel; turn round and round
> Without a pause, without a sound:
>   So spins the flying world away!
> This clay, well mixed with marl and sand,
> Follows the motion of my hand:
> For some must follow, and some command,
>   Though all are made of clay.

Various scrolls intertwined with flowers decorate the remaining surfaces of the jug and upon these scrolls are inscribed the titles of some of Henry's more popular poems. Henry, receiving the jug, writes a pleasant letter of thanks to the inspired Briggs. How many New England households secured this jug and placed it where all eyes could feast upon the poet's countenance?

It is too early for Henry to be immortalized by having a cigar named after him, so he must be content with a jug. This jug, however, is but the precursor of many photographs, small busts, ink-wells, plaques and even embroidered heads, for the aspect of Henry now becomes a part of the heritage of New England. His features become as familiar to the child as the chromo of the Pilgrims landing at the Rock. It is in such ways that the magnitude of his popularity must be impressed upon him. He is not the darling of esoteric schools or rarefied groups but the familiar pleasure of that enormous bourgeoisie that craves definiteness and simplicity. He belongs almost with the leaders of the Republic, the presidents and generals who are household words. As the wheels of his career revolve with a lessening celerity he finds that he has almost become a symbol for poetry, as the wooden Indian has become a symbol for tobacco. There has been nothing like him in the American scene.

II

The year 1880 is, on the whole, the last season of any particular activities on Henry's part. He sees his book come out, he is pulled about outrageously during the summer from Nahant to Portland, where he passes a week each season with his sister, Mrs. Pierce, to Nahant, to East Greenwich, where he takes part in wedding festivities at the Greene windmill, to Nahant and so back to Craigie House; and he takes a minor part in the 250th anniversary of the founding of Cambridge, appearing at Sander's Theater with Holmes and so making his last appearance in public. It is not the Cambridge of his youth that hurries to this celebration but a bustling city. Still for Henry there must be many faces, unseen to others, thronging the crowded theater.

At the close of the anniversary exercises his beloved children crowd about him and he writes his name again and again in the anxiously upheld albums. He even goes so far as to make a brief speech. The affection bestowed upon him by children is immense and intense. It is during this year that his birthday is celebrated in the public schools of Cincinnati and some 15,000 children, from the primary grades to the high schools, take part in ceremonies that include addresses, biographical sketches and the recital of poems. Henry is delighted with these evidences of affection and he keeps a scrapbook wherein he pastes the accounts of the celebrations that occur this year and the next. It is easy to see why he should occupy so high a place in the hearts of children, for the bulk of his work has been of that simple nature that appeals to the child and does not leave him discomfited with mysteries. There are no mysteries in Henry's work. It is bright with daylight, simple as the stream that purls through its sedgy banks, and as pellucid as the clear springs of Maine. The child need not go beyond himself in elucidating the message which Henry gives his world, for he stands somewhat apart and below his contemporaries in point of comparison. The depth of feeling implicit in Bryant's best work, the rarefied moral ether of Emerson, the strangely mature human sympathy of Whittier, the "barbaric yawp" of Walt Whitman, the macabre imagination of Poe, these things may puzzle the child, who, while he enjoys the measures, can hardly read the secret hieroglyphics between the lines; but there is none of this mystery in Henry. His feeling is sincere but it is not deep. His moral approach is pleasantly colored with sentimentality. His human sympathy is always simple. His strains are ever felicitous and unmarred by the barbaric. His imagination is sweet and limited. And best of all, his work is garmented in mellifluous music and bright colors. Unconsciously perhaps, his nature has shaped him into the child's poet, and because of this generations of school children will rehearse his lyrics, the hexameters of *Evangeline* and *The Courtship of Miles Standish* and the ceaseless flow of *Hiawatha*. When he strives to fly beyond the sphere of childlike simplicity as in *Christus: A Mystery*, and the posthumous *Michael Angelo*, his failure is obvious. It is with good reason, therefore, that the children adore him. He has beaten in upon their receptive minds. Several generations will grow to maturity knowing his name as a household word.

As 1880 draws to a close Henry grows sententious. Like all aged men of professional training he enjoys concocting adages, tame epigrams, concentrated tablets of moral wisdom. There are moments when the spirit of Martin Tupper descends upon him. "It is not the possession of a thing, but the use of it, which gives it value," he notes, sagely enough, and with the New Englander's delight in an implied moral. And again, "A censorious critic is often like a boy sharpening a pen-knife. The blade suddenly closes and cuts his fingers." So to the last he maintains his attitude toward carping critics, the attitude that has been his since the days of Margaret Fuller and Edgar Allan Poe. It is better to praise than to blame, seems to be his idea of their function. So with poems, friends, adages and a dwindling series of forays into the world he passes the quiet months. The Mapleson Italian Opera Company comes to Boston and Henry, as usual when music is at hand, partakes largely of the pleasures which they have to offer. He prefers the music of the past to the music of the future and Boito's *Mefistofele* leaves him somewhat astounded. It is wild and weird beyond conception to him. The cold weather bites as it never bit before and the heating of Craigie House becomes a problem. He clings to the fire and his friends observe with some consternation that he is really an old man, after all. The spring in his gait is missing and his face is lined. He is more careful of his health, not so willing to venture into wintry blasts. It cannot be said that he relies more on books for amusement, for he has always relied on them. But he seems more immersed than ever in the written word. On Christmas day General Sherman calls and Henry's thoughts go back for a moment to the strenuous Civil War days. He lives in memories and ruminations now, unconsciously comparing the old with the new, to the utter confounding of the new. The particulars of Ole Bull's death are brought to him, the flags of Bergen at half mast, the telegram from the King, and the funeral oration by the poet Björnson, and he notes, "No Viking ever had such a funeral." The year slides away and it is 1881 and bitter cold weather.

His days are merely a matter of repetitions. Visitors, letters, requests for autographs, honors. Salvini, the Italian tragedian, comes to lunch, comes again and reads a paper he has written on *Hamlet, Othello* and *Macbeth*. Luigi Monti, his old college confrère, plays *Sonnambula* to him in the evening. He receives word that forty or more schools are about to celebrate his seventy-fourth birthday and obligingly enough, he sends them all a stanza, with a signature and good wishes. A woman in Ohio sends him one hundred cards with the request that he write his name on each as she desires to distribute them to her guests at a party she is giving on his birthday. He is tempted forth to a birthday dinner at Houghton's where he meets Holmes, Howells, Aldrich, Miss Bates and Miss Jewett, and sits late, glowing in his honors. His seventy-fourth birthday dawns and the Craigie House is heaped with roses and lilies. Letters and felicitations flow in. The school children recite his poems and sing his songs. These seemingly inconsequential notations might be added to profusely, but there is little need of it. They serve to show the caliber of these days.

It is true that there is a more somber side to all this. Age continues to steal upon him and slow his movements. His friends slip out of his life. James T. Fields dies on a Sunday and is buried on Tuesday; Dr. Palfrey dies on this Tuesday and is buried on Friday. Two old comrades in a single week. Henry is disconsolate for a short period; then his buoyant nature reasserts itself. He goes to Portland and dreams in its charm during a few sunny days, sitting on the piazza and smiling at the townsfolk who pass. The assassination of President Garfield rouses him to a sonnet and he busies himself with the index to Charles Sumner's *Works*. But he grows feebler daily now and for the most part absents himself from public view. All October, November and December find him confined to his room in Craigie House with nervous prostration, following upon a severe attack of vertigo. He creeps about the chamber, looks out the window at the autumn foliage, and reads Miss Berry's *Journal and Correspondence*. He goes to bed early and gets up late and finally relinquishes the attempt to keep up with his mail, having a card printed which explains that he can do no more than acknowledge letters. A French delegation, among them the grandson of Lafayette, present in America to attend the centennial of the surrender of Cornwallis at Yorktown, call upon him, but he is unable to see them. His thoughts must go back to Lafayette himself now, to the old General whom he met during his first visit in Paris and found so mildly exciting. And so 1881 ends wearily, on a note of sickness.

These two years, although Henry certainly does not know it, are periods of dissolution. The springs of being have run down, and as their blithe and busy whir diminishes he depends more and more on the sedentary delights of Craigie House. To sit in his study, to hold a new—or, for the most part, old—book in his hand, to gossip with Greene, who visits him frequently, or Luigi Monti or John Owen, to greet visitors with just the proper degree of benignity, to write the few scattered utterances of his weary poetical being, to listen to the sound of the sea at Nahant, or to dream away the hours at Portland, these are the things that are left. They are the pleasures of an old man; they are complicated to some degree by various ailments but he makes the best of them. He relishes his days, tasting life now as he tastes the Falernian from his cellar, as he draws in the rich aroma of his Havana cigar, with a deliberate and unexcited zest. The months pass and these two years dwindle down to a sick room and a man, old and weary in body but urbane in spirit, suddenly sampling the rare seclusion that has come to him through the doors of illness, almost reveling in the escape from the more and more importunate obligations and onerous duties. He begins to belong to himself for a little, although the curious and unreasonable public which has so claimed him has yet to bankrupt his generosity. To the very last he will give himself as well as he may to whoso may desire him. Possibly he recognizes the fact that he has evolved into a sort of monument, a sight to be seen, much like Bunker Hill monument or the Craigie House itself. It is, perhaps, not without a mystical forethought that Time inter-

venes with these months of illness. He reads but little
now, writes but few letters (always to Greene, of
course), and receives hardly any friends. He is like
an anchorite sitting just outside the walls of the city
of life. His townsmen pass through Brattle Street and
Cambridge continues to grow into something rather
monstrous and commonplace, but happily he is unaware
of this. The old graciousness of the ante-bellum New
England is implicit in him and his immediate scene, and
it suffices to carry him through unstained to the end.
Though shops and factories may spring up and the
wheels of commerce may steadily accelerate he is safe
in his little oasis bulwarked with tradition and history.
He passes the evenings playing backgammon with his
daughter. He watches the lamplight dance on the
walls. His books, those treasured friends of his long
years, stand in their serried rows on the shelves and he
gazes at them fondly, although he takes down but few.
"My ornaments and arms of other days," he dubs
them in one of the infrequent poems that now creep
from his pen. It is all quiet, hushed, drawing ever
nearer to its calm dénouement.

III

The dawn of 1882 finds him a trifle better in health.
In January he writes *Mad River* and in February
he achieves some verses for Decoration Day. But his
writing years are over and he seems to suspect it. The
long regiment of his works is assembled on the shelf.
It is in many uniforms, some of them unduly elaborate
and others in the simplest of simple garments. Here
is his first effort of all, L'homond's *French Grammar*
which he edited for his students at Bowdoin, and here
is the elaborate collected edition which aroused Mar-

garet Fuller's ire. Here, too, is that *Waif* that pricked the angry Poe to battle and here is *Hyperion* in which he pleaded so successfully for a fair young wife. They are all here, the major works, *Evangeline, The Courtship of Miles Standish, Hiawatha, Christus: A Mystery,* and *The Poets and Poetry of Europe.* Sandwiched between the stouter tomes are the books of lyrics, *Voices of the Night, Ballads and Other Poems, The Belfry of Bruges and Other Poems.* There are trial editions and odd printed pamphlets and even leaflets. It is an impressive regiment, the work of a long lifetime of copious effort. Henry assuredly sees in them his bulwark against the insidious encroaches of oblivion, and to a limited degree his instinct is correct. They will save him for posterity but not for themselves alone. They will reveal him for what he is, a curious summing-up in himself of the simple literary urge of a new land that must draw its sustenance from ancient and foreign springs. Like the shaft of stone on Bunker Hill he will stand for something, and it is of no importance at all if, like the shaft of stone, he stands eventually for something that has died and ceased to exist in this land that grows so enormously within such small periods of time. It is not alone for simpleness and Victorian serenity and purity that Henry stands. He represents in himself, also, the gentility of an old tradition. It is that that proves to be finest in him, for Victorian purity after all is rather a matter of many smugnesses and self-deceits and thin-lipped evasions. Henry is smug from the beginning to the end, but he is absolutely unconscious of the fact, and this divine unconsciousness becomes an inherent portion of the tradition wherein he exists because of the gentility that informs it. His writings are the visible aspect of this tradition, but one must look

further than them to find the tradition unflawed in itself. Henry may not be the perfect example of it but
he goes a long way toward revealing its best side.

In January Henry is apprized that the city authorities
of Portland have passed resolutions regarding his sev-
enty-fifth birthday, that it is to be celebrated by the
Maine Historical Society, and he writes to William Sen-
ter, Mayor of the city, thanking his birthplace for the
honor to be conferred upon him but indicating that
the state of his health will not permit him to be present
in person at the public reception offered him. However, the Maine Historical Society goes ahead with its
plans and the anniversary meeting is held in the rooms
of the Society in City Building on Monday evening,
February 27. The library is adorned with Longfellow
material, letters of the four Stephens (they look down
from the wall somewhat blankly on this gathering in
honor of a mere writer), portraits, autographed poems,
early printed books, even the fierce physiognomy of
Gen. Peleg Wadsworth in silhouette. The crush is so
great that the meeting is adjourned to the Reception
Hall where before an audience which includes two of
Henry's sisters and a brother various orators hold forth
in extolling their poet. W. G. Barrows of Brunswick
delivers the opening address, James Phinney Baxter of
Portland reads a poem, and the Reverend Henry S.
Burrage of Portland reads a paper on *Henry W. Longfellow and His Paternal Ancestry*. Hon. William
Goold of Windham follows this with a paper on
*General Peleg Wadsworth, and the Maternal Ances-
try of Henry W. Longfellow,* and Edward H. Elwell
of Portland augments these ancestral notations with
The Portland of Longfellow's Youth. Pride of
birth is strong in these New Englanders and blossom-
ing genealogical trees bear rich fruit for them. The

foundations, as it were, thus being established, the orators turn to more personal considerations and there follow in rapid succession *Longfellow as a Student and Professor at Bowdoin College* by Professor Packard and *The Genius of Longfellow* by Hon. George F. Talbot, which comes in a poor fifth. Letters from J. W. Bradbury and Israel Washburn are read and the evening draws to a triumphant close.

While the city of his birth is thus making a gentle little holiday over him and basking in the light of his reflected name Henry is quietly moving about the Craigie House, not too much concerned with the fact that he is seventy-five years old. On March 12 he writes *The Bells of San Blas* and three days later he adds a final verse as an afterthought. It runs:

> O Bells of San Blas, in vain
> Ye call back the Past again!
>   The Past is deaf to your prayer;
> Out of the shadow of night
> The world rolls into light;
>   It is daybreak everywhere.

He puts down the pen. It is the last rhyme he is to write.

IV

On Saturday forenoon, the eighteenth of March, four schoolboys from Boston, ardent youthful disciples, come to Craigie House at the express invitation of the poet, who to the very last reveals his unaffected pleasure at sincere adulation. They are shown through the many rooms so redolent of a calm and mellow past, halted before the various objects of interest—the chair made from the old chestnut tree that waved above the village smithy, the pen made from a link of Bonnivard's chain, the inkstand of Coleridge, the fragment of Dante's coffin, the ancient books, the many pictures and busts—and eventually depart, each bearing in his album an autograph in the clear round handwriting of their god. They are probably rather mute boys, hushed by their awe of the white-bearded and kindly-eyed gentlemen who accepts their stammering praise so benignly. It is a feeble man with a lined face who walks slowly beside them as they turn awkwardly toward the door, but there is an exalted glint in the blue eyes turned upon them. After their departure Henry strolls about his eastern veranda wrapped in his long, fur-lined, Italian coat and the afternoon passes slowly. Shadows lengthen over a land that is just beginning to push forth the tentative blooms of spring. A bluebird flashes in the shrubbery. In the air is a rawness, the icy aura of departing winter, a reminiscence of those freezing days in Brunswick when the little blaze in the fireplace fought so valiantly the baying hounds of winter. Henry notices it and returns indoors complaining a little of the cold that creeps through his bones. Luigi Monti dines with him and noticing that he seems indisposed leaves immediately after the meal. Henry is put to bed, and the pulse of anxiety quickens in the household. His children who have lived with him so long, the married ones returning with frequency, sense a dark figure standing outside the door in the wind. Violent pains assail Henry in the night but he is unwilling to disturb the household and it is not until Sunday morning that Dr. Morrel Wyman is sent for. A diagnosis is made and the illness proves to be peritonitis. Opiates are administered and Henry passes into a drugged sleep.

When he awakes he seems improved and there is some degree of optimism amongst the startled children.

There is yet a chance that he may pass out of danger if no further setbacks manifest themselves. But with the advent of Monday new disasters befall the body that is now so feebly functioning. Unlooked-for symptoms arise and increase during the day and night. Henry has but little to say. The sight of his sister, newly arrived from Portland, rouses him to, "Now I know that I must be very ill, since you have been sent for." By Tuesday morning it is apparent that he is approaching his end. In the meantime the world proceeds on its disordered way. The cold spring creeps toward the warmth of a seasonable atmosphere. In Cambridge and Boston the businesses of life are accelerated. The friends of the poet, in spite of brief reports of illness in the daily papers, continue unalarmed. He who has been so long among them, white and gentle, will continue to be so still. The vast public that has grown up on his smooth lyricism and simple sentimentality, his vague and kindly appeal to the heart, knows nothing of what is happening.

Wednesday and Thursday pass and the patient lingers. Slight improvements are offset by the inevitable approach of the end. On Thursday evening he is desirous of conversation and throughout a brief rally he discourses with some degree of animation on various subjects. His mind functions rationally, that mind that has been always so simple and rational, but toward midnight his ardor collapses. Unconsciousness, a troubled unconsciousness, sweeps over him and carries him through the night until the morning, when he revives. He does not complain of pain but he appears anxious that others should realize that he is nearing his Ultima Thule. Slight incoherences mark his conversation through the day.

Of what is he thinking when he does not speak? To

what places and faces does his mind turn as he discovers himself at the end of that long and placid triumph that has so endeared him to a world which, on the whole, is not especially thrilled by literature? It is possible that he turns back to the Portland of his youth, to a strange little town where relicts of a bygone day still walked forth in cocked hats, bush wigs and knee breeches. The "Spanish sailors with bearded lips" of his boyhood dreams may hover about the bed. And then there are the days at Bowdoin with the logs tumbling down the Androscoggin and dark-eyed Nathaniel Hawthorne frittering away his time in the ominous silence of youthful meditation. It is certain that no comparison between Hawthorne and himself enters his mind, no realization of that Nature that fastened all his roots of being upon the surface and not in the dark soil of the New England which produced *The Scarlet Letter*. We may imagine the dying man observing his life like a ribbon of pictures and finding much that is good, much that is well intentioned, and much that failed only because the reach exceeded the grasp. The law office after graduation and the impatient wait to start forth on his destiny; the appointment to a professorship when he is but nineteen and the journey to Europe to prepare himself for it; the various scenes and aspects of the Old World so eagerly assimilated, impregnating him to such a degree that his essential self becomes Europeanized; these, too, must swim before his dim eyes. Towers, palaces, crumbling châteaux, German rivers, the plains of Granada, the Coliseum, the dark eyes of Tennyson and the hand of Victoria, the feel of Europe, the curious placid sense of domination. And through it all the desire to draw his native land back to the deep springs of European culture, a desire that becomes almost an apostolic mission to him.

The calm years as a professor at Bowdoin follow preceded by the bright interlude of courtship in the rose-garden at Portland and then unfold the long seasons at Cambridge with their multitude of activities and friends, seasons that witness the steady growth and umbrageous spread of a talent which is colored and informed with felicity, charm, mellowness and melody. It is all a trifle thin, perhaps. Not once have the deep springs of life been touched in living verse. Not once have the passionate eagernesses and sorrows of existence been plumbed. Yet tragedy has visited him. The Dark Face has turned her burning eyes upon him. And possibly a thought of that tragic Christmas so long ago when he enveloped his burned and perishing wife in a rug comes back to him. He has known terror and pity and he has been incapable of projecting them in any single line that he has written. But even so he has spread like the day's broad sunshine over the land of his birth. He has touched the universality of an era and perhaps it is too much for him to fling his mind into the veiled future and discover that his universality of utterance does not stretch so very far beyond the eventual lustrum of his days. He has lived like a kindly sage. His leonine head is the head of a Homer emasculated by a simple kindliness that is the pleasurable outgrowth of Puritanism. He has been pure. He has been calm and facile and religious. And so musing, at ten minutes past three o'clock on that Friday afternoon of March 24th, while the loud winds raced across the Cambridge marshes, his gentle spirit passes away to the bewildered sorrow of half the world.

· · · · · · · ·

The snow falls softly on Mount Auburn while the Reverend Samuel Longfellow reads slowly from the Scriptures. The mourners bow their heads silently as

the casket with its crossed palm leaves is deposited in its
last resting-place.   Ralph Waldo Emerson, standing
feebly by his daughter, lifts his vacant eyes.   "I cannot recall the name of our friend," he murmurs to
a mourner near him, "but he was a good man."

THE END